# Bollywood's India

# Bollywood's India

*Hindi Cinema as a Guide to Contemporary India*

Rachel Dwyer

REAKTION BOOKS

*To the memory of Yash Chopra, 1932–2012*

Published by Reaktion Books Ltd
33 Great Sutton Street
London EC1V 0DX, UK
www.reaktionbooks.co.uk

First published 2014

Copyright © Rachel Dwyer 2014

Printed and bound in Great Britain by Bell & Bain, Glasgow

A catalogue record for this book is available from the British Library

ISBN 978 1 78023 263 8

# Contents

# Preface

*Bollywood's India* is an investigation of the imagined worlds of mainstream Hindi cinema, whose interpretations of India over the last two decades are, I argue, the most reliable guide to understanding the nation's dreams and hopes, fears and anxieties. This book explores the nature of Hindi cinema – now best known as 'Bollywood' and whose non-realistic depictions of the everyday are often dismissed as 'escapist entertainment' – by considering how escapism and entertainment function and are mobilized to think about life and the world.

India is changing rapidly, and in the last twenty years following liberalization in 1991 social and economic transformations have been occurring at an unprecedented speed. Long acknowledged as one of the world's greatest and most ancient civilizations, and notorious too for being home to many of its poorest people, India now enjoys a new and unaccustomed role as a potential emerging superpower, and is producing some of the planet's richest individuals and one of its largest middle classes. These changes have been so rapid and so pervasive that their impact can barely, as yet, be understood. While journalists and other writers have examined these transformations, tracing their causes and their impact in the social, political and economic realms, it remains difficult to know how people have adapted to the changes, how they interpret them, what their hopes and fears are, how they see their future and how they look at their pasts. Indians know that they are now serious players on the international stage, but how do they see themselves as having

Chaudhry Baldev Singh (Amrish Puri) feeding birds in Trafalgar Square in *Dilwale dulhaniya le jayenge.*

changed and how do they see the world and their lives – how do they make sense of it all?

As cinema does not reflect society but rather imagines it, and Hindi cinema does so in ways that often eschew the values of realism, *Bollywood's India* emphasizes the role of the imagination, suggesting that cinema plays a highly significant role in creating a way of comprehending the way society is and how it should be. This way of thinking about Hindi cinema is also a way of looking at India, and this book is concerned with the present as India changes: what are the rights and duties of the individual and their responsibilities to one another; how do pre-modern hierarchical ideas interact with modern political ones; how does individualism relate to society?

Like other arts, cinema is about standards of behaviour and their consequences, a way of understanding the self and the world which can be interpreted in many ways. However, the Hindi film is also a mighty cultural product, consumed by millions of people in India and world-wide as a global media form. As a 'new' postcolonial nation, India created new myths and national texts. Some of these took shape in movies which have become myths, reaching out beyond the cinema halls into everyday life as they inculcate beliefs and offer ways of understanding the world.

Hindi cinema has itself been transformed since 1991, particularly with the formation of what is now known as 'Bollywood', the high-profile, globalized mainstream cinema which lies at the heart of the growing entertainment industry. This is the focus of this book, not the other forms of Hindi cinema which have emerged recently, notably the multiplex/independent (*hatke* or 'different', offbeat, indie) films. These have different economies of production and content, being less star-oriented and more realist, and have other circuits of distribution – mostly limited viewings in multiplexes or at festivals and through other media. While it is widely acknowledged that these films are not viewed universally in India, whether by choice or by need, it is also undeniable that Bollywood permeates India's public culture more significantly than the viewership of the films themselves. The use of Bollywood dance rather than folk or classical forms in the closing ceremony of the Commonwealth Games in Melbourne in 2006 signified its cultural dominance and coming of age, yet many regarded it as a nail in the coffin of traditional Indian culture.

*Bollywood's India* does not see cinema as a direct reflection or representation of society – indeed it would be foolish to believe this – but rather as a series of symbols and meanings which are created between practice and theory. It thus looks at cinema as a repository of imaginaries and imaginary worlds, showing ways in which change is visualized in films, depicted in narratives, images and sounds where meanings are condensed, displaced by star images and intensified by melodrama. It also considers how Hindi cinema in turn shapes the way that people see modern India and interpret it – how its images, words, music and affects generate or regenerate images of India across many media forms.

This is neither a sociological profile of Hindi cinema nor a potted history of the cinema industry. The largely undocumented history of Indian cinema deserves many more books devoted to it, but this one aims to examine what the imagining of India in the last twenty years has to say about the new and emergent India, rather than it being about Hindi cinema itself. It is nonetheless based on a study of this cinema – to inform its understanding of the cinematic imagination – and thus investigates arguments and aspects of cinema such as narrative, audio and visual forms which have been discussed by scholars of film studies. Nor is *Bollywood's India* an encyclopaedia or a gazetteer; instead it looks at a selection of key films as a way of understanding India over the last twenty years: at the invitation to dream, at the imagining of India by Indians, at the collective dream and at Indian cinema itself. The films discussed in this book were released up to July 2013, when the manuscript was completed. They have been chosen because of their popularity, as many of them have become part of new mythologies – endlessly told, retold, quoted and imitated in everyday speech and elsewhere.

## A Personal Note

The book covers my own period of major Hindi film viewing and marks something of a personal journey. It was wonderful to have the opportunity to rewatch the older films and to feel a great nostalgia for the time when the new India was on the horizon and the changes all felt so exciting and seemed to bring freedom. Now the new seems to be destroying the old that first brought me to India. I had enormous fun rewatching films which I first saw on terrible VHS copies, many during the curfews in Bombay in 1992, when my Hindi was very limited and my friends, Rekhi, Monisha and Sonal Shah, had to explain much of what was happening and who was who. As I rewatched clean prints, my Hindi better, the films subtitled, they seemed very different from the first time I saw them – many of them are now historical documents of fashions and star style. One of the great pleasures in seeing them again was hearing long-forgotten songs which I had followed to try to improve my Hindi, the words of which I still remember.

Indian film drives me and has been the best way I have found to understand contemporary India. My own study of India began with learning Sanskrit, and its lyrical traditions were the forms with which I have the greatest affinity, having been brought up in a world of classical scholarship at home and at school. A shift to modern India, or late medieval India, as I began my doctoral research, was new to me as I knew only what I had studied at school as part of British imperial history and from reading the Indian English novel. My decades of travelling in India supplemented this imaginary world, though I continue to find Indian texts, whether film, literature, history or religion and classicism, powerful tools with which to imagine and think. It is only in this imaginary world, and the world of 'facts', that I have heard the voices of the poor, the deprived, the rural. My years in India have been among elites and emerging or aspirational elites. My actual sphere has been mostly Anglophone, as this is the language of the elites among whom I have spent my time, with less time in Gujarati and Hindi spheres, although the texts I have read and studied have been decreasingly English, in the sense of British English. This is not because I am turning my back on those who are not part of the elites, but because this is the way my professional and social world has formed over several decades. Yet the people whom I have found the most interesting are by no means confined to this world, as their religious, private and other lives reach beyond it and have informed our encounters.

Hindi films have illuminated all my understandings of India, and *Bollywood's India* brings together the ways in which I have found the films rewarding, insightful and critical, as well as unpleasant and alarming, in the ways in which they present a worldview and imaginary world. I hope that the understandings I present in this book will prove of wider interest and that no one will ever say to me again that Hindi films are all the same and 'unrealistic'.

# Introduction

Hindi cinema, now often referred to loosely by the term 'Bollywood', is one of the best-known and most widely appreciated features of contemporary Indian culture. It makes its presence felt beyond the screen throughout wider media, whether the Internet, television, news, art, literature or music, and has become synonymous with a style of excess, melodrama and kitsch. Yet the films of twenty years ago now seem impossibly remote, dated even, as they, the cinema audiences and the industry that produced them have been overtaken by the massive and deep-rooted social and economic changes of the period, which have revolutionized sections of India. This introduction examines the background to these wider changes in society before looking more closely at the transformation of Hindi cinema and the emergence of Bollywood, and lastly at the changing dynamic between cinema and society in the last two decades.

## From National Postcolonial to the Global

It is hard to overestimate how much life in India has changed in the last twenty years. New social groups have emerged, notably the new middle classes; politics have shifted from the national to identity politics; and the Nehruvian dreams of a united nation and of planned modernization have been replaced by those of globalization and a weakening of the boundaries of the nation with the importance of the diaspora being reflected in new categories of Overseas Citizenship. India sees itself as an emerging global power, as one of the world's largest economies, and it seeks a permanent seat on the UN Security Council. These changes, which have mostly been welcomed in India, have been unequal and uneven and have not directly benefited some of the most vulnerable in society, notably children and the poor.

After independence from the British in 1947, India followed the model laid out in the early years in its 1950 Constitution. It was founded as a democracy, with the qualifications socialist and secular being added in 1976, while foreign policy was largely one of non-alignment. The economy was state-driven and the state played a major role through nationalization, the 'Licence (or Permit) Raj' (government regulation of the private sector by the issue of licences or permits) and protectionism, with the economy being almost closed to multinationals. Though India had a very positive image as one of the first countries to become independent from European rule and a democracy, it was also perceived to be desperately poor, despite its high-profile princely, business and political elites.

British institutions and structures of democracy shaped the postcolonial state, and India was governed by a service elite who were mostly educated in schools, colleges and universities modelled on the British system, including an administrative cadre who had studied overseas, usually in the UK. This postcolonial bourgeoisie, though not wealthy by international standards, enjoyed great privilege within India. Their cultural tastes were dominant – at least until a new middle class began to emerge in the 1970s, their prosperity fuelled by agricultural development ('the Green Revolution'), remittances from migrant workers, especially those in the Gulf, and the entrepreneurial skills of its businessmen.

*Bollywood's India* takes 1991 as its point of departure: the onset of economic liberalization. P. V. Narasimha Rao, who became Prime Minister after Rajiv Gandhi's assassination in 1991, was faced with an economic crisis. His Finance Minister, Manmohan Singh, negotiated a structural-adjustment loan from the IMF which required the devaluation of the rupee, the easing of restrictions on foreign investment and the end of the

'Permit Raj'. It could be argued that the changes triggered in 1991 were just as important a watershed in India's history as 1947.

These economic changes and the opening of markets were major contributory factors in the rise of the 'new middle classes', an emerging social group formed from the petite bourgeoisie and upper working classes. Many of these people came from groups with a business background who operated in the private sector – often in small businesses which profited from the new deregulation – and who seized the advantages of a rising consumerism in which they played a major role. These new middle classes are the main focus of this book, as those who make and consume Hindi cinema mostly come from their ranks.

In the years since Independence in 1947, average life expectancy has doubled from 32 to 65, while literacy has risen even more spectacularly, from 12–16 per cent to 74 per cent. These statistics are still behind those of more developed countries and show a vast and entrenched difference between social groups. Nevertheless, they are a good index of development and suggest that the overall standards in India have been improving in part due to the economic changes outlined.

The major market for entertainment is the young, and India has a huge youthful population. Over 350 million people, or around one third of India's population, are under twenty and were born during the period on which this book focuses: 1991–2014. They are one of the major groups consuming media from this era. In 1991, India had been independent for 44 years, long before any of them was born, so nearly all their parents were born in independent India, and perhaps even some of their grandparents were. The parents of many of today's young people first became consumers and started their working lives after liberalization.

While liberalization changed the whole economy and is often said to have benefited the middle classes, legislation has also favoured the lower castes, who are often India's poorest. Although caste discrimination was made illegal in the 1950 Constitution, social mobility among the lower castes has been negligible. One of the most significant political events in recent decades was the creation of the 'reservation' system – positive discrimination – in public-sector jobs and educational institutions, brought in after the 1990 Mandal Commission Report. Although proportions vary in different states and for different positions, the most famous outcome was the creation of a reservation quota of 27 per cent for low castes ('Other Backward Castes', or OBCs), who form over half of the population. Together with the reservations for Scheduled Castes and Tribes (including Dalits, formerly called 'Untouchables'), this means that 49.5 per cent of places in government-funded higher education and public-sector jobs are reserved. Post-liberalization has also seen the general rise of OBCs and then Dalits – especially in the north, where they have come to power by mobilizing caste politics, in particular with Mayawati's Dalit party, the BSP (Bahujan Samaj Party).

In an avowedly secular state, India's religion and politics are inexorably intertwined, and events associated with politicized religion have brought the nation to crisis at several points since liberalization – notably the communal riots and subsequent retaliation after the demolition of the Babri mosque in 1992 and the massive communal carnage in Gujarat in 2002 in the aftermath of the Godhra train fire. Although some tried to find underlying economic causes for these clashes, political scientist Christophe Jaffrelot says they are manifestations of militant ethno-religious ideology whereby political parties exploit communal issues. While Muslims form a minority, at around 12 per cent of the population, Hindutva, or Hindu nationalist, sentiments have voiced fears on the part of some Hindus that they are divided and weak, and the rise of global Islamophobia after 9/11 bolstered this rhetoric of fear about Islam's 'encircling' of Hinduism. Hindutva governments were elected in Delhi and in several states for the first time during the period considered by this book, most notoriously Gujarat's charismatic Chief Minister, Narendra Modi.

Other terrorist attacks, in particular those on the Indian Parliament in 2001, the various bomb blasts in many cities and the 26/11 (2008) attack on Mumbai by Pakistani members of Lashkar-e-Taiba, led to more anti-Islamist rhetoric in some quarters, although economic and other factors seem to have played a larger part in electoral politics of late than communalism. The regions of India manifest very different political cultures, with the north most caste-based and the west most pro-Hindutva, while the Shiv Sena, a local chauvinist party, has been powerful in Mumbai despite its lack of national electoral success. Bengal has seen the decline of communism, while Maoist insurgents have been increasingly active in parts of the east and centre of India.

The worlds of education and work have also changed. Caste-based reservations are commonly blamed by the middle classes for the increasing difficulty with which their sons and daughters can access government-sponsored higher education, but this may be due to inadequate educational provision for India's growing population. The new middle classes have tried to bypass this, and the state's inadequate healthcare provision, by patronizing private schools and hospitals, with those who have the financial resources even travelling overseas to obtain such facilities. Once, these privatized resources were possible only for the rich, but they are now accessible to growing numbers of the middle classes who have benefited from financial deregulation, including the opening of private banks and the availability of credit cards, mortgages and loans, as well as the rising Indian stock market, coupled with their growing incomes from new fields such as Business Processing Outsourcing (BPOs or call centres, mostly from overseas companies), media industries and the information technology (IT) sector. The latter now employs around 14 million people, although this is still far fewer than the 21 million people in government employment, whom the new middle classes generally resent for alleged idleness, wasting public money and being susceptible to corruption.

The middle class has transformed as these new *desi*, or non-Anglophone, elites have emerged with different backgrounds and different tastes. However, while they speak Indian languages other than English themselves, they want their children to learn English as a social marker and for career advancement. As privileged consumers, they are educated and often well travelled, but remain keenest on India's public culture, enjoying Bollywood rather than Hollywood and preferring Indian food to Western. It may be that they are not cosmopolitan but are rather conservative, despite their global networks. Typically, they work in the private sector and are segmented by new divisions of education, health and employment which seem to supplement, rather than replace, the old categories of class, caste and religion. The one social distinction which seems to be more firmly entrenched than ever is the division between the urban and the rural, even though post-liberalization has seen the rise of rich farmers in hinterland (*mofussil*) towns who have formed a small-town elite with massive consumerist clout while the majority of the rural population is still very poor.

Many members of the new middle classes are ambivalent about democracy, which they regard as mob (for which read lower-caste or poor) rule, and favour strong leaders – as was manifested in their support for Anna Hazare's anti-corruption campaign in 2011. They prefer to keep apart from poor India, shopping in the malls which only they and their like may enter, many of which have opened since the pioneering example set by Mumbai's Crossroads Mall in 1999. They are committed to a new India which has modern facilities and an improving infrastructure but which is otherwise neo-conservative. This class feels good about itself and about India and celebrates the global visibility of India and Indians. They have a desire for change and self-improvement which they will have to find outside politics and seem to be making choices at present as to whether to entrench their traditional values or embrace new ones. For example, a rise in alcohol consumption is being accompanied by an enforcement of hitherto-neglected permits for drinking on licensed premises.

Consumerism and economic growth do not benefit everyone and actively disadvantage others. The poor are excluded from this world and India still has parallel universes of modernity and feudalism. Poor Indians are barred from entering both the malls and the growing gated communities, unless they are workers or servants. Their wages may have risen but growth has sparked years of inflation, undermining the benefits. Adivasis or indigenous people (defined as 'tribals' by the Indian government) are often displaced by mining companies, for example, as they often do not have legal title to their land. Industrial development has moved farms away from cities and out of sight – and mind – of urban India. The massive agricultural labour force receives little government funding and has mainly come to wider attention through the issue of farmer suicides, portrayed in the film *Peepli (Live!)* (dir. Anusha Rizvi and Mahmood Farooqui, 2010).

One of the most important changes in India during the twenty-year period examined by this book is the advent of new-media technologies. The telecommunications revolution and the spread of mobile/cellular phones, plus the rise of the Internet and cable and satellite television have all occurred during these two decades. These have permitted a new kind of globalization and a new interconnectedness between India and the rest of the world.

Television has seen almost unprecedented growth. In the late 1980s there were two state television channels, but in 1991 STAR TV (bought by News Corporation in 1992) launched in India, bringing MTV, BBC, Star Plus and sports. Now there are hundreds of commercial channels which have penetrated the entire country, and television forms a bigger part of India's entertainment industry than film. Its content has seen the growth of new genres such as 24-hour news channels, domestic/female-oriented soap operas, reality shows and quizzes, as well as music- and film-based programmes.

Current affairs can be found on Internet news sites and via social media, but printed newspapers maintain a vast circulation and are in fact growing in all languages. Advertising has spread from print and state television to a range of commercial television channels as well as Internet and other sites, and its personnel often work in film and television, creating strong links between the media.

The poor and uneducated have less access to the media, which focus on large cities and metropolitan areas, with very little penetration of rural and poorer markets. However, they have mobilized cheaper technologies in unexpected ways. For example, cheap mobile phones are imported from China to be used as handheld devices that can be loaded with data and music, rather than for making expensive telephone calls.

India has a small readership for books in terms of population and certainly in comparison with cinema, but English-language publishers regard India as a potentially enormous market and, after some tentative steps in the early 1990s setting up local divisions of international firms, major multinational houses are now opening up, among a proliferation of local publishers. Despite the immense success of some best-selling authors, such as Chetan Bhagat, the non-English markets are larger, especially for Hindi, but these have not had the profile of the English-based press.

While cricket remains India's most popular sport, the days of listening on the radio to leisurely test matches have been replaced by one-day matches, and the IPL (Indian Premier League for cricket) is the focus of the Bollywood/business nexus of 'sports as entertainment', notably where cinema stars are owners of teams as well as the guests providing glamour in hospitality boxes.

Films have benefited from the media networks, with advertising – in particular for products endorsed by film stars – encouraging product placement, television boosting awareness of new films (especially through music) and the Internet and social networks being used for publicity by stars and production houses as well as for reviews. These various changes outside the film world have had a major impact on the making and viewing of Hindi cinema as well as shaping the film texts themselves. While later chapters pick up many of these issues for further discussion, the massive changes in the film industry itself require further discussion.

## The Hindi Film Industry

Mainstream Hindi cinema has never been quite a national cinema. It has had very little backing from the state, which has supported more realist forms of cinema, often known as 'festival cinema', through its funding bodies, notably the National Film Development Corporation and the National Film and Television Institute in Pune. There is still no film academy in Delhi. However, the government allowed the industry some access to insurance and funding by officially recognizing it in 1998, this late recognition date reflecting the old elites' disdain for mainstream film. This cinema does have some claim to being a national form, though, as it is funded and produced in India, made in the official language, Hindi, and consumed largely in India, too. Although Hindi cinema circulated worldwide from its earliest days, it became transnational or globalized during the period with which this book is concerned, not just in the sense of an increase in its overseas circulation and market penetration but also in that some films were made entirely overseas, and the overseas audience became increasingly important, especially financially, to producers. To this day Bollywood retains its private funding and its unique resistance to Hollywood, as Indian audiences who now have access to other cinemas still prefer their own, even while its content may be influenced by Hollywood. Indians are consuming a wide range of global media alongside film, and these have also influenced the film industry, the films and their audiences.

As well as having realist and other forms of cinema, India also has other major film industries, which are often referred to as 'regional'. It is true to say that the other cinemas have a more limited national reach, though they are immensely popular wherever the relevant language is spoken and in the overseas diaspora markets, and the viewership for their films can be as large as, if not larger than, their Hindi counterparts. Many successful Hindi films are remakes of south Indian language films, especially the comedies, which usually have a Telugu, Tamil or Malayalam original – or have even been made previously in more than one of these languages.

These other cinemas, notably Tamil and Telugu, target more closely imagined audiences, and so have a different sphere of reference among which the clear association with state and regional politics is clear. It is curious that the south Indian cinemas have been given relatively little scholarly attention (at least in English), considering the passion they arouse in critics, fans and others. Tamil cinema is flourishing and has produced a host of new, critically acclaimed film-makers. Marathi cinema, which has been making high-quality films since the early days, has recently made some extraordinary films examining, for example: contemporary issues of land and displacement (*Devrai/Sacred Grove*, dir. Sumitra Bhave and Sunil Sukthankar, 2004); farmer suicides (*Gabhricha paus/The Damned Rain*, dir. Satish Manwar, 2009); romances featuring senior citizens (*Uttarayan/ Journey to the Other Side*, dir. Bipin Nadkarni, 2005); and gender in the context of history and performance (*Natrang/Actor*, 2010, and *The Story of Balgandharva/Sound of Heaven*, 2011, both dir. Ravi Jadhav). No work could claim to be about Indian cinema without taking these other cinemas into consideration, and *Bollywood's India* deals only with mainstream Hindi cinema, in spite of connections that exist between the various cinemas, their makers and their audiences.

A wider study of Indian cinema would also include the country's realist cinemas, made in most of India's languages. Most famous of these are Satyajit Ray's Bengali films, many of which are adaptations of Bengali literary classics, negotiate between the old and the new and examine the worlds of different social groups, both contemporary and historical. Other forms of Hindi cinema have their own imagined worlds, whether that be the middle-class Hindi cinema of the 1970s and '80s made by Hrishikesh Mukherjee, the 'parallel' or 'middle', more realist cinema exemplified by the films of Shyam Benegal from the 1970s to the present or the 'indie' or *hatke* cinema made today, whose leading figure is the producer/director/ writer Anurag Kashyap.

Whatever its claims to being a national cinema, Hindi cinema has been important in shaping a national culture in India. Indian cinema before Independence operated under British censorship, but nationalist ideas circulated and also began to shape ideas of Indianness that had been forming in other media, from literature and theatre to visual culture. The new nation needed new mythologies, and cinema supplied these via the great film-makers of the 1950s, in particular the films of Raj Kapoor and also in Mehboob Khan's *Mother India* of 1957. In the former, the hero seeks romantic love and to create a new family after the fragmentation and disappointment – or just plain absence – of his parental family, but in the latter the woman embodies the divine nation and is rewarded by the state for her sacrifices. However, other film-makers queried the sacrifices made for the new India – poverty and rejection afflict the heroes of Bimal Roy's and Guru Dutt's darker films. Mainstream films rarely engaged with the problems of India, although wars and the frequent presence of the armed forces hinted at problems, while the Amitabh Bachchan films of the 1970s brought in a hero whose loyalty to his family led him to actions which were in conflict with the law and the modern state.

The films of the early 1990s were a range of melodramas about the family and the private sphere, concentrating on the heteronormative romance and how to bring the couple into the family structure. There were comedies of confusion over identities, especially in those directed by David Dhawan, and jokes about getting up to mischief in the family, but the main topics explored were the quest for partners, love and the boundaries of relationships – in the context of families threatened by other family members, notably the maternal uncle and stepmothers, who often used institutions such as the law to their advantage against the powerless good. It is Aditya Chopra's *Dilwale dulhania le jayenge* (often called *DDLJ*)/*The Braveheart Takes the Bride* (1995) that is really the point of departure for a new type of cinema and film practice that came to be called Bollywood.

Bollywood is currently the internationally recognized term for popular or mainstream Hindi cinema made in Mumbai (Bombay prior to 1995). Although the term is much disliked by many in the film industry, it has spread from its origins in the 1970s or 1980s, and being used mostly by the diaspora, to becoming the standard term in journalism and beyond. Most people limit the term to the popular Hindi cinema, but its historical reach is more nebulous. In academic circles, Bollywood is usually restricted to the last twenty or so years, when it became part of the wider globalized entertainment industry and in particular the glossy films aimed at the overseas market, which is more about branding India than about film. The Bollywood form of film was at the top end of the economic spectrum for both makers and audiences by the late 1990s, but in the 2000s it became the dominant form for even the aspirant classes. However, the old Hindi cinema has not vanished but carries on in the comedies, even as they get glossier and glossier, while regional films such as those made in Bhojpuri (spoken in Bihar) continue traditions of the lower-class

Raj (Shah Rukh Khan) and Simran (Kajol) on their European rail holiday in *DDLJ*.

Raj (Shah Rukh Khan) and Simran (Kajol) are reunited in Punjab in *DDLJ*.

films and the seeds of an 'independent' cinema are being sown by makers such as Anurag Kashyap and Dibakar Banerjee. Other forms of Hindi cinema have also emerged during these years, notably the multiplex/ independent (*hatke*) films, with their different values – more realistic and less concerned with being star vehicles – and different distribution networks, mentioned above.

Indian cinema is now a global phenomenon, though different in scale from that of Hollywood. Outside western Europe and the USA, it is hugely popular and is often preferred to local and Hollywood cinemas, celebrated as a non-Western form that upholds different traditions and values, in particular in its depiction of love within the larger family and a changing, often Westernizing, society.

Hindi cinema had little recognition in the West (Europe and North America) until the 1990s. Hindi films were screened there only for the diasporic Asian markets, but since the 1990s they have begun to find a niche interest and are now viewed in multiplex theatres, although they have only a limited penetration into mainstream audiences in Europe and America. This move was part of the massive changes that occurred in the India of the 1990s, including the media explosion, the shifts that took place within films and the cinema industry and a reorientation of government policy towards its relations with the global Indian diaspora.

## Producers and Makers

The Hindi film industry itself has changed from very loosely organized family ventures to corporate and professional ones. My own research with Yash Raj Films began shortly after the release of *DDLJ* (Aditya Chopra's *Dilwale dulhania le jayenge*, 1995), which changed the whole equation for the company. The production house went from a comfortable house in a smart residential complex to a vast integrated studio with offices, sound floors, screening theatre and so on and began to produce many more films. However, creative and business control of the company has remained within the family, although the founder, the late Yash Chopra, bemoaned the change from the family nature of the film unit to a corporate and impersonal set-up. Other production houses have also 'corporatized', notably UTV Motion Pictures – they are part of the wider media company UTV, which was partly bought by Disney after a valuation rumoured to be U.S.$900 million.

While the corporate changes may have allowed foreign investment and collaboration and provided a more professional basis to the industry, the view is not entirely positive. The unregulated and personal nature of relationships within film-making has changed, and the 'holiday' feel of an outdoor shoot has been replaced by a more clearly defined working relationship. The effect on the actual films is not clear as yet but is part of the professionalization of the industry, whose sometimes shambolic nature may well have generated its own form of spontaneous creativity.

Film-makers, as well as distributors and exhibitors, have their eye on the market and have to make their films with some calculations regarding finding their target audience. The powerful director–producers have to have a sound economic sense, and they want people to pay to watch their films, however much they see themselves as romantic artists, expressing themselves through cinema. Most of them imagine their audiences and speculate what will and will not work with this imagined audience in mind. Film-makers are increasingly aware of other cinemas, although they are often ignorant of Indian realist or art cinema and its history. The older generation of film-makers was economically distant from their audiences when the latter were the urban working class, while the younger generation of mainstream film-makers, who may seem distant from their audiences as mostly an educated, metropolitan elite, have an emotional understanding of their audiences which is essential to their success.

In the early 1990s, film-makers talked of their audiences as 'classes' and 'masses', and films were thought to appeal to one of these categories – the classes, also called the 'gentry', being the more upmarket segment who attended the more prestigious cinema halls – while the 'masses' were the lower-class audiences. The film-makers are primarily interested in the wealthy markets of the metropolitan cities and the diaspora, who provide the greatest revenue. The cinema audience in India has always been primarily urban, but revenues from the 'B' and 'C' circuits, where ticket prices are lower, are of decreasing significance to producers and distributors, whose major revenue comes from the expensive multiplexes and from selling television and DVD rights. Some of these audiences are now so remote from Bollywood that they are making their own local productions, whether that be the expanding Bhojpuri-language film industry or tales such as that of film-makers in the town of Malegaon told in *Supermen of Malegaon* (dir. Faiza Ahmad Khan, 2008).

Multiplex cinemas, mostly located in new malls, have become elite destinations, while the single-screen cinemas, despite their striking, often Art Deco, architecture, are falling into disrepair. These new multiplexes show that the audience's urban viewing space is also about one's place in the world, as space, buildings, economy and taste are part of consumerism and advertising.

While Indian film audiences are proportionately quite low as regards the ratio of cinema halls to population, nothing is known about how many people see pirated films. Piracy is rampant in India, and pirated films can be found across the entire country. The audience is also often fragmented, with individual spectators viewing films on small screens, usually televisions or computers but also tablets, mobile phones and other devices. The Internet, too, has had a huge impact on the film world, with people able to watch forms varying from pirated or legally downloadable films (with some films even being premiered online) to YouTube extracts. While Indian cinema audiences have long been known for their 'audience participation' at screenings, and also for the circulation of film songs in other social settings, from *antaksharis* (a kind of singing competition) to weddings, Internet viewings are also far from being just passive consumption. The Internet has allowed film (or rather its digital form) to enter into the highly popular forms of social networking, with YouTube extracts posted on networking sites and reviews appearing on newspaper pages or blogs, while stars and other film personalities are active on Twitter and marketing sites.

Hindi cinema pervades other forms of media, too. Even the English novel set in India seems to have its Bollywood section, mostly to show a bit of local colour and reference some of the kitschy features, although a few make a genuine tribute, notably most of Salman Rushdie's novels after *Midnight's Children* (1981). Films about India often refer to the world of Hindi film; for example, *Slumdog Millionaire* (dir. Danny Boyle, 2009) refers directly through mentioning the stardom of Amitabh Bachchan but also indirectly through its stars (notably Anil Kapoor) and its music (A. R. Rahman), including a pseudo-Bollywood dance at the end. In other words, Hindi film, or rather Bollywood, spreads beyond its actual audiences.

The non-film media are also major sites for consolidation of the stardom created by films. Superstar Shah Rukh Khan's considerable wealth is built on many non-filmic activities, such as owning an Indian Premier League cricket team, having a substantial property portfolio and being a brand ambassador via advertising premium products as well as endorsing many FMCGs (fast-moving consumer goods). Aamir Khan Productions makes few, but highly successful, films and he is now building on his image to make television programmes – his acclaimed talk-show series *Satyamev jayate/Only Truth Prevails* has engaged with social issues from female foeticide to pesticides.

The stars have remained the major focus for gossip and their sexuality lies at the heart of the discussions. The film-makers and stars are imagined by the audiences through gossip, which circulates in famous star magazines such as *Stardust*, but also through the Internet, whether official newspages or social media. The three major Hindi film stars of the period covered by this book, Shah Rukh Khan (SRK), Aamir Khan and Salman Khan (who are not related), all have fan followings according to their images, created by the media and themselves. Shah Rukh is the diasporic superstar and the face of the new India; Aamir is the thinking one; Salman is the eternal kid, the ideal body and the Everyman. There has not been a major female superstar during this period as roles for women in mainstream cinema have become more marginalized and they have become celebrities on account of their beauty and style rather than because of their films.

Much of the discussion around films circulates in English, which is the metalanguage of the Hindi film, used widely throughout the production process, whether in the offices, during direction or in legal documents or censorship. However, although the Hindi film in some ways seems part of the elite English aspect of globalization in India, English has encroached little into the films themselves, although there are key stock phrases, such as saying 'I love you', and English also filters into lyrics, while the protagonist of *English Vinglish/English, Whatever* (dir. Gauri Shinde, 2012), for example, silenced by her lack of English, pursues its study as the main story of the film.

Bollywood films have retained their popularity with the educated elite, who watch the top-quality films of Yash Chopra, Karan Johar and Mani Ratnam alongside *hatke* films and foreign films ranging from mainstream Hollywood to world cinema. India remains the only country outside the USA which prefers its own cinema to that of Hollywood, so it is not surprising that the Hollywood studios have tried to produce Hindi films, such as Sony Pictures' *Saawariya/Beloved* (dir. Sanjay Leela Bhansali, 2007) and Warner's *Chandni Chowk to China* (dir. Nikhil Advani, 2009), but these were box-office flops and the companies soon withdrew. Disney, after the unsuccessful *Roadside Romeo* (dir. Jugal Hansraj, 2008), has now invested in UTV, while Reliance Big Pictures have bought into Steven Spielberg's DreamWorks.

However, Hindi film does not exist in isolation. Its makers watch Hollywood, and increasingly films from other parts of Asia such as Korea and Hong Kong, from which they draw inspiration (or even copy directly), keeping the hybrid nature of the Hindi film, and its music in particular.

Although it would be difficult to avoid Hindi cinema culture in India, at least in the urban north, not everyone in the country watches the films. Many choose not to view them, preferring Western cinema or other forms of entertainment and the arts. This is not the cinema of the have-nothings, who rarely see films and, if they do, do not see these ones. This is for the world of the haves, the know-they-will-soon-haves and the aspirants who are still far from having. These are people who can make economic choices. This film viewing links them to the world of the trans-national Indian middle classes who see these films elsewhere in the world, alongside other forms of international and local media. These classes choose what to watch and this shapes how they see the world. The worlds traced in *Bollywood's India* are not restricted to the Indian nation but focus on these transnational middle and upper middle classes.

In 1998, the social and cultural critic Ashis Nandy said that the Hindi cinema represented the 'slum's eye view', but films during the last twenty years have become more closely associated with the new middle classes, who were initially from a lower middle and upper working class. Films at the beginning of this period showed fantasies of rich lifestyles, but the super-rich seen in contemporary films are now living out these dreams in India. The films have mostly avoided the depiction of the lower classes themselves, with even the 'poor' looking fairly prosperous and usually ending up wealthy by the end of the film. Films which have realistic depictions of the poor and key social issues are rarely found within the mainstream, but only in the realist/art/'festival' cinema and the new forms of 'indie' cinema, which are watched mainly by the urban elites.

Political films or those which directly seek social change are mostly confined to realistic cinema. That said, Hindi cinema is not as reactionary as it is often thought to be, but it is primarily an entertainment cinema which seeks to maximize its audiences through having a broad appeal, unlike some of the south Indian cinemas, which are closely connected to state politics. However, given the cinema's feeling for the zeitgeist, as the 1950s were 'Nehruvian' at least in part, a connection with the current political climate, as well as broader social issues, cannot be ignored. Hindi film mostly espouses vaguely liberal political views but sees electoral politics as corrupt; it has little interest in the concept of universal rights but is concerned with the politics of everyday justice, mostly within the family, which is regarded as a benevolent institution.

## Cinema, the Imagination and Dreams

A history of films in the period covered by *Bollywood's India* – that is, 1991 to the present – is yet to be written as changes have been rapid, trends may lead to dead ends and success is unpredictable. *Bollywood's India* aims to interpret the films and to contextualize them within a study of contemporary India and its wider culture. It does this by focusing on the films themselves and their analysis, while making connections with other films and non-cinematic events. It draws on observations acquired from repeated viewings of films, reading about films in books, online and in newspapers, talking to people and spending time with directors, producers and actors, but it does not draw on detailed interviews and instead keeps the focus on the films themselves. It also seeks to gain cultural understanding by looking at the imagined worlds created within the films, which shape elements of people's understanding of themselves and their lives in different ways. It would have been wonderful to have had audience ethnographies to work from, with details of who watched which films, what they thought of them and why. While the chance for initial views on the older films has gone, even responses in interviews with current audiences would need considerable unpacking and analysis. Audiences have different ways of watching films. Sometimes they are just watching to see the star, or they may be watching ironically, or watching and feeling bored. They may be watching the afterlife of a film in other media. But, for many, these films are a passion, a way of dreaming about the world; a way of seeing how topics may be raised and how they are dealt with along lines that can be shaped into narratives, into modes of viewing, emotional responses, stardom, words and lyrics that then form part of everyday life.

Cinema is often regarded as dreamlike by scholars such as Siegfried Kracauer, who see it as daydreams about society where reality is foregrounded. Hindi cinema can also be seen as a modern mythology, a unique repository of India's public imaginings, shaped by fantasy, nostalgia and desire, and it is one of the most productive arenas for discerning clearer patterns of India's social imaginaries, which show how India sees itself today, how it hopes to see itself in future and how it views its past. However, these imagined worlds of cinema are not unique to India, nor is this in any way implying oriental fantasies and dreaming. The imagination, as Arjun Appadurai argues, is different from fantasy and escapism as it is an active force, fuelling action and creating fields of possibility for the individual. It can also be collective, playing a key role in what Benedict Anderson calls 'imagined communities', where a people imagine themselves as a community or nation. *Bollywood's India* looks at Hindi films as a collective imagined text, as both art and culture and also as part of the everyday world of ordinary people.

The imagining seen in Bollywood offers an understanding of how an important section of modern India sees itself and shapes ideas of how things are and how they could or should be. It is neither revolutionary nor conformist, but it may show elements of how new conceptions of the world are being shaped by the film-makers, who turn these conceptions into films which allow others to share them as part of a larger public. This massively popular cinema seems a good source to access for looking at imagined lives and worlds, as it offers an invitation to dream rather than holding a mirror up to society. Like the image itself, one can look close up or in long shot. It can bring the audience into reality and moves them away from it, too.

The imaginary worlds of mainstream Indian cinema have changed rapidly. For example, although many classic Hindi films are about failed struggles against society where the hero dies (*Devdas*, 1955; *Mother India*, 1957; *Sholay*, 1975; *Deewaar*, 1975), recent Bollywood films depict Indians feeling good about themselves. They are a younger generation, people from 'middle India' who have known little else other than success. Yash Chopra's films from the 1960s onwards were striking for showing modern wealthy lifestyles, which has now become standard in many films as well as being an actuality for the few.

Consuming media is everyday and ordinary, but it may also be actively creative if it changes and challenges existing ideas and beliefs or if the texts are read negatively or in imaginative and unlikely ways. Media may connect people in unexpected ways while they also divide them by drawing them into other imagined worlds. Cinema provides cultural capital for upward mobility. Audiences borrow from and mimic characters in films rather than their peers to create a style that they can use to resist other worldviews. An example in India would be Amitabh Bachchan's 'angry young man' films from the 1970s and '80s, where he uses style and language as means of resisting humiliation and oppression. Although there is a huge market in self-help books in India, film remains a guide to life and lifestyle, from what to wear and how to speak to how to fall in love and live a family life.

Hindi films are about hopes and dreams, fears and wishes. Films create dreams but they are also dreams or fantasies themselves. There is no clear link and no reflection between these worlds. Cinema allows the viewer to fantasize, to imagine new possibilities, new lives, new looks, new ways of doing things, as they enable narcissistic pleasure by eliding boundaries between the viewer's body and the rest of the world.

The melodramatic mode focuses on emotion and feelings in a world that is ultimately just. The moral dilemmas, the fantasies, the ideals and crises may be culturally specific. Indeed, cinema may be a new mythology, albeit one located in its predecessors. The *Mahabharata*, the great Indian epic poem, deals with a dysfunctional family and the machinations of power – themes taken up in Hindi films and TV soap operas today. The epic is told in self-contained episodes, each of which has a conclusion, while the whole story finishes with the end of a *yuga* ('aeon'), the most definitive ending of all. Films, which need a resolution, tend to be more conciliatory, the fantasy greater, with the focus on how to restore moral order, while television dramas show the problems of ongoing conflict in their continuous and episodic narratives.

*Bollywood's India* explores some key aspects of films in order to think about what these imagined worlds are and how they relate to the real world. It offers a way of looking at them as entertainment to see what makes some entertain and satisfy their audiences. What are the fantasies they show? Why do people go to see these films? Some of it is 'timepass', just something to do to pass the time, but why do audiences prefer certain films over others? Some films offer a way of thinking about things, raising issues every bit as serious as those dealt with by the various surveys carried out across a wider India – and indeed most countries – that ask selected interviewees direct questions and collect facts. Here the questions are raised by the films themselves, but often in ways that are subconscious yet are important to the interaction of the audience and the film, why the film becomes popular and how the audience reacts. Audiences differ, with some being fairly passive while others actively construct meanings, or they may copy or emulate styles and manners from the film and prefer certain stars to others. The most successful Hindi films interest people by focusing their attention through emotions, spectacle and music and allow them to think and feel about people and situations in ways in which they can form new concepts themselves.

Hindi films are often discussed as if they were bad films in terms of aesthetics, coherence and even sense, but *Bollywood's India*, which is based on a deep appreciation of these texts, is interested in why some have a particular appeal to the audience, seeking to see if they create particular fantasies and how those fantasies are sometimes transformed into dreams in everyday life – if not into life itself. Most people have rather dull lives, unlike those depicted in films.

The method of exploring films in *Bollywood's India* is shaped by a very loose interpretation of psychoanalysis, a way of looking at films and making links into a plausible narrative – a narrative which is productive in itself, more than just watching the films, rather opening up the subtexts, other stories and possibilities (including both those that the films hint at and those that they present in such a blatant way that they might be ignored out of embarrassment). Psychoanalysis, which has dominated film studies for much of its history, has been the major way of reading melodrama, while star theory has used this and gone beyond it to include economic and other bases in the theories of stardom developed by Richard Dyer.

The films discussed here, like literary texts, develop meaning in excess of what the makers intended. The latter presumably always intend to make a path-breaking hit film, but this is rarely what happens. The film's director and the team create meanings, but not necessarily those that the audience shares. Film-makers themselves can be cynical and stars can be complacent. The film takes on meanings which are shaped by its audiences over time. Films get the audience to do certain things (sit down, be quiet, watch), but Indian film audiences – at least outside the expensive multiplexes – also rebel against such behaviours by participating: shouting, whistling and so on as if it were a live performance.

There is no consensus that underlines the films, but there are commonly held values. Readings are only suggestions of possibilities rather than absolutes. The films do not set out to give an analysis of the questions raised in this book – or not all of them. Some films do, as they raise questions about marriage, love and the family; films may skirt certain issues or not answer them fully, but at least they invite the audience to enter into a debate. Often, the issues raised deliberately may not be of much interest, while those raised unintentionally are. There is a two-way dynamic as social changes also influence the films – so evolving views on beauty are not shaped just by the films but by fashion, advertising and so on. The films not only celebrate the wealth and leisure of the new India but look at new anxieties raised by consumerism such as competition and the need for recognition.

Throughout, *Bollywood's India* looks at the bare minimum of components of film as being audio, visual, narrative and the star. The stars are the focus of ideals of beauty and romance, and, like the other key elements, they are discussed throughout the book. The characters that build up the star text may amount to something greater than the films. So, just as Amitabh Bachchan was Vijay from the 1970s, so Shah Rukh Khan was Rahul from the 1990s, and their characters, often confused with the star text, also become part of the public imagination.

The narratives are discussed not as plots but as myths which tie together the world of the film, reaching out to people to shape their emotions and thoughts as the films live in memory, imagination and dreams. Cinema shapes lives, offers cinemagoers ways of thinking along with providing a guide to living – a way of examining emotional and moral issues, a guide to life itself. If a Hindi film does not do this then it is not working. The films provide representations, emotions and narratives from which the audience has to decide what they want, choosing to allow some films to work on an emotional level.

Hindi film songs are mentioned throughout the chapters, so here it must be said that they have a central importance. This is not for breaking up the narrative but for bringing together music, language and images to give a special depth and concentration to the imaginary, whether in the repetition of words in choruses, the outfits worn for the songs, the locations or the dancing and display of emotions and sexuality – all of which can be recalled later when just the humming of a tune evokes an imagined world. While 'The American Dream', so-called, is widely acknowledged, 'The Indian Dream' is not. *Bollywood's India* hopes to provide an initial exploration of this by looking at Hindi film, the major source of India's dreaming.

## The Selection of Films

The films which were chosen for my book *100 Bollywood Films* (2005) are used mostly as the reference for the pre-1991 films, while *Bollywood's India* concentrates on 1991 to 2012. For the main period discussed in this book, the major source has been the list of hits according to www.boxofficeindia.com, one of many websites to report cinema ticket sales for Hindi films and which seems as (un)reliable as any other. However, discussions sometimes include films which fall more into the *hatke/* multiplex genre whose audiences also include India's new middle classes. Although these films were not major hits, and are very different from the mainstream, they were successful with the niche audiences and created much critical debate in the mainstream media as well as on Internet sites.

As with other mass media, there are some statistics but it is hard to profile cinemagoers sociologically, especially given the current rates of piracy and viewing practices beyond the cinema halls. Popularity is one of the means used here (box office), but films are remembered differently and form a history of contemporary cinema even when not box-office hits in their time. For example, *Silsila/The Affair* (dir. Yash Chopra, 1981), while not hugely popular at the time of release, is now a classic, whereas other films that were hits are barely remembered today.

The comedies of the 2000s have been some of the greatest hits, yet they have not been discussed by scholars and are often disparaged by critics as they are seen as vulgar embarrassments which display the awkwardness of the emerging middle class. However, these films are important in terms of their depiction of 'the good life' and other values, showing us aspirations, ideals, obsessions and fantasies.

Some films are included simply because I like them and I have seen them several times. It is not surprising that I am not fond of rape or vigilante films, while I love religious dramas and silly comedies as well as the romance, social and *hatke* films. I have favourite stars, as is quite clear from the text, as I count myself as what Henry Jenkins calls an 'acafan' (www.henryjenkins.org) – that is, an academic and a fan of Hindi cinema at one and the same time. I hope I have conveyed my passion for these films and am sure that debates about my choices and interpretations will be lively.

ONE

# Unity: The Nation, Its History and Trans-nationalism

Hindi films are often concerned with what it means to be 'Indian' in a way that exceeds the official definition of citizenship. They query the concept of Indianness – Does one have to be born in India? Believe in 'Indian values' (defined within the film)? Have parents who were born in India? Can one stop being Indian? Such questions are in large part to do with domestic changes that have altered the definition from the understanding of the term that was formed up to and after 1947, famously explored in Nehru's book *The Discovery of India* (1946), where national boundaries and limits of Indianness were well-defined, to one which is no longer bound by the nation state. This chapter examines how Bollywood defines Indianness, relating it to ideas of the past and ideas of the future and looking at how overseas Indians are part of this Indianness and how important Indianness is today.

## Understanding the Past as a Guide to the Present

The late 1980s was a critical moment in the history of Indian media and also transformative in public understandings of Indian history and culture. India's state television, Doordarshan, broadcast two lengthy series of the two great epics. Ramanand Sagar's *Ramayana* was first transmitted in January 1987 and ran for 74 episodes. It was soon followed by B. R. Chopra's *Mahabharata*, which had 94 episodes and broke all records of viewing statistics with its audience penetration. Serials based on often-told stories or myths were viewed as Indian history that provided lessons for the present. The massive impact of these series on Indian politics is undisputed: they helped mobilize Hindu nationalism as stories of the new postcolonial nation were displaced by the mythological origins of India as Bharat. The television serials were a new way of telling the epics, and although they drew on earlier versions, they came to be seen as the standard view, watched by all communities across the length and breadth of India at the same time every Sunday morning.

The mythological film, India's founding film genre, presented ideas of the past which were read as history by many people who view the *Mahabharata* as ushering in the current aeon (*yuga*) and who believe that Rama ruled Ayodhya 5,000 years ago. By the late 1940s, the mythological film had moved into a b-genre and fewer of them were being made, although there was the occasional success of one of these in the mainstream, notably the huge hit *Jai Santoshi Maa* (Hail Santoshi Maa, dir. Vijay Sharma, 1975). However, it was the two television series mentioned above which conflated history and mythology in new ways and reached such enormous audiences. Films throughout the century have also reconsidered history via their historical genre. Film is one of the most powerful media from which to learn history and is often the only way that people know about history at all.

Hindi cinema interprets Indian history, telling stories about the nation whether under threat or victorious, looking at sexuality and gender, looking at great figures of the past, implying a contrast with the present, and considering other such themes – rather than trying to represent accurately the given historical moment. The past is used, then, as a heterotopia, or another place, more often than as a heterochronia, or different time. The past shown in the film can then tell us more about the present than the present itself can.

These are not the official views of history, based on facts and archives or research monographs written by professional historians. Indian cinema's history belongs instead to another kind of history – a popular view of the past, sometimes called 'bazaar history', whose stories and images derive from epics, poems, theatre, and folktales. This kind of history is closely linked to the urban theatre that emerged in the nineteenth century, the Parsi theatre, and to the mass-produced image enabled by calendar art (chromolithography) and photography.

The power of cinema's history is that it often replaces academic history in the public imagination. Indian cinema's history is not about truth nor is it an enquiry into truth. It is a presentation of the past built on images, words and the imagination. It is interested in rumour and gossip, to which facts are subsidiary. History must be told as plots, not events. Cinema is created imaginatively, using image, music and dialogue as the foundations upon which its own poetry and metaphor are developed and elaborated with gesture and costume to create a sensibility. History has to be shown in ways that suit the features of the films and their genres.

The form of the Hindi film, with its attractions of spectacle and star power, lends itself well to the demands of the historical genre. Indian cinema audiences like familiar stories and historical stories allow for ritualization, repetition and overvaluation of the past. These historical narratives suit the melodramatic mode of the Hindi cinema as they focus on crises and conflicts over power, legitimacy and identity through encounters with sickness and medicine, morality and the law and ethics and religion in a way that stirs up emotions. The films focus on topics that are common to historical narratives of struggle, sacrifice and patriotism. The historical film is particularly skilled at depicting the nation in crisis, so the films are about the melodrama of the nation itself, not just its heroes and heroines who are struggling and often sacrificing their lives in its cause.

Hindi films are often 'star vehicles', and so the historical film is often history as the story of individuals and families, where a well-known historical figure is played by a major star. The star embodies national sexual and gendered values, thus the historical film allows societal and economic values from the present to be transferred to the past as those associated with the star are ascribed to the historical figure and vice versa. The star is a melodramatic figure known beyond their films and brings to film his or her other characters, as well as lending iconicity to the historical character while being part of history her/himself.

Cinema itself is also part of India's history, and it does not just reflect official or academic history but supplements it. The Hindi film, with its enormous audiences, is closely connected to other forms of culture such as theatre, literature and television, which helps to create a common-sensical, consensual view of history. The historicals are not the products of directors who are historians manqués but rather the products of commercial film-makers aiming to reach the widest audiences using the form of the film. Although some film-makers do carry out historical research, it is the film form and its requirements which dominate.

## The Historical Film in Hindi Cinema

Indian cinema's genres are notoriously fuzzy. They are hard to define, but producers, audiences and critics seem to have no problem in identifying each one when they see it. The historical is loosely defined as any film set in the past. The Hindi historical film has many forms, themes and sub-genres, which overlap with other Hindi film genres. Some of these sub-genres are shared with Hollywood, others not, and include the social drama set in the past – often called costume drama, the war film, the biopic and patriotic films. In other words, there is no narrow generic definition.

The historical genre in particular adapts and alters its form according to when the film is made as well as the time in which the film is set. For, while historical films are about contemporary sensibilities and a present understanding of the world, the genre also looks at historical issues, connecting the present to the past.

The historical has always been closely linked to ideas of nationalism, and in India it has created new myths for the new nation by reinterpreting the past. Interesting regional nationalisms also play their part. While Indian cinema favoured the historical as one of its genres, different regions have focused on different subjects, so films about the iconic leader Shivaji

(1627–80) were particularly popular in what is now Maharashtra from the 1920s.

Many arts reconsider history as a way of dealing with change in society. In the modern world, we seek narratives that deal with change, though the representation of vanishing ways of life, while engaged in modern activities, can make displacement feel more like mobility and rootlessness feel more like liberation. Viewers may also indulge in the pleasure of nostalgia, which, as Svetlana Boym argues, is not only 'a sentiment of loss and displacement, but . . . is also a romance with one's own fantasy'. Nostalgia, this longing for another place and another time, finds particular scope in the historical film, whether the viewers are in India or perhaps even more if they are in the diaspora, and it is immaterial whether or not they have experienced the time and place depicted on-screen.

The historical genre's imagining of India has changed as India has changed. At Independence, when the country needed new ways of thinking about itself, the historical genre helped to create new foundational myths for a new nation. Just as *Cleopatra* (dir. Joseph Mankiewicz, 1963) brought at least a temporary end to the great historical epic in Hollywood, so *Mughal-e-Azam/The Great Mughal* (dir. K. Asif, 1960) was the last of the great historical epics in India for a long time: the genre became too expensive to make and too risky for producers to back. Audiences turned to the new musical romances in colour, whose high fashions and exotic locations mark nascent consumerism in Indian cinema in the mid-1960s. Although there were still films being shot with historical settings and references to recent historical events, as well as mythologicals, it took 40 years for the A-grade historical epic to return.

It seems that this revival was partly to do with new technology and partly to do with trends in Hollywood, to which Hindi cinema is closely linked. The epic historical film re-emerged in Hollywood around the early 2000s as CGI (computer-generated imagery) allowed the recreation of great spectacle, as seen in *Titanic* (dir. James Cameron, 1997). Although this was one of the most expensive films ever made, its huge success inspired other historicals, including the hit *Gladiator* (dir. Ridley Scott,

2000). The relation of these to the Indian historical epic is close and there have been many jokes that *Titanic* was really a Bollywood film made in Hollywood.

As the 'new India' has emerged in the last decade, yearning to be a global power, it needs new ways of viewing its past as it plans its new future. The historical Hindi films being made today are helping to lay the foundations for a history aimed at their viewership's class, forming part of what could be called a new middle-class history of India, which is also being shaped in school texts and political discourses. These films are peopled by their own types rather than by historically accurate figures. They feature religion, family, tradition, modernity and how India relates to the rest of the world – all working around the Hindi film form itself.

The year 2001 saw the sudden revival of A-grade historical cinema with several films: *Asoka* (in which the great Buddhist emperor romances and dances; dir. Santosh Sivan); *Gadar – ek prem katha/Turmoil: A Love Story* (a Partition story with our Sikh hero single-handedly taking on the Pakistan army; dir. Anil Sharma); and the Oscar-nominated *Lagaan: Once Upon a Time in India* (featuring a cricket match which lasts longer than a Hollywood film; dir. Ashutosh Gowariker). A series of biopics such as Mani Ratnam's *Guru* (2007), whose central character shares many features with business tycoon Dhirubhai Ambani, and several films about the freedom fighter Bhagat Singh, were also made during the early years of revival – a revealing litmus test to indicate which individual's biographies are deemed to be interesting and how the films reveal history through the lives of real people.

## Ancient India

The founding genre of Indian cinema was the mythological genre, which draws on tales of gods and goddesses and heroes and heroines, mostly from Hindu sources. This love of mythology is hardly unique to Indian cinema – Cecil B. DeMille said 'God is box office' and the first Indian film was made in 1913 partially because its director, D. G. Phalke, was directly inspired by seeing a film called *The Life of Christ* (probably a film of a Passion Play). However, given the popularity of the previously mentioned mythological television series, interpreted as the history of India and its culture, it is surprising that, beyond television screenings of the epics, historical stories of ancient India feature rarely in films. Myths do not show ancient India but mythological India. This is despite attention being given outside film to politically motivated discussions about sacred geography where mythological and historical narratives are conflated, for example the Ram Setu, the bridge to Lanka in the *Ramayana*, and the contested connections between ancient archaeological sites and Vedic texts. Myths and legends were often used in cinema in the service of Indian nationalism, especially before Independence. A striking example is Vijay Bhatt's *Ram Rajya/The Kingdom of God* (1942), whose title evokes Gandhi's vision of India as the Kingdom of God.

Sivan's *Asoka* featured the superstar Shah Rukh Khan in the role of the Indian emperor Asoka (or Ashoka) the Great, who united much of India in the third century BC. Asoka's greatness is founded upon his unification of much of what is now modern India, which was followed by his conversion to Buddhism after experiencing a series of terrible

The romance of Ashoka (Shah Rukh Khan) and Kaurwaki (Kareena Kapoor) in *Asoka*.

wars. His edicts, inscribed on pillars and rocks, are the oldest writing in India that can be read, and the Asoka *chakra* ('wheel') features on the flag of India, representing the turning of the wheel of *dharma* – that is, law and virtue. The film focuses on the warrior prince and his romance, taken from folktales, with Princess Kaurwaki and barely features his conversion and renunciation. *Asoka* follows the pattern of a typical Hindi film, with Shah Rukh Khan fighting, romancing the star Kareena Kapoor and dancing. Ancient India is portrayed as the land of warriors rather than religious thinkers with Buddhism only mentioned right at the end of the film. *Asoka* was not, however, well received, as audiences felt it was disrespectful to a national hero and of little historical interest.

## Medieval India

Also popular in early Indian cinema was another religious genre, the devotional, which overlaps closely with the historical film. These are biopics about religious devotees, or *bhaktas*, from the medieval period who often challenged contemporary orthodoxy. Some of the most famous examples were made by the Prabhat Studios in Pune and were closely tied to Maharashtrian history. In the 1930s these contained an overt Gandhian message, usually concerning caste. They also incorporated Mahadev Ranade's nationalist vision of the *bhakti*/'devotional' medieval Hinduism movement, bringing the heroic leader Shivaji into the *bhakti* cult and showing him as a man of God, not just a fearless warrior. In perhaps one of the greatest films ever made in India, *Sant Tukaram/Saint Tukaram* (dir. Damle and Fattelal, 1936), Shivaji is portrayed as listening to the guidance of Tukaram (early seventeenth century), showing his acceptance of a low-caste, saintly form of religion.

This devotional genre has not been popular in recent years, and medieval India is usually represented by the Mughal film. This is a sub-genre of the Islamicate film – that is, films which show the culture of India's Muslims, rather than films which examine Islam in India. The

Islamicate historical films show the integral role of Muslims in India's intertwined culture, rather than seeing them as a discrete minority. They reveal nostalgic affection for the figure of the Muslim as a cultured ruler who enjoyed good relations with his Hindu subjects. They are not about the history of Muslims in India but instead celebrate a particular way of promoting composite culture. Thus, while we have films about many of the Great Mughals, including Humayun, Jehangir and Akbar, there is none about Aurangzeb, who promoted a more narrowly Islamic vision of India.

The story of the Great Mughal, Akbar (r. 1556–1605), has been told through numerous media, not least nineteenth-century Parsi theatre and many film versions. These draw on the history of the bazaar rather than the large chronicles and archives of Akbar's reign, such as Abu'l Fazl's *Akbarnama*, the *A'in-i Akbari* and Bada'uni's *Muntakhab at-Tawarikh*. The images are much more those of tourist India, in particular Agra and Fatehpur Sikri, rather than the illustrations of the *Akbarnama*. The story of Akbar had its greatest moment with 1960's magnificent film *Mughal-e-Azam*, whose narrator is India personified, telling the story of the new nation. Again, however, the narrative here is of romance and family

Akbar (Hrithik Rosha) at the darbar in *Jodhaa Akbar*.

history about the love of Prince Salim, later Emperor Jahangir, for a court dancer, Anarkali, rather than the social or political impact of Akbar's rule.

*Jodhaa Akbar* (dir. Ashutosh Gowariker, 2008) dealt with the other famous story about Akbar, namely his marriage to a (Hindu) Rajput princess, Jodhaa. Although seen as a strategic alliance to consolidate his unification of India, this marriage is also celebrated as showing his respect for Hinduism and other religions in an early form of Indian secularism – that is, equal regard for all religions. The film also presents Akbar as very much an Indian rather than a Persian-speaking central Asian outsider, as the Great Mughals are regarded by Hindu nationalists. Like the other films about the Mughals, *Jodhaa Akbar* engages with present-day debates, notably that on intercommunal marriage and the role of Muslims in shaping India's history.

*Jodhaa Akbar* features two of Bollywood's biggest stars, Hrithik Roshan and Aishwarya Rai. Despite displaying skills in elephant training and martial arts, the royal couple is played as a middle-class unit. The Hindu wife wants to feed her husband as part of her wifely duties, cooking a vegetarian feast (although Rajputs are non-vegetarian) to establish herself as a good Hindu wife as well as the power behind the throne. Although Akbar's mother is very welcoming to her daughter-in-law, the

Preparations for Jodhaa's feast in *Jodhaa Akbar.*

evil wet-nurse, Maham Anga, plays the wicked mother-in-law in a manner familiar from the popular *saas-bahu* (mother/daughter-in-law) genre of Indian television. The film allows for much Bollywood spectacle, from Akbar's taming of a rogue elephant to the huge song-and-dance number, 'Marhaba' – performed by Akbar's grateful subjects on the lifting (at Jodhaa's suggestion) of the *jazia* tax on Hindu pilgrims and featuring a display of national diversity and unity and a show of weaponry and power in the format of the present Republic Day parades.

It is not entirely clear whether Jodhaa ever existed, as Akbar had many wives, yet even biopics of possibly fictional characters, based on bazaar history, can be contested. The Karni Sena (a Rajput group) claimed Jodhaa was not the daughter of Bahrmal of Amer and was married to Salim, Akbar's son. This led to a ban on the film in several north Indian states, while Hindu nationalists objected to the benign portrayal of Akbar as protector of Hindus and demonstrated against its screening.

## A Struggle for Freedom

Epic historical films – that is, those with known historical characters, made on a grand scale, with battles, palaces and elaborate costumes – were never common, not least for financial reasons, but they include some remarkable movies. In Hindi cinema this sub-genre was very much in the service of Indian nationalism both before and after Independence. Sohrab Modi's films were always nationalist portrayals of heroic figures of freedom, such as Porus, who fought Alexander the Great (*Sikandar*, 1941), Emperor Jehangir (*Pukar*, 1939) and Rani Laxmibai of Jhansi (*Jhansi ki rani*, 1952), also released in English as *The Tiger and the Flame*. These films emphasize the nobility of Indian kings and aristocrats, while Muslim rulers and Rajput nobles are shown working together for the good of the country.

Even rarer is the costume drama – that is, a historical which does not feature real people. The revival of the historical film in the 2000s began with another major star, Aamir Khan, producing and acting in *Lagaan* (2001), which was shortlisted for an Oscar as Best Foreign Film. The film's story of heroic struggle, familiar from many other types of film, had numerous features that were unusual for Hindi films at the time. The film is set in an ordinary village rather than in spectacular locations around the world. *Lagaan* contains no references to bourgeois and Western values, having a subaltern viewpoint and upholding the peasant perspective rather than that of the merchant or businessman so popular in 1990s films. One of the greatest differences is that *Lagaan* upholds inclusive community values, rejecting divisions of caste, region and religion, rather than focusing on family values or tub-thumping patriotism. There are villains among the British but it is the villain's sister who teaches the Indians how to play cricket. The film also pays less lip service than was usual to religiosity and ritual, except for the folk songs and dances with their religious references, with the temple seen as a public space rather than one of worship.

Yet this film did not set a trend for other films and the biopic, or biographical movie, became the major form of the historical after *Lagaan*. While 'middle' or 'parallel' Indian cinema has produced biopics on several of India's political leaders, this genre has not been popular in mainstream Hindi cinema. The Bollywood film form has a problem with showing nationalist leaders on screen as they are seen as being too revered, saintly and uncontroversial, and it would be inappropriate for them to sing or dance. A film made about the Emperor Shivaji would be an example of an impossible subject for a biopic, unless he were shown as

*Lagaan*: the eleven cricketers.

he is in Bhalji Pendharkar's Marathi classic *Chhatrapati Shivaji* (1952) – a great heroic leader with no shades of grey, who can state that minorities must conform to the culture of the majority. Moreover, plans to make biopics of Indira Gandhi and Jawaharlal Nehru have been cancelled due to fears over the controversy they would generate, including court cases – all of which would delay the film's release, not to mention perhaps cause actual violence. The only leader of the anti-British freedom struggle who has been a popular subject for the biopic is 'Shaheed' (Martyr) Bhagat Singh. A leader regarded in his time as more popular than Gandhi, Bhagat Singh is barely mentioned in official histories though he is still much cited by establishment figures and revolutionaries and his image is present all over India, especially in Punjab and the north, from vendors' stalls to the offices of radical lawyers and certain trade unions.

Bhagat Singh (1907–1931) was a real-life popular hero and a romantic figure, martyred at a young age. This means he can sing and dance and fulfil all the requirements of a Hindi film hero, although as he is revered as an unmarried martyr, he does not usually romance a heroine. These versions of his life play down his role as an intellectual, a writer, an atheist and a committed Marxist; instead they concentrate on his short, heroic life, his fearless and valiant nature and his use of violence casting him as a romantic hero who appeals to the young.

The year 2002 saw the release of several films and a television biopic of Bhagat Singh. These films, which criticized Gandhi, appeared at the time when the Hindu Right was in the ascendant and Gandhi's Congress Party seemed to be in decline, but they were not commercial successes. They may have paved the way for 2006's *Rang de Basanti/Colour It Saffron* (dir. Rakeysh Omprakash Mehra), which was one of the biggest hits of the year, later selected as India's entry for the Oscars. This film, named after Bhagat Singh's favourite song, shows a group of disillusioned metropolitan youths who are inspired to action when acting in a play produced by an English girl about Bhagat Singh. Said to be influenced in structure by *Jesus of Montreal* (dir. Denys Arcand, 1989), *Rang de Basanti* reflects on politicized youth and anti-corruption themes in parallel with the story of Bhagat Singh. The biopic forms one of the streams of the film as the modern-day protagonists gradually take on the ideology of the characters they are playing and respond in character to their disillusionment with modern India, its corrupt politics and discrimination against minorities, with their struggle driving them to their own martyrdom. It ultimately shows the futility of violent protest, but the film became a cult among youth – as did Bhagat Singh himself.

The next major biopic again starred Aamir Khan, who had consolidated his status with *Lagaan*. He played Mangal Pandey in *The Rising: Ballad of Mangal Pandey* (dir. Ketan Mehta, 2005), the story of an Indian sepoy who is a semi-legendary hero of the 1857 uprisings which led to the British Crown taking control of India. The film develops the story by having Mangal Pandey befriend an Irish/British soldier, rescue a *sati* from a funeral pyre and visit the house of a dancing girl. The film ends with footage of Gandhi to tie the freedom struggle into one narrative from 1857 (dubbed by V. D. Savarkar, the architect of Hindu nationalism, the First War of Independence) to the end of British rule in 1947.

Political parties such as the then-ruling Bharatiya Janata Party, and the state government of Uttar Pradesh, sought to ban the film on the grounds of errors amounting to falsehood in the story and for showing a national hero visiting a courtesan's house. In the area from which Pandey came, there were protests and demonstrations against the film. These served as further reminders that showing great leaders and national heroes as men and women with feet of clay was to prove controversial and unpopular with audiences. *The Rising* remains Aamir Khan's only flop of the last decade, his other films including the most commercially successful Hindi film of all time (*3 Idiots*, dir. Rajkumar Hirani, 2009).

It is not surprising that the most famous biopic made in India was about the most celebrated Indian of the twentieth century. This was the Indo-British production Richard Attenborough's *Gandhi* (1982), which won eight Oscars. This biopic, which starts with Gandhi's life in South Africa, has the tagline 'His triumph changed the world forever' and shows him as a saintly though wily figure. Recent films have depicted Gandhi as a more troubled figure, but we have been spared the Gandhi of political histories – it would hardly make good cinema – or of the alleged crank highlighted in recent controversial biographies.

There have, however, been a number of films in mainstream commercial cinema in which Gandhi features, though not as the lead character. These include several which were not major box-office successes, such as *Hey Ram* (dir. Kamal Hassan, 2000), *Maine Gandhi ko nahin maara/I Didn't Kill Gandhi* (dir. Jahnu Barua, 2005), *Gandhi My Father* (dir. Feroz Abbas Khan, 2007) and *Road to Sangam* (dir. Amit Rai, 2009). Among them, though, was the massive all-India hit: *Lage raho Munna Bhai* (*LRMB*)/*Carry on Munna Bhai* (dir. Rajkumar Hirani, 2006), the publicity tags for which included: 'What happens when the present meets the past? What happens when our very own Professor of History encounters a figure from History?'

Munna Bhai was a new film hero who first appeared in 2004, reaching out to one of the biggest audiences in India in *Munna Bhai MBBS* (dir. Rajkumar Hirani, 2003). Munna is a loveable rogue, a petty gangster who aspires to a middle-class education and falls in love with upper-class girls. He has appealed across audiences, across classes, across regions and to viewers of all types of cinema. This is in part because he is one of the few heroes to represent a national fantasy, accessible to all classes and ages: even though Munna Bhai is a gangster, he has the right aims – to please his parents by becoming a doctor in the first film, for example; he simply focuses on the ends rather than the means.

*LRMB* is the fairytale story of a good-hearted thug led by love to pretend to be a professor of history and a Gandhian. In this film Munna is now fatherless and lacking an authority figure. The father of the nation comes to fulfil this role in his life, perhaps making Munna – whose name means simply 'kid' – the 'Aam Hindustani' or the Indian Everyman.

This film also marks a popular rehabilitation of Gandhianism as an Indian way of thought, albeit originally hybridized from global influences. Although Gandhi himself was famously anti-consumerist, his other values remain strong in India; even the most avid consumers in India put religion and family first – at least as ideals – and consume *as* Hindus and *as* family.

*LRMB* does not deal with tricky or difficult points concerning Gandhi but shows how, by adopting one of his strategies, *satyagraha/victory through truth*, there can be an ethical resolution of conflict. Munna Bhai calls this 'Gandhigiri' (Gandhianism), a formulation which echoes his own practice of *dadagiri*, or thuggery. This ethical stance, combined with Munna's devotion to his beloved Jhanvi, his desire to do good and his ability to suffer, are seen to be more valuable than education. His understanding of Gandhi is shown to be superior to that of a history professor. We soon find out that these hallucinations of Gandhi are, in fact, manifestations of the inner conscience of this Indian Everyman. Indian cinema is concerned with a moral vision, which, however much hokum it may be, still lies at the heart of Bollywood: love requires a moral reformation and honesty.

Munna's Gandhigiri had real agency, as people began to follow it as a non-political, moral way of behaving. This new presentation of Gandhi is more powerful than anything we've yet seen and has led to a revival in talking about Gandhi, especially among the young. There have been many imitations in real life of Munna's Gandhigiri, as people now imitate Munna by sending flowers with cards, saying, 'Get well soon' to the morally corrupt.

Yet there is a great ambivalence at the heart of this film. Although it is critical of 'today's values' (the obsession with money and consumerism, not looking after old people, superstitious beliefs, the corruption of business and so on), ultimately Munna is an upwardly mobile street guy. He moves up the social ladder by marrying the English-speaking DJ and hosting a radio programme himself. He does not achieve his middle-class aspiration of becoming a history professor, but he teaches Indians history and morality and rewrites their history and Gandhi's in the popular imagination.

*LRMB* typifies the way in which history is used in Bollywood cinema. This is less a new history and more a new mythology which is not as

concerned with facts and truths as it is with morality. Ashis Nandy argues
that myths and legends are open-ended views of the past and use 'prin-
cipled forgetfulness'; they do not separate the past from ethical meaning
in the present and so are at odds with history, which remembers. More
than history, myths have ethical meanings in the present – though they
also have religious elements, which the secularists fear.

Now is a time of radical social change in India, one that is seeing the
creation of new histories and new mythologies, so it is not surprising that
figures from the past such as Gandhi are reappearing to answer questions
that Indians are being presented with today. Although Gandhi is back,
it is not the historical Gandhi, a challenging and difficult figure who urges
us to abandon consumerism, but a Gandhi of India's new middle classes.
This is not a political Gandhi, but a Gandhi who is an inner conscience
and moral guide, as well as a fairy godmother who will help us to realize
our dreams.

Its depiction of a new historical Gandhi for a more confident, assertive
India is only one way in which the Bollywood film creates new traditions
which are part of the wider Indian social imaginaries. All cinemas trade

in and create mythology, especially national mythology, and Hindi cinema as a national cinema also binds together the global Indian middle class. In the process it reveals the imaginary of this increasingly important social group, who are determining the future not just of India but also of the wider world. It makes perfect sense that Munnabhai's next adventure is to be filmed in the USA, where he is likely to demonstrate what India can show the world in this new, globalized century.

## The Partition Film

Along with Independence in 1947, the Partition that took place the same year, creating an India flanked by West and East Pakistan, was a defining moment in the region's history. Tragedy inaugurated the new nation in the form of forced migration and war between the new states. Relatively few films mention the Partition of India, the period of the worst communal conflicts in Indian history, which saw the largest movement of people in history – ten million men, women and children migrated as Pakistan was created alongside the secular republic of India. Some film-makers try to show that Hindus and Muslims are 'really the same', so a Hindu extremist has to come to terms with the fact that he was born a Muslim in *Dharamputra/Son of Religion* (dir. Yash Chopra, 1961) and *Tamas/Darkness* (dir. Govind Nihalani, 1986) shows how other bonds were broken in the upsurge of violence of this time. Much use has been made of documentary footage, notably of straggling columns of migrants, which is spliced into the main film.

In public life, little was said about the Partition – perhaps a trauma too great to mention – until its fiftieth anniversary in 1997. Four years later, one of the biggest hits in Indian film history chose Partition as its subject. *Gadar – ek prem katha/Turmoil: A Love Story* (dir. Anil Sharma, 2001), which is a Punjabi film in all but language, has a Sikh rescue a Muslim woman during the Partition riots in Delhi. They marry and have a child but her father, whom she visits in Pakistan, tries to marry her to a Pakistani. The Sikh hero goes to Pakistan to try to persuade his in-laws

*Gadar – ek prem katha* – the hero singlehandedly fights the Pakistani army.

to allow his Muslim wife to return to India. Surrounded by the Pakistani army, the hero is willing to convert to Islam, but risks his life by refusing to praise Pakistan and curse India. He more or less single-handedly takes on the Pakistani army and brings his family back to India.

This film was an all-India hit but found particularly large audiences in Punjab, the area of India where there was a massive exchange of Muslim and Hindu populations in 1947 and where around a million people died. This was the first Partition film to find a large audience. It was popular for its self-sacrificing and decent hero, played by the Punjabi superstar Sunny Deol, who was brave, strong and gentle – never asking his wife to convert, allowing her to travel to Pakistan and willing to take on the role of protector of his neighbours and family but not willing to dishonour his country. This allows a way of looking back at the Partition with a sense of loss but also with one of pride in the honourable behaviour of one's own community, while it also shows the mixed behaviour of the Muslims, with the 'good female Muslim' staying in India and the 'wicked male Muslim' migrating to Pakistan.

War films are not a popular genre of Hindi cinema, despite greats such as *Haqeeqat/Reality* (dir. Chetan Anand, 1964), about the Indo-Chinese war. Most other incidents are to do with the three wars India has fought with Pakistan (1947/8, 1965 and, though less frequently, 1971). Perhaps there are so few such films because they would exacerbate tensions with Pakistan, or lose a sizeable part of the non-Indian audience, or perhaps war is not a topic which interests film audiences who have little experience of it. At the time of writing there have been no major films in Hindi on the Indian Peace-keeping Force (IPKF), deployed in Sri Lanka between 1987 and 1990, which is seen, rightly or wrongly, as very much a 'Tamil issue' (pointed out in *Kandukondein Kandukondein/I Have Found It*, dir. Rajeev Menon, 2000), although *Madras Cafe* (dir. Shoojit Sircar, 2013) was based on the assassination of Rajiv Gandi. Several war films were made following the Kargil encounter between India and Pakistan in 1999, from *Lakshya/The Target* (dir. Farhan Akhtar, 2004) to *Deewaar/Let's Bring Our Boys Home* (dir. Milan Luthria, 2004), which came at a time of growing tensions between India and Pakistan. None of them was a major hit.

Hostilities between India and Pakistan have been central to their histories, but only very recently have Hindi films mentioned Pakistan by name or shown agents of that state, previously mentioning only the 'hidden hand' and such like. One of the first to do this was *Sarfarosh/The Willing Martyr* (dir. John Matthews Matthan, 1998), in which a *ghazal* (light classical music) singer acts as an agent for a Pakistani arms-smuggling team. The film tries to show Indian Muslims positively, with a Muslim police officer complaining that he is tired of proving his Indianness, while the star, Aamir Khan, a Muslim, plays a Hindu police officer. One of the few war films made since Independence, *Border* (dir. J. P. Dutta, 1997), is based on the Battle of Longewala in the 1971 war, but shows the Indian army's respect for Islam in the daring rescue of a Quran from a burning house. Such films may show Muslims in a negative light, not because of their religion or culture per se but because they are Pakistani.

The India–Pakistan conflict has largely focused on the Kashmir region, dispute over which has existed ever since the Partition in 1947; some parts are controlled by India and some by Pakistan. The Indian-administered area is part of the state of Jammu and Kashmir (Jammu, the Kashmir Valley and Ladakh); it holds a special status in the Indian constitution and is India's only majority Muslim state. Kashmir has been the location for many Hindi films from the 1940s onwards and has had a fascinating filmic history, from its depiction in tourist films of the 1960s to films from the 1990s which have examined the conflict as one of the problems of Indian secularism as well as part of the nation's internal crisis.

Following the assassination of Rajiv Gandhi in 1991 by a female suicide bomber, there were several 'human bomb' films in the 1990s, including Santosh Sivan's *Terrorist* (1999), set in Tamil Nadu, and Mani Ratnam's *Dil se/From the Heart* (1998), which dealt with separatism in India's northeast. This latter film is part of Mani Ratnam's 'trilogy' dealing with points of crisis in the Indian nation, the earlier two films being *Roja/Rose* (1992) and *Bombay* (1995), which deal with Kashmir terrorism and the riots in Bombay in 1992/3 after the destruction of the Babri Masjid in Ayodhya by Hindu nationalist extremists. Unlike *Dil se*, Mani Ratnam's first Hindi film, these two earlier movies were both made in Tamil, although Hindi-dubbed versions became national successes. These are among the few films that have engaged with contemporary issues about the Indian nation state, and it is striking that they were made in the Tamil cinema, which had earlier concerned itself more with the local political issues of Dravidianism and anti-Brahminism. It has been suggested that these films, made after the assassination of Rajiv Gandhi, represent a venting of collective guilt by subsuming Tamil nationality into an Indian one. They all feature high-caste, if not Brahminical, figures who travel throughout India rehearsing a high-caste Hindu nationalist identity. The first two films have quite unjustifiably led to Mani Ratnam being attacked as a supporter of Hindutva (Hindu nationalism).

Much of *Roja* is set in Kashmir, which until the 1980s was the major shooting location for romance in Hindi movies, drawing on its associations as an earthly paradise. During the 1990s, political unrest in the region made it too risky for film crews to work there, so they switched to other tourist locations, notably Switzerland, whose lakes and hills were similar but which had added associations of wealth and glamour. The Hindi-dubbed version of *Roja* was a huge hit, not least because of the new style of music, composed by A. R. Rehman. The film was the love story of a couple from southern India who spend their honeymoon in

Kashmir, as so many earlier film heroes and heroines had done – but this time Kashmir is a hell peopled by separatists. They kidnap the Indian code-breaker, Rishi, taunting him before burning the Indian flag. Rishi throws himself on it in an effort to save the flag, to the words of a song by the nationalist Tamil poet, Subramania Bharati: 'India is dearer to me than life.' The film cuts to Rishi's impassive Muslim captor at prayer, reinforcing the image, feared by Hindutva followers, of the disciplined, self-controlled Muslim linked to millions of other Muslims praying in a regimented manner.

The commercial success of *Roja* was accompanied by critical acclaim. It won the National Award for the film that best promotes national integration, gained tax-exempt status (which makes the tickets much cheaper) and is regularly screened on Doordarshan (Indian state television) on Independence Day. This happened under the Congress government, though many associate *Roja*'s success with the rise of the new middle classes and Hindutva ideology of the early 1990s.

Numerous other films about Kashmir have been made during this period, including *Mission Kashmir* (dir. Vidhu Vinod Chopra, 1998) and *Fanaa/Oblivion* (dir. Kunal Kohli, 2006), but despite the severity of the problems in the Valley, it is considered a remote region by many of the audience, plus, now that there is little actual fighting, the focus is more on Pakistan and global issues of Islamism rather than the politics of Kashmir, which are raised only in films like *I Am* (dir. Onir, 2010). Even *Fanaa* was concerned not with the lives of Kashmiris so much as the spreading of terrorism outside of Kashmir, with a nuclear attack being planned by Kashmiri separatists. However, Yash Chopra's *Jab tak hai jaan (JTHJ)/As Long as I Live* (2012), which showed the army in the Kashmir Valley and in Ladakh, also restored it as a place for love and romance.

The couple in Roja.

*JTHJ* – the Indian army in Kashmir.

# Politics and Hindi Films

Independent India's earlier generation of politicians are still revered, so Gandhi, Nehru, Ambedkar and even Indira Gandhi have superhuman status. However, this is not true of today's politicians – it is often remarked that they are usually shown in films as khadi-clad hypocrites, which reflects wider views that they are old, out of touch and corrupt. While politicians can be extremely powerful (and dangerous), at least to the poor, the lack of respect which they are afforded is partly because of endemic corruption but also because many of them are low class and low caste, voted in by their particular constituencies or vote banks. This is reflected in the rise and fall during 2011–12 of Anna Hazare, whose anti-corruption campaign consisted largely of the new middle class forming a movement to bypass electoral politics.

Politicians are often enthralled by the film industry, though it seems that the film-and-politics nexus is much weaker in the north than it is in the south, despite the fact that several former Hindi film stars have gone into politics, whether briefly like Amitabh Bachchan and Govinda or more permanently like Shatrughan Sinha or Vinod Khanna. In Mumbai there are some closer links between the two arenas, such as the star Riteish Deshmukh, who is the son of Vilasrao Deshmukh, a Union Minister and the former Chief Minister of Maharashtra.

Hindi films are mostly mass entertainment and do not want to ally themselves to a political party or, it seems, even to make a political point. Under the Congress consensus, many films featured images of Gandhi or Nehru, while Manoj Kumar, the great nationalist, paid tribute to Lal Bahadur Shastri in *Upkar/Helper* (1967). Indira Gandhi features less often, though Gulzar's famous *Aandhi/Storm* (1975), the story of a female politician whose work leads to the breakdown of her marriage, was banned during Indira Gandhi's lifetime. Few, however, noted the missing initial G of the title (Gandhi rhymes with *Aandhi*).

Although the 1990s saw a rise in support for Hindutva ideologies, films continued to avoid making direct political statements – many, however, read the rise of Hindu Family Values in the films of this time as being political. The television epics whose screenings mark the rise of Hindutva ideology in the media are about highly dysfunctional families which literally go to war with each other – in the *Mahabharata* – and exile the ideal son – in the *Ramayana*.

Hindutva ideology, which is overtly anti-Muslim, would not get past the censors (although the films discussed in the Islamicate section show how films may be read as covert statements) and would alienate important parts of the audience at home and overseas, as well as be contrary to the views of many in the film industry, not least its substantial Muslim personnel. However, there were films which showed characters who espoused Hindutva only to reject it, including *Hey Ram* (dir. Kamal Haasan, 2000) – not a success – and *Rang de Basanti*, which rejected it.

In recent years, although films tend to gloss over political issues, some that engage with politics and politicians have appeared, in particular those made by Prakash Jha, which also depict violence, often based on real events. Hindi cinema is obsessed with violence, but this is usually focused on verbal abuse and violence as a marker of manhood, as well as the failure of the state to prosecute wrongdoers, allowing heroes to pursue their own moral codes. Many films, especially in the 1970s and '80s, showed the hero beating up villains, who frequently threaten any women he is protecting. The hero himself may be attacked, often in a masochistic display of his self-pity. Few films deal with actual violence and the fear of it. In older films, the police may arrive too late, showing that they do not do anything, but today they are seen to be corrupt and are themselves feared by the public in films such as *Dabangg/Fearless* (dir. Abhinav Kashyap, 2010). Terrorism has been raised as an issue, though mostly Islamist, often located overseas and with no mention of Hindu terrorism, dowry deaths, caste violence, riots or domestic abuse.

Films which show realistic violence in the family are often outside the mainstream. This may be partly to do with considerations for what is suitable for entertaining a family audience as well as having an eye on the censors. The mainstream has largely ignored political events. Mani

Ratnam's *Bombay* (1995) is the major film on the Mumbai violence of 1992–3 and the events of 2002 in Godhra and Gujarat feature only in documentaries and in 'realist' (non-Bollywood) films such as *Firaaq/ Separation* (dir. Nandita Das, 2002) and *Parzania/Heaven and Hell on Earth* (dir. Rahul Dholakia, 2007). The bomb blasts in Mumbai were central to the story of *Mumbai meri jaan/Mumbai, My Love* (dir. Nishikant Kamath, 2009), and a citizen's anger at the state's inefficiency in thwarting terrorism is dealt with in *A Wednesday* (dir. Neeraj Pandy, 2008). There have been a few major films about 9/11 and Islamist terrorism (to be discussed in the section on the Islamicate genre in chapter Three) and the only film about the attacks on Mumbai of 26/11 is Ram Gopal Varma's *The Attacks of 26/11*, released in 2013. Another film that has affected the discourse on terrorism is *Maachis* (dir. Gulzar, 1996), based on the Punjab insurgency.

There are two major voices in this comparative silence. One is that of Anurag Kashyap, who has sought and been anointed with the status of the angry young man of today's Bollywood, and who is willing to raise these issues, even though it has led to a number of his films being stalled by the Censor Board. *Black Friday*, his film about the bomb reprisals in 1993 for the 1992 riots by members of the Muslim community following the demolition of the Babri Masjid, was stalled several times, while his earlier film, *Paanch/Five*, is yet to be released. His later films have been released, including *Gulaal/Vermilion* (2009), which dealt with an imagined Rajput secessionist movement and student politics, and *DevD* (2009), his reworking of the Devdas story in the new context of drugs and alcoholism, multimedia messaging (MMS) scandals and prostitution. Kashyap's most recent *Gangs of Wasseypur* (split into two, Parts I and II; 2012) is a family saga of the twentieth-century coal-mining area of Dhanbad (formerly in Bihar, now in Jharkhand), showing a world of mafias, dons and sexual relations with snappy and humorous 'dialogues' (as set-piece lines of dialogue are known in Indian English), brilliant music and outstanding performances. It has enthralled metropolitan youth but came under heavy censure from critics from the Dhanbad area for being an unrealistic fantasy – so showing the disconnect in the imaginaries of the different areas and indeed of cinema.

Prakash Jha, who himself stood for election in Bihar, is one of the few film-makers to make overtly political films (which raise issues of violence), all of which have been commercially viable throughout the period dealt with in this book. While his first film, *Damul/Bonded until Death* (1984) is little seen, his *Mrityudand/Death Sentence*, about violence to women and starring the then top star Madhuri Dixit, hit the festival circuit in 1997, followed by two films featuring major stars, both of which won National Awards although they were not major commercial successes. Both raised issues of violence in Bihar; the first, *Gangaajal/Holy Water* (2003), was a police drama dealing with the Bhagalpur blindings and *Apaharan/Kidnapping* (2005) was about kidnapping in Bihar.

However, Jha's *Raajneeti/Politics* was the biggest Hindi hit of 2010. This story of a family dynasty involving politics, murders and dysfunctional relationships blended with the epic mythology of the *Mahabharata* and the new mythology of Coppola's *The Godfather* (dir. Francis Ford Coppola, 1972). His next film, *Aarakshan/Reservations* (2011), which examines caste politics, was a less successful film, perhaps because it touched directly on the issues of the New Middle Classes (NMCs) and other elites who are virulently anti-reservation. His latest movie, *Chakravyuh/Battle Formation* (2012), engages with Maoist insurgents but has been the least successful, in part because the Maoists are active far from the metropolises and barely feature in the imaginaries of Hindi film viewers.

Over the period in question, big-budget Bollywood films have become part of the metropolitan imaginary, open to those who are or who aspire to be metropolitan but far removed from the *mofussil* towns and small towns, except where there is a burgeoning middle class. While the metropolitan audience has much in common with parts of the diasporic audience, this imagined world may be Indian but it is not necessarily located in India, as discussed below.

## India and the World: A Global Nation

Although Indianness remains a major theme in films today, the concept itself has changed. In the early 1990s, Indians often felt inferior to the West, obsessed with being slighted and angry about being regarded as 'backward' due to the real poverty of the masses and the relative poverty of their elites, who did not have access to the same resources as their Western peers. Today, Indians are proud of their Indianness, as India is now seen as an important place with the potential to become a major power given its educated workforce and economic dynamism. Indianness is no longer about being a 'son of the soil' but is about a global category rather than a local citizenship. The rising middle classes, indeed, regard the state itself as an obstruction to giving Indianness full play, and many of them try to withdraw from the state by living in gated communities which draw on non-state amenities for everything from water to education. They are often more connected to other parts of the world, particularly to the diaspora, among whom many of them have family members or which they aspire to join. The national has become the trans-national and Indianness is now part of this borderless, imagined world. In the mid-1990s, the diasporic film had extended the notion of Indianness within the film itself by mixing Indian and overseas locations, but now overseas locations are Indianized and the differences between the two have been reduced. Indians who live in India may inhabit the wider world in their dreams, while Indians who live overseas make their own India there and travel freely between the two places.

This shift in the imagining of Indianness was also due to the acceleration of already rapid social changes in Indian society that had begun in the 1990s. Economic liberalization led to the influx of global capitalism and to Indians becoming part of the international workforce (from multinationals investing in India through to overseas companies establishing Indian call centres). There were also massive shifts in various spheres as disparate as education, ideas of culture and identity, the rise of lower castes, the growing cultural dominance of the new middle classes, the coming to power of parties whose ideology was Hindutva, the emergence of the diaspora as part of Indian politics and the idea of India as a global superpower. The swift and enormous expansion of electronic media also transformed social networks both within India and beyond.

The world has always been interconnected but globalization today is about a speeding up of this process and the denser links of its networks. India is itself at the heart of global networks with its large overseas population. Empire established many of the nineteenth- and early twentieth-century migratory routes for Indians across parts of Southeast Asia and Africa, but the migrations to Europe from the 1960s, along with the migration of skilled labour to the USA, have also been hugely significant. As well as people, goods and objects are also part of this circulation, from trade to finance to consumer items. Once the Indian markets opened, it was not long before it became clear that this was too big a market to be ignored by global capitalism. This affected everyone, even those who do not participate directly, as everything was transformed.

Of all the global flows, one of the strongest and most massive is that of the media. The media have been flowing into India with no or little respect for the boundaries of the country and have changed the local media as well as providing new ways of viewing the world. English is spreading as a language of such media and is transforming into a more Indianized variant, often called 'Hinglish'. The Internet as well as satellite channels bring in new forms of entertainment, such as gaming and sports (football looks set to become a major sport), and are transforming existing sports – even cricket, which is now also available as the Indian Premier League (IPL), or cricket as showbusiness.

Film has been hugely affected by these media flows in almost every conceivable way. Western media have presented new values, some of which have been adopted, some rejected, sometimes creating divisions. The possibility of viewing global cinema in India opened up, along with the increased circulation of Indian films around the world. Moreover, Bollywood films wanted to reach the widest – and most lucrative – markets.

India's new middle class is part of a trans-national group closely linked to the Indian diaspora, whose role and presence in India has shifted – as recognized by government policy. The 'Overseas Indian' became the 'NRI' (Non-resident Indian) when new monetary policies were introduced; then the new category of 'PIO' (Person of Indian Origin) was added when further financial benefits were supplemented with changes in citizenship and visa requirements. In the 1990s, the NRIs were often dubbed 'Non-required Indians', but changes, largely associated with the post-1998 'Hindutva' Government, led to an increase in the importance of the diaspora, as they came to be seen as important political lobbying groups in their countries of settlement. The Indian Government began to court them with investment possibilities and economic trading zones, and then with the promise of dual nationality to PIOs and the celebration of Pravasi Bharatiya Divas (Overseas Indians Day). A government minister was allocated to deal with PIOs, thus increasing the diaspora's influence on India's internal politics. Many PIOs chose to live in India for at least part of the year and many more talk of returning. Many have joined the new category of OCI, or Overseas Citizen of India, to make travel easier. They, like the new middle classes in India, elide the image of poorer India and are themselves more visible, given that the diasporic Indian is omnipresent, although not in a 'realist' manner. The films underline the fact that the diaspora are still Indian and that India is set to surpass the rest of the world in economic terms.

## The Diasporic Hero: Shah Rukh Khan and Karan Johar's Films

There is a long history in Hindi cinema of stories of Indians returned from abroad, from *Bilat pherat/England Returned* (dir. D. N. Ganguly, 1921) in the silent era to today. Overseas locations, mostly used to show the glamour of travel, became popular with colour film in the 1960s, and this wallpaper still continues as an attraction of the Hindi film which adds spectacle, gloss and an air of cosmopolitanism – but is not a space inhabited or explored by the characters. Another group of films shows Indians who have gone to live overseas – that is, the Indian diaspora – but at this early stage these films were about bringing the family home to escape the material West and return to the spiritual East.

In the 1980s, the diaspora began to make its own films, not in the traditions of Hindi cinema but in those of realist cinemas, exploring the lives of south Asian characters who live outside India. They are watched in the diasporic countries by large audiences but are not popular in India except with groups who watch foreign films.

In the 1990s, one of the most popular genres in India was the diaspora romance, which began a long and continuing representation of the Indian diaspora – or at least the diaspora in the UK and the USA, as Indian cinema has barely glanced at the twenty-million-strong Indian diaspora beyond the West. The landmark was Aditya Chopra's *DDLJ* (*Dilwale dulhania le jayenge/The Braveheart Takes the Bride*, 1995), which many have argued also inaugurated the new type of Hindi cinema known as Bollywood (see Introduction). Henceforth the diaspora began playing a key role in Indian cinema both as audiences and as characters within the films, no longer Hindi-speaking exiles waiting to return to the motherland, but the second generation born and brought up in the West. In *DDLJ*, the father dreams of returning to the homeland but the children have no such intention. Although the daughter is taken to India for her wedding, there is no indication of a return otherwise. Yet these films do not present the characters as realistically diasporic: these are Hindi-speaking Indians whose fantasies, styling and interiors are those of Indians, or at most recent migrants, even if they display no dreams of a 'return'. This means that while the parents may be convincing (as first-generation migrants), the children are not. This goes hand in hand with the lack of realism and the violence done to geography seen in *DDLJ*: the father feeds pigeons daily in Trafalgar Square though he lives in Southall, the heroine returns from the Eurostar at Kings Cross via Angel tube station and an open-topped tourist bus – and so on.

Shah Rukh Khan (SRK) is one of the biggest stars of the Hindi cinema since the mid-1990s, both at home and abroad. However, in the overseas market he is the biggest star, starring in eleven of the 25 top overseas grossers of all time, including five big-budget family romances closely associated with Karan Johar's Dharma Productions (ranking by box-office sales shown in brackets):

(2) *My Name Is Khan* (*MNIK*), 2010

(4) *Kabhi alvida na kehna* (*KANK*)/*Never Say Goodbye*, 2006

(11) *Kabhi khushi kabhie gham* (*K3G*)/*Sometimes Joy, Sometimes Sorrow*, 2001

(20) *Kuch kuch hota hai* (*K2H2*)/*Something's Happening*, 1998

(23) *Kal ho na ho* (*KHNH*)/*There May or May Not Be a Tomorrow*, 2001

(Source: www.boxofficeindia.com)

These films are set partially or wholly in an imaginary diaspora, usually in the UK or the USA, yet one in which the lead character, played by Shah Rukh Khan, has his lifestyle and language marked as Indian rather than as diasporic, and plays a young, international, emotional and desirable hero. Although many of Khan's roles were not as a diasporic hero, it is these roles which form a significant body of his work and have involved the biggest banners or production houses, as well as being some of the all-time greatest hits of Hindi cinema at home and overseas. He plays a diasporic hero in *Pardes* (dir. Subhash Ghai, 1997) as he saves Ganga, the pure Indian woman, from her violent fiancé, gets her back to her family in India and wins them over by showing that he is the one who really understands Indian values.

One of Shahrukh Khan's more realistic films was *Swades: We the People* (dir. Ashutosh Gowarikar, 2004), a Gandhian film which specifically refers to activist Rajni Bakshi's book on neo-Gandhianism, *Bapa kuti* (1998). In this film, Khan plays a character called Mohan (note the similarity to Mohandas Gandhi) who returns to India, leaving behind his job at NASA. He has no family in the USA but finds himself a place in India by locating himself within a family and a community in a village as he reunites with

Mohan's visit to a village by boat in *Swades*.

his adoptive mother and falls in love with a teacher, tellingly named Gita. Mohan becomes involved in promoting education for all and anti-caste activities. Although he needs to be in India to find himself as an Indian, he uses his overseas experience, just as Gandhi formed his ideas of Indian nationalism in South Africa but experimented with them in India.

In *Kuch kuch hota hai/K2H2* (1998), Rahul (Khan) does not even go overseas, but foreign locations are used to stand in for India for romantic songs and for the location of the college. The film has a strongly American feel, with its summer camps for children and its world of fun and colour. The film raises questions about the family which are often raised in the diasporic film, notably concerning remarriage, the duties of parents to children and children's love for their parents.

Karan Johar's next film, 2001's *K3G*, is a great family drama and perhaps the film that defines the Bollywood style. It is inspired by Yash Chopra's 1976 intergenerational family romance, *Kabhi kabhie*, which it partly locates in a diasporic setting, with the emphasis in the film on the parent–child relationship, shown by its slogan: 'It's all about loving your parents.'

The first half of *K3G* is set in Delhi – though the family house and the school in 'Mussoorie' are clearly in Europe – with the only specific location in India a studio set which recreates Delhi's famous Chandni Chowk, where the poorer characters live. Locations are used as decorative settings for songs, such as the Pyramids for 'Suraj hua maddham'/'The Sun Dimmed', which establishes the romance between Rahul and Anjali; or when the family migrates to the UK, where well-known public buildings such as Blenheim Palace are used for a college and a wealthy family reunion happens in a bland mall. When the second son arrives in London, the nationalist song 'Vande Mataram'/'I Praise Mother [India]' plays; it is unclear whether this is a nationalist reclaiming of London or whether it is 'I Praise Mother [England]'.

Overseas locations are used as part of the spectacle of wealth and glamour in *K3G* and a location for romance, placing consumerism and lifestyle at the heart of romance. London is a location for education and work but it is also a place for the new India to win admiration for

The Pyramids form a romantic backdrop for 'Suraj hua maddham/The Sun Dimmed' in *K3G*.

its style, dancing and being cool, as well as a place to feel a specific Indian nationalism and indulge a nostalgic view of India. However, it is a place, too, where the broken family in the film begins to reunite. The exiled family adds a nanny as a mother figure and a brother pretending to be a lodger and lives under a massive photograph of the parents. The death of a grandmother reunites the family in the sacred city of Haridwar as the two brothers and the father hold the torch to light her pyre. Overseas is a site of exile, a temporary place, and the brother's quest to bring his older brother home is a clear reference to the *Ramayana*, with the film's first song reminding us of the images of Rama, Sita and Lakshman, while the reunion is marked by the Gayatri mantra and the image of Radha-Krishna. This image overrides resonances of the adopted child as Karna in the *Mahabharata*, whose birth condemns him to exile from his family. India is a sacred space in the film, where the family has its *khushi*/'happiness', while overseas marks the years in the wilderness – the *gham* or 'sorrow'.

Although Karan Johar was only the producer of *Kal ho na ho*/KHNH, directed by Nikhil Advani, his former assistant, the style and content mark it as a Karan Johar film. An unhappy, fractured Indian family in NYC prays for an angel and Shah Rukh Khan arrives to mend their broken hearts and teach them how to live again through talking, understanding, forgiveness and coming to terms with the failure of the father, who committed suicide. Once the angel has united the diasporic family and created a new family for his beloved by getting her to marry her best friend, he dies.

In this film, Khan is not diasporic but he brings his magic from India to mend broken hearts, while he himself has a poor actual heart and comes to seek medical treatment. The diasporic family tread the paths of other diasporas by taking over a restaurant in NYC that was run by an earlier generation of migrants.

In *Kabhi alvida naa kehna*/KANK, the families are settled in NYC, although it is unclear how long they have lived there, why they all speak Hindi and why Shah Rukh Khan is a soccer star. Popular opinion has it that while the film did very well with overseas audiences it had only

Aman (Shah Rukh Khan) the Angel arrives in New York in *KHNH*.

moderate success in India because divorce is not so widely acceptable in India. However, its reworking of *Silsila/The Affair* (dir. Yash Chopra, 1981) highlights issues of mixed feelings, confused loyalties and not knowing what to do when living in a society that emphasizes romance and easy divorce without having the networks of jobs, friends and community that would be available in India. In the film, the couple suffer and are forgiven by their former partners, and it seems that the case for divorce that the film makes may, like *Silsila*, give it later success.

In Karan Johar's *My Name Is Khan/MNIK*, Shah Rukh Khan plays Muslim Rizwan Khan, who is autistic but with special talents for repairing machines, and even people's lives. He migrates to live with his brother in the USA because communal (Hindu–Muslim) troubles kill his mother. However, Muslims face problems there, too. Rizwan's brother throws him out because he marries a Hindu, and then he has to face the wider issues of being a Muslim in the post-9/11 world. His stepson, who is a Hindu, is killed by Islamophobes, and his wife leaves him as she doesn't want to be associated with Islam. Rizwan's goal is to tell the U.S. President, 'My name is Khan and I'm not a terrorist', encountering racism and helping flood victims in Wilhemina on his way. He finally meets the President, who understands Muslims are not all terrorists, before reuniting with his

Aman (Shah Rukh Khan) sings a version of 'Pretty Woman' on 4 July in *KHNH*.

Khan's tears in *KANK*.

wife and his brother. (See also chapter Three for material on the Islamicist terrorist film.)

Hindi films are shot overseas for spectacle as well as for business and production reasons, while overseas markets remain important. But it is also because they allow outdoor shooting with major stars and can show wealthy lifestyles by shooting in parts of London, New York or San Francisco where poverty need not be shown and consumerism can be celebrated. This new space is imagined as Indian, and what India itself is poised to become.

Indian modernity is something that is shaped overseas and then imported to India. This is created in a space where the hero may face family problems, which are often seen to be to do with change, largely brought about by modernity and Westernization. Also, the diasporic Indian in Hindi films, who has been most exposed to these threats, is removed from the pressures that affect the modern Indian elite – including urban squalor, traffic congestion, dreary work and inefficiency – by living a life of privilege which it is hard to have in India without the 'old', poor India seeping through. Characters in these situations focus on the family and romance, yet they may still suffer as they seek to negotiate these relationships. In such films, public life overseas is meaningless beyond garnering recognition for the self and for India.

These films show the life of the super-rich Indian overseas, creating an aspirational lifestyle for Indians who increasingly want to have an Americanized existence, supplemented by servants and Indian food. Although Hindi films have long avoided issues of caste, these films, at least post-*K3G*, also move away from representing class differences, as the lead characters are all from the super-rich business group.

Shah Rukh Khan is the figure who makes the transition between India and the West, as well as between the old and the new India. This is seen most closely in *KHNH*, where he is the Indian who comes to NYC ostensibly seeking treatment but in reality he has gone there to die. Self-sacrificing, loving and more than a little divine, this Indian angel unites broken families and couples and even unites fractured American communities on the fourth of July. He is the figure who represents the modern Indian, at home in India and the world, the cosmopolitan or truly global citizen.

Khan's casual style makes him seem classless and ageless. His attractiveness is coupled with extraordinary charm and charisma, so he appears sophisticated, creating a new image of today's Indian as simultaneously Indian and global. Khan is the modern hero, an emotional man who, in particular in these family melodramas with Karan Johar, expresses every nuance of his feelings throughout the film and in particular in song and dance. These films foreground the tender sentiments and pain which are not usually aired in public in the West, and certainly not by men, but they link the audience to Indian sentiments and emotional worlds where these are not only expressed but admired.

Khan's songs usually have a particular emotionality, from their plangent music to their picturization. He is often shown feeling the emotionality by reacting to the music with his whole body, stretching his hands in the air and gesturing expansively. There are songs of pain and love as well as some fun dance songs.

It is striking that in all these films Shah Rukh Khan suffers from some form of disability or disadvantage, which means that although he remains good-looking, he does not play a powerful male but a victim – widowed, rejected, ill, injured or disabled – where it is never his fault. Although many may read this as having gay references, it certainly presents him as a more 'feminized' male, emotional and not seeking – indeed, even having lost – alpha status. Rather, this suffering and pain show him weeping, melancholic and facing a threatened loss of status and respect. This pain is beyond his control but he adds to it through his own self-sacrifice, as he aims to redeem himself through suffering. Shah Rukh Khan's characters do not display the noble sentiments of Amitabh Bachchan's star roles but are inclined towards the more 'feminine', tender sentiments and a quest for romance. These characters give meaning to pain and suffering and may lead to the 'pleasure of tears' in his audiences, whether through empathy or identification. Khan represents a modern Indian emotionality, appealing to his audience as a gentle, suffering person who responds with tears and only occasionally with anger. Indeed, in many films, Shah Rukh's emotions are opposed to those of Amitabh, which are driven by an anger based on reason rather than emotion. This is perhaps a sign that emotions are

The tears of Rishi (Abhishek) and Maya (Rani) in *KANK*.

valued differently by the new middle classes and the diaspora in their negotiation of new values in India and overseas.

The confident new Indian that Khan portrays has now become a standard Hindi film type. Others may also play international Indians – Akshay Kumar in comedies, often as the small-town innocent in unexpected settings (*Singh Is Kinng*, dir. Anees Bazmee, 2008), or Saif Ali Khan playing Agent Vinod (*Agent Vinod*, dir. Sriram Raghavan, 2012), India's James Bond – but Shah Rukh Khan was the hero of the newly liberalized India. As a diasporic hero he embodied the new transnational Indian that is emerging and which is dreamed of for the future.

Nationalism and obsession with the wrongs of the past are the most important aspect of history today in India. However, these are not really about pre-1947 and British colonialism but have much more to do with India in the globalized world today. It can be said that India has moved out of the postcolonial phase of its history into a new era where its imagining of itself has changed, as its new dominant social groups have little interest in the past beyond a sense of the former glory of India and a feeling of grievance at the injustices of 'invaders'.

There is an undeniable shift in the concept of Indianness, in the ways in which India sees itself and how Indians see India in the world today. This is what the films show and what is hard to access elsewhere. Before the 1990s, India saw itself as a poor country with a glorious past, out of which Indians had often been cheated. This view of the past, shown in the films, by and large remains, but how India sees the present has shifted enormously. Indians sometimes felt ashamed of themselves, mostly because of poverty. This applied both on a national level – in terms of feeling able to take on a role in the world at large, despite India's non-aligned status and feeling that it inhabited the moral high ground – and on a personal level, with regard to the lack of opportunities to be consumerist and stylish. Indians now see India as a major global player, an English-speaking, modern country which has not forgotten its roots. It has also changed its views of other countries, with Westerners no longer seen as alien or sexually depraved but as admirers and friends of the new Indians.

The denouement
as laughing gas fills
Buckingham Palace
in *Housefull*.

Although this new vision of India is seen throughout the films mentioned in this chapter, it is also summed up by social journalist Shobhaa Dé in her book, *Superstar India*: India's pride in having three World Heritage Sites; its shame at the squalor, frustration; but the comfort of the generous hospitality on trains, the anxieties about needing to be bicultural, to look sophisticated for the West and the sensitivity of Indians to possible slights from Westerners in ways which suggest that they think Westerners are obsessed with finding fault with them. As Dé points out, her generation grew up with very little and the transition to the new, consumerist India and the rise of a new kind of wealthy class does indeed make many Indians feel unsure of the present.

The hit comedy film *Housefull* (dir. Sajid Khan, 2010) is set in London, with each character representing a different Indian community but uniting as Indians in an overseas setting, despite jokes about each other's names, diet and behaviour. A hotelier says at the beginning of the film that the British have exploited us (meaning Indians) for 200 years and now is the time for us to show them who we are. However, the climax of the film occurs when the diasporic Indians attend a party at Buckingham Palace, meeting the Queen, the Prince of Wales and the Duchess of Cornwall, direct descendants of the former (British) Emperors of India, showing a deep ambivalence here to the historical legacy of colonialism.

The British left India in 1947, meaning that the vast majority of the current population was born since Independence, with many being second or third generation in this regard. The rhetoric about the British and the West in general is not about pre-1947 but rather about the idea that others are always out to demean India and Indians and that India still has to prove itself. Stories in the Indian press featuring the misadventures of overseas Indians or negative reports about India often carry implications of racism and colonialism, at least for the older generation of Indians, although cities that are much loved by the Hindi films, notably London, are now multiracial.

Samar busks in tourist locations in London in *JTHJ*.

Yet even as a new Indianness forged from trans-nationalism and pride in India have emerged, divisions within Indian society have remained deep and may even have been exacerbated. These fissures are formed around a range of categories, including caste, region and class, which are examined in the next chapter.

TWO

# Diversity: Region, Caste and Class

In the early years of Independence, the single and all-important category of identity was meant to be 'Indian', a view upheld in Nehru's *Discovery of India*. In the intervening years, the region, no longer subsumed under 'unity in diversity' and parades at Republic Day, has become the focus of regional nationalisms and linguistic difference. The category of caste, which was contested by India's nationalist leaders in the hope that it would fade, is now heavily reinforced by the state, which addresses it in the context of positive discrimination (reservations), keeping around 50 per cent of government positions for the lower castes. Class, once based on wealth, education and employment, has extended its reach to be defined also by consumerism as India's new middle classes have risen and expanded.

In the post-Independence period, Hindi cinema, aspiring to be India's national cinema, aimed to address the new Indian citizen. The impossibility of creating an ideal modern Indian citizen led to an awkward avoidance of caste, viewed as pre-modern or even anti-national. Cinema upheld the policy of a national language through its use of the lingua franca of Hindi/Urdu/Hindustani, playing a role more important than that of the state, which, although promoting *shuddh* or 'pure' Hindi, was meanwhile shaping the new nation into linguistic and regional states, thereby entrenching regional differences.

Although the Hindi cinema industry itself has never been located in the Hindi Belt of north India, the north, largely Uttar Pradesh and

*79*

Punjab, has remained the imaginary homeland for many Bombay-based Hindi films. While the films of the last twenty years may be set in Mumbai or overseas, often in London or New York, the main characters of the films reveal by their language and their names that they are north Indians. Just as Hollywood sought to appeal to a pan-American public by flattening ethnicities through using vaguely WASP norms and stereotyping minorities (such as Irish, Italian and African-American), so Hindi cinema shows the north Indian high-caste Hindu as the 'normal' Indian. Other populations become 'minorities' and the rest of India 'regions', which are marked as divergent from the mainstream. Defined by Hindi cinema, this figure has become, by default, the average Indian. As in other cinemas, the principal male role is usually the lead figure, seen in the narrative but also reflected in the pay. Female divergences from this norm of the Indian are found more frequently than male.

In an attempt to create the Indian 'Everyman' in the 1950s, heroes such as Raj Kapoor's onscreen character, Raj, were only vaguely 'north Indian' or Hindustani. Caste was eschewed, with characters not having full names to avoid mentioning region and caste – so 'Mr Raj' or 'Kumar' could be added. Raj Kapoor, like many other film stars, looked nothing like an 'average' Indian, being tall, well built and fair with blue eyes – features which marked him as upper caste and class as well as belonging to the north. Yet, in *Shree 420/The Trickster* (dir. Raj Kapoor, 1955), where Raj experiments with identity partly through changing clothes to switch from tramp to businessman, he also plays a laundryman without any reference to the traditional (low) caste of *dhobi*. Raj's fluid identity is not shared by the villain of the piece, Seth Sonachand Dharamanand, whose name and dress are among the markers of a traditional *baniya* or merchant although his actual caste and region are unspecified. In recent films, the mention of caste names such as 'barber' and 'cobbler' led to protests from these communities, with, for example, the film originally called *Billu Barber* finally being released as *Billu* (dir. Priyadarshan, 2009).

This chapter examines three major intertwined social and ethnic markers – region, caste and class – as part of a shifting idea of Indianness from the 1950s concept of a homogeneous – or hegemonic – national unity onwards, before looking in subsequent chapters at core values which enable the Indian to hold his, and less often her, place in the new world, based on some idea of emotion, religiosity and relationships, especially a commitment to the family. Lately, a shift towards ideas of being true to oneself and one's feelings has become more central, especially in the more upmarket films.

## Region

*Chak de! India/Go for It, India!* (dir. Shimit Amin, 2007) was premiered in London as part of India's 60th anniversary celebrations. Its rallying call is not just for the Indian women's hockey squad but also for Indian unity itself, as the film shows that national success depends on bringing the regions together in order to work as an effective team.

In the film, Kabir Khan (Shah Rukh Khan), a Muslim hockey star, is sacked as Captain of the Indian team after his missed penalty leads to their defeat by Pakistan, thereby questioning his loyalty to India. He later coaches the Indian women's hockey team, which is seen as being of little importance compared to the men's team, knitting together a squad comprised of women from all over India in what seems to be a lost cause. The women's changing-room squabbles echo regional politics, notably over

The hockey team training at India Gate in *Chak de! India.*

the city of Chandigarh, joint capital of Haryana and Punjab, or internal racism as the team's northeasterners from Manipur and Mizoram face the 'non-Indian' jibes that are commonplace in Delhi. Two players are bullied by their partners to quit sports, further underlining India's ongoing struggle over gender. The primacy of national unity is underlined by the absence of any romance for Shah Rukh Khan, for whom integration and devotion to the country are all that matters.

Although the action in a Hindi film is often located in Mumbai, London or New York or some composite place, the characters are usually of north Indian, vaguely UP (Uttar Pradesh) or Punjabi origin, wherever they live. The Hindi cinema's new national image is not the diversity of India but the old 'Hindustan' – the Gangetic plain – and Punjab.

## The Importance of Language

Hindi cinema is considered to be India's national cinema, which is in large part due to its being made in Hindi, the most spoken language. The majority language of India's north Indian cities before Independence was a lingua franca that could be variously described as Hindi, Urdu or Hindustani. Much has been written about the intricate and entwined emergence of these languages and their separation in north India. The terms have been used differently over time but, in short, Hindi and Urdu, though almost identical at some levels, have very different scripts (Hindi being Devanagari, the script widely used for Sanskrit; Urdu, Perso-Arabic) and diverge considerably at higher registers, where Hindi draws on Sanskrit and Urdu on Persian and Arabic. The separation of Hindi and Urdu from the mid-nineteenth century is due in part to political reasons, with Urdu becoming seen as a 'Muslim language' due to its association with Muslim courts and its close ties with the Persian language and Persian literature (see also chapter Four). While this may have been true for parts of north India, Urdu was also the language of culture of the Punjab for Hindus and Sikhs living there, until 1947, and it was a language of public culture and the bazaar in other Indian cities, such as Bombay, from the nineteenth century. After Partition, Hindi became the national language of India and Urdu of Pakistan so 'Hindi' is the term used as shorthand for the language of the films.

In the colonial period, once 'talkies' were established in the 1930s, the Hindi/Urdu/Hindustani lingua franca was the major language of the Bombay film studios. The Bombay Talkies studio, for example, made Hindi films, although it was staffed mostly by Bengalis as well as Germans, who, it is assumed, communicated in English. Studios outside Bombay made films in the local language as well as Hindi, so Calcutta's New Theatres made Bengali and Hindi films, and Poona's Prabhat Film Company made Marathi and Hindi films. Prabhat used a north Indian *mise en scène* for their Hindi films, showing that the association of the language with north India remained.

After 1947, many Punjabis and Bengalis migrated to work in the film industry, where Hindi and English are now established as the working languages of the business. Given the history of Hindi as the urban lingua franca, the status of Delhi as the seat of political power and the sizeable potential audiences of the north Indian cities, as well as the language skills of the new migrants, Hindi flourished as the language of Bombay/Mumbai's cinema – even though the largest part of the population speaks Marathi and a substantial minority Gujarati.

The 1950s saw the creation of new states in India, many of whose boundaries were those of language. Bombay State became Maharashtra and Gujarat, with Bombay as the capital of Maharashtra, where Marathi, the official language of the state, has yet to become a lingua franca despite local attempts, with Hindi(-Urdu) retaining this function. Hindi, now the official language of India, also remains the language of the bazaar and a wide variety of Hindi is spoken in India today. However, Hindi films mostly use a north Indian variety of the language, whose best speaker is usually said to be Amitabh Bachchan, who is also a mimic of regional varieties and Bambaiya (Bombay's colloquial Hindi). The son of one of India's most famous poets, Amitabh is from UP, where Nehru insisted Urdu was taught in schools after Independence; it became the second official language in 1989. All this is changing today as many of the younger stars speak only Mumbai-inflected Hindi, even if they are playing north Indians, and do not attempt to modify their speech.

Mainstream Indian cinema is not interested in promoting any language in particular but wants to reach the widest audience possible. However, some films do show sensitivity to different types of language, with *Mughal-e-Azam*, for example, featuring Hindus more prone to speaking Sanskritized Hindi and its Muslim ruling classes tending to speak Farsi-inflected Urdu. Also, the language of Hindi cinema, with its flair for style and quotability and grandiloquent rhetoric, often draws on the strong association with Urdu, and in particular the Urdu lyric. Many of the screen's most famous writers were firmly based in Urdu literary traditions, such as the Salim-Javed writing duo (Salim Khan and Javed Akhtar), who scripted many of the blockbusters of the 1970s and '80s – famed for their quotable dialogues. However, it seems today that Hindi and Urdu are diverging and Persianized Urdu, while admired for its grace, is less understood and less well suited to the characters of contemporary cinema.

Hindi is taught in school, where it is often a much-hated subject, especially by the English-speaking middle classes. Films such as *Main hoon naa/I'm Here for You* (dir. Farah Khan, 2004) poked fun at the frumpy Hindi teacher, who teaches Sanskritized Hindi. When Munnabhai (in *Lage raho Munna Bhai*), who speaks very little English, decides to woo the more sophisticated Jahnvi, he attempts *shuddh* ('pure' – that is, educated or Sanskritized) Hindi in inappropriate phrases, resulting in general hilarity. Accented Hindi, rather than *shuddh* Hindi or Urdu, has been used for a long time. Bhojpuri/Bihari accents, for example, are associated with dacoits, as with Dilip Kumar in *Gunga Jumna* (dir. Nitin Bose, 1961), Gabbar Singh in *Sholay/Embers* (dir. Ramesh Sippy, 1975) and now in the new wave of films set in the badlands of north India, such as Anurag Kashyap's *Gangs of Wasseypur*. Accents are sometimes used to give authenticity, hence Western UP Hindi was found in Vishal Bharadwaj's *Omkara* (2006), although some actors deployed this accent considerably better than others. Salman Khan always keeps his Mumbai Hindi accent intact even in these situations, but given that his star image disrupts reality, this switch rarely invites comment.

Hindi films are popular in south India, at least in the cities where the Telugu and Tamil industries flourish, the local industries finding larger audiences despite the smaller number of people who speak those languages in comparison with Hindi. India has also retained another bridge language other than Hindi, namely English. The Official Language Act 1963, amended in 1967, gave English the status of the 'associate official language' of India. From 1968, the three-language formula was brought into the education system to encourage north Indians to learn a south Indian language and vice versa, but this was mostly ignored. English gives access to a global language as well as the global media, so the desire to acquire it is strong. It is estimated that around 5 per cent of the population speak it, but this may be increasing, despite a resurgence in the prestige of Hindi among the new middle classes. *English Vinglish* is the delightful story of a middle-class housewife who sets out to learn English in order to improve her self-esteem. Language remains a contested issue in India but it seems that many languages are thriving in the new media as well as in their more established domains.

One of the striking features of language in India is the switching between English and Hindi (or other languages) – whether this be words, phrases, sentences or just changing languages several times during a conversation. A frequently heard example in the film industry is when the director tells the story of a film to the actors and others in English but speaks the dialogues in Hindi. The reasons are complex, being more than simply shifting domains and ranging from the expression of a concept one knows only in one language to emphasis and style.

In the older films, English was the language of colonialism and the elites who stepped into their shoes (frequently used commands in films included 'Shut up!' or 'Idiot!'), but by the 1990s it had become a more widespread language associated with privilege, education and class. The meeting of English and Hindi has also spawned words, phrases, sentences or dialogues that are called 'Hinglish'. Hinglish seems to have developed in

*85*

advertising and in the film magazines of the 1970s founded as advertising opportunities, in particular *Stardust* under the editorship of Shobhaa Dé, and it became known in literature most famously with Salman Rushdie. Hinglish has now spread through advertising, with campaigns such as Pepsi's 'Dil maange more'/'The Heart Wants More', to film titles such as *Jab we met/When We Met* (2007) and *Love aaj kal/Love Today* (2009; both films dir. Imtiaz Ali).

Hinglish is seen in both speech and lyrics, one of the most striking examples being in an 'indie'-style film from 2011, *Delhi Belly* (dir. Abhinay Deo), a film about cool urban style, in which English and Hindi are 'rhymed' for comic effect – 'Go to hell, jaa chudail'/'Get lost, witch' – while the Hindi is replete with innuendo and double entendres, which were famously overlooked by the censor board. *Gangs of Wasseypur* uses English extensively in its song lyrics, such as: 'Moora'/'Stupid' – 'Jo bhi wrong-wa hai usse, Set right-wa karo ji'/'Whatever is wrong, put it right'. English connotes style as well as class but knowledge of cool Hindi is now just as essential and the blend of the two has to be hip, from quoting old Hindi dialogues to new English expressions, such as throwing in 'whatever' and 'like'. Knowledge of English is increasing in India, not least through the desire to be cosmopolitan and advance socially but also due to the availability of English in various media. However, Hindi holds its own and films remain one of the major places where new forms of urban Hindi are developing.

English is often used for comedy, whether this is the use of English by unlikely people or getting English wrong, such as the taxi driver who repeats, 'You come come, Memsaab' instead of 'You're welcome' (*Raja Hindustani/Indian King*, dir. Dharmesh Darshan, 1996). Other characters like to throw English catchphrases around, so in *Karan Arjun* (dir. Rakesh Roshan, 1995), the villain keeps saying, 'What a joke!'

English is also the language of stock film 'communities' such as Christians. Hence, in *Ajab Prem ki ghazab kahani/The Amazing Story of Wonderful Prem* (dir. Rajkumar Santoshi, 2009), Katrina Kaif plays Jenny, a Christian whose mother tongue is English (Kaif does this in many other films, presumably in part to cover up her English-accented Hindi). The lead, Prem, speaks very little English – to show that he is middle class and a poor student. When praying to Jesus in church, however, he speaks (very bad) English to 'Jesus-ji' in order to cement this association with the religious community. In *JTHJ* (Yash Chopra's *Jab tak hai jaan/ As Long as I Live*, 2012), Samar (Shah Rukh Khan) addresses 'Sir Jesus' in English, which he learns from his Christian girlfriend (again played by Katrina Kaif).

The only other widely spoken language in Hindi films is Punjabi. There are many important Punjabis in the industry, including the Kapoors and the Chopras, and the Punjabi identity is associated with masculinity, the military and a community which lives life to the full. Punjabi is also the language of other forms of public culture in India, notably a sizeable non-film music industry which is also closely tied to the diasporic Indian audiences.

In other words, the imaginary world of Hindi cinema is largely articulated via Hindi, English and a mixture of the two. Films have to respect their domains and follow appropriate usage, whether this is marking religion, intimacy, ways of being modern or connecting to a global culture by saying things such as 'I love you'. Hindi is now becoming as hip as English, and its use is no indicator of ignorance, as perhaps it once was. Rather, the imaginary worlds associated with the language are changing, so while differences in the type of Hindi and the level of English may still mark region, religion, education and class, they also indicate choice and self-definition through style and its knowledge of English. The question may yet arise as to whether a Bollywood film can be made in English.

Regional difference in film is marked in ways other than language and performance, through the ethnicity of the stars and the texts of all the various media discussions about these stars that occur outside the film itself. Most stars are popular in particular regions or among certain groups. Dharmendra and Sunny Deol find their biggest fan-following in Punjab, whereas Shah Rukh Khan is popular in the diaspora, as he often plays diasporic roles. Some female stars are celebrated for their regional diversity, so Bengali women such as Sharmila Tagore may have nicknames – hers was the 'Bengal tigress'. Similarly, female actors with south Indian backgrounds, for example, may have this fact picked up on. Vidya Balan, whose family was originally from Tamil Nadu, though she was brought up in Mumbai, has played a south Indian, Silk Smita, in *The Dirty Picture* (dir. Milan Luthria, 2011); however, the performance seemed more remote from her normal character roles than her Bengali role in *Parineeta/The Married Woman* (dir. Pradeep Sarkar, 2005). There has never been a major south Indian male star in Hindi films, with only Kamal Haasan playing leading roles, although 'superstar' Rajni, India's biggest star, acts mostly in Tamil films but is a byword for superstardom even in the north.

Regionalism within the films themselves is rare among the male heroes. The hero may well live in Mumbai, the location for so many films, or he may now live outside India, but he usually has a north Indian name. Yet other Indian ethnicities are seen, usually drawing on those essentialized in the public imagination. Apart from the north Indian, upper-caste Hindu male, these are nearly all exaggerated, performative roles.

While the hero is usually vaguely north Indian, it is also popular for the hero to be Punjabi (see text above on the language). The Punjabis dominate much of India's public culture, whether the film or music

Women dancing in the yellow mustard fields of Punjab in *DDLJ*.

industry. They were labelled a 'martial race' by the British, who created Punjabi regiments in the Indian Army, and this tag is proudly upheld even today. In the 1950s, the Punjabis created much of the style of the modern Hindi film, and, perhaps following the troubles in the Punjab in the 1980s and the anti-Sikh riots in Delhi in 1984, many of the biggest hits of the last two decades have been specifically Punjabi in theme and were reconsiderations of the nature of Punjabiyat (Punjabiness). While the hero may play a turbaned Sikh, as in *Rocket Singh: Salesman of the Year* (dir. Shimit Amin, 2009) or the Rishi Kapoor/Saif Ali Khan shared role in *Love aaj kal*, the Punjabi hero is more usually a Hindu or a clean-shaven Sikh.

The film which is said to be the first 'Bollywood' film, *Dilwale dulhania le jayenge*, is about the imagined Punjab, set out at the beginning of the film as the migrant's dream-of-return location. Europe is where the film's couple get together, but they have to go to Punjab to enter the world of the Indian (Punjabi) family, although it is one peopled only by Hindus. In Aditya Chopra's later film, *Rab ne bana di jodi/A Match Made by God* (2000), the setting is Amritsar, the holy city for Sikhs. Another of the biggest hits of the last two decades was *Gadar – ek prem katha/Turmoil: A Love Story* (dir. Anil Sharma, 2001), whose hero is a brave Sikh who marries a Muslim woman for whom he will do anything other than agree to her father's command to abuse India. Yash Chopra's *Veer Zara* (2004) has an Indian airforce officer, Veer, fall in love with a Pakistani Muslim, Zaara, where their common Punjabiness overrides any religious or national difference.

Although Gujaratis form a substantial proportion of the Indian diaspora, they are closely associated in the public imaginary with Mumbai's Gujarati mercantile classes, and are shown mostly as miserly and conservative, obsessed with money and with the particularities of their diet. Just before the Hindi/Punjabi song 'Mahi ve'/'Beloved' in *Kal ho na ho*, the Gujaratis attempt a song and dance where they mention their famous vegetarian food (*gaathiya* and *undhiyu*) and are seriously uncool. In *Housefull*, the Gujaratis are shown to have their stereotypical strong women and money-loving men.

South Indians (usually lumped together) are frequently comical figures, wearing traditional clothes, speaking heavily accented Hindi and exclaiming 'Aiyo'/'Oh!', as Shah Rukh Khan's home production *Ra.One/The Demon* (2011) had him do when he acts as a 'south Indian' – typically highly educated, wearing a curly wig and eating spaghetti and yoghurt with his hands. He visits the south in *Chennai Express*, a huge hit in 2013. Rani Mukherji stars as a Maharashtrian girl who falls in love with a Tamil and with Tamil cinema in *Aiyaa* (dir. Sachin Kundalkar, 2012), where South Indian cinema is seen as bright and vulgar, as in Milan Luthria's *The Dirty Picture*. The comic Mehmood was famous for his impersonation of Hyderabadi Muslims but also for his south Indian musician in *Padosan/Neighbour* (dir. Jyoti Swaroop, 1968). This established the south Indian as a comic figure in Hindi cinema and was followed by many others, including Satish Shah in *Saajan chale saasural/Double Trouble* (dir. David Dhawan, 1996). Mithun as Krishnan Aiyer in *Agneepath/The Path of Fire* (dir. Mukul Anand, 1990) was initially made fun of as the lungi-wearing coconut seller but turned out to be a true friend to the film's embattled family. The mocking of the south in films seems strange as the south offers a good market for Hindi films, at least in the big cities, while film-makers such as Mani Ratnam are highly respected in the north and where his bilingual and dubbed films are known. Kerala's Priyadarshan is also renowned in north India for his remakes of south Indian films, many of which have been huge hits.

The British classified Bengalis as effeminate and thus lacking in hero material. They are also seen as formidably intellectual, normally wearing dark-rimmed glasses and preferring to speak Bengali and English to Hindi. *Vicky Donor* (dir. Shoojit Sircar, 2012), depicts the prejudices of Punjabis and Bengalis towards each other as a Punjabi man marries a Bengali. Perhaps this is why there have been relatively few Bengali male stars in Hindi film, with none playing a major role during the period of this book, although Saif Ali Khan is half-Bengali, while Bengali female stars include Rani Mukherji, Bipasha Basu and the partly Bengali Kajol.

As the film industry is based in Mumbai, it is not surprising that many of the lead characters live in Mumbai and speak Mumbai-accented Hindi, even if they are north Indian. Mumbai is usually shown as the most modern Indian city, in terms of its liberal values, its architecture and its mixing of different communities. However, it is also the seat of one of the most strongly regionalist groups, the Shiv Sena, who feature occasionally in films, or rather groups which are usually identified as representing them do, in movies such as Mani Ratnam's *Bombay* and Ram Gopal Varma's *Sarkar* (2005) and *Sarkar Raj* (2008).

These regionalist groups figure in the imaginary of the film-makers and exhibitors, as they have acted as unofficial film censors – for example the regionalist group Maharashtra Navnirman Sena disrupted screenings of Karan Johar's production *Wake Up Sid* (dir. Ayan Mukherji, 2009) for using 'Bombay' rather than 'Mumbai'. The Shiv Sena tried to prevent screenings of Johar's *My Name Is Khan*, not because it was a Hindu-Muslim love story, but because its Muslim hero, Shah Rukh Khan, recently made a statement about letting Pakistanis play in the IPL.

Hindi films now try to create an Everyman not by avoiding mentioning region but by sticking to regional stereotypes. The most successful of these is Munna Bhai, who features in two films, *Munna Bhai MBBS* and *Lage raho Munna bhai*. Although Munnabhai could be from any north Indian community (Munna means 'kid'; -bhai means 'brother' or 'gangster'), we know he is not a street kid, but he is a migrant and his real name is Murali Prasad Sharma, suggesting a north Indian Brahmin. He is no educated Brahmin, however; rather he is a thug and a speaker of Bombay street slang. The film takes the latter to new heights (from its development in cinema from the 1950s onwards by writers such as Abrar Alvi, through the personae of Amitabh Bachchan, Aamir Khan and others), creating quotable dialogues and phrases such as '*Bole to . . .*'/'Like', celebrating the local 'Bambaiya' dialect, the speech of the ordinary man.

Munnabhai became one of the few national heroes, someone who could be hero of one of the rare all-India hits. Its star, Sanjay Dutt, is himself from a mixed background. He is the son of Sunil Dutt, a Punjabi migrant to Bombay who became a leading cinema star, and Nargis, one of India's greatest-ever film stars and the daughter of Jaddan Bai, a Muslim and one of India's few female film-makers, and a Hindu doctor. Nargis' greatest role was in, and as, *Mother India*, and she was later an international representative of India as well as a member of the upper house of the Parliament of India (Rajya Sabha). Sanjay Dutt's troubled life seems to add to his popularity in this film as the *aam aadmi* or regular guy who struggles to find his place in the world.

The decades since Independence have seen continued stereotyping of non-north Indians. It is impossible to make a character region-neutral, but while there have been small attempts in some more realist films to present on screen-characters that are less performative of their region, mainstream films create stereotypes that many dub racist, as with *Housefull*. In this comedy, everyone's regionalisms are exaggerated apart from the hero, who seems to be vaguely north Indian, while his girlfriend Sandy is a south Indian – Soundarya Bahgyalakshmi Venkateshwari Basappa Rao – and his friends include Maharastrians and Gujaratis, Sindhis, Punjabis and a Muslim (in the last, the category of religion seems to serve the same function as region), plus the half-Italian character Akhri Pasta, who supplies an Italian stereotype. Apart from Pasta, other differences include exaggerated portrayals of a traditional older generation versus a younger generation shown as a modern cosmopolitan, sophisticated group.

During the 1950s, Hindi cinema may have played some role in enabling the imaginary of the nation by addressing audiences as Indian citizens as well as by creating figures who have come to represent the modern Indian. In the early 1990s, many films examined threats to the integrity of the nation, mostly from domestic separatist movements but also from Pakistan. This anxiety seems to have abated lately, perhaps as the boundaries of the state seem less important to the concept of 'Indianness', which now can include the diaspora, and now that the hero, while still usually a north Indian, upper-caste Hindu, can be shown to differ from more traditional models by living overseas or being associated with a region without undermining the idea that he can be a national figure.

## Metropolitan India

Perhaps more important than the regions for the Hindi film-makers and their audiences is the division between metropolitan and non-metropolitan India. The Hindi film audience is overwhelmingly urban, so this is the audience the industry seeks to address rather than the traditional village Indian who is hardly ever likely to view the films.

The 'metros', or modern metropolitan cities, may be situated far apart and be capitals of particular regions, but in many ways they are more similar to one another than they are to their hinterlands. Some cities hardly seem to belong to their hinterlands – such as Mumbai, despite attempts to make it more Maharashtrian. These days, differences between metropolises are marked less by state and language and more by lifestyle and other choices.

Some metros seem to have become deregionalized and for many people Mumbai is *the* Indian cosmopolis. It looks out to the Indian Ocean and the Gulf (it is a major exit port for the Hajj) and now increasingly to the USA, seeming to turn its back on its hinterland. Regional differences remain (so one can be a Punjabi in Mumbai, even after many generations), but other factors can be more defining than region or one's language (Hindi and English are only the dominant bridge languages in the city). These factors include the fact that Mumbai is the media centre of India, not only for film but also for music, television and advertising. India's rich, who have long lived here, are building new towers for themselves, including the world's most expensive home (for the Ambani family). However, Mumbai is often used as wallpaper or a meaningless backdrop in films.

Delhi has begun to feature more frequently in films, as the seat of politics and history in politically charged movies such as *Rang de basanti* or as a real home for north Indians who attend its universities – examples include *Rockstar* (dir. Imtiaz Ali, 2012) and *Band baaja baaraat/Bands, Horns and Revelry* (dir. Maneesh Sharma, 2010) as well as new 'indie' films such as Dibakar Banerjee's.

Calcutta features as a city for intellectuals in *Kahaani/The Story* (dir. Sujoy Ghosh, 2012) and in Anglicized historicals such as *Parineeta*, but it appears less often than London and New York, which feature so frequently in Hindi films that they seem to be Indian metros. As India's changes began during the 1990s, the question of national identity re-emerged as a central concern, questioning the Indianness of the Indian born and raised overseas. Over the last twenty years, the idea of the trans-national Indian has become fixed and now seems to be as simply another cosmopolitan or metropolitan Indian rather than a foreigner.

The 'small town', which has begun to feature in Indian cinema recently, would be a large city by non-Indian standards and is distinguished just by being non-metropolitan. These 'towns' are usually in UP, including major ancient cities such as Allahabad or Varanasi, or in Punjab, such as Bhatinda in *Jab we met*. Choosing a small-town location may offer film-makers a different type of storyline, as in *Bunty aur Babli/ Bunty and Babli* (dir. Shaad Ali Sehgal, 2005), in which the young couple are running away from just such a stifling small town to Mumbai, or in *Tanu Weds Manu* (dir. Anand L. Rai, 2011), in which the heroine is determined to escape from Kanpur. However, the small town is usually inauthentic. So, for instance, Bihar might be referred to or stories grounded there, but films are rarely shot in Bihar and the actors' accents are not local – Prakash Jha's films are an example of this. Non-metropolitan India may isolate the action from the city and present problematic social issues that hardly affect metropolitans, while also highlighting more traditional categories such as region, caste and class.

The village, where most Indians live, is seen as being 'authentic India', but it is not where most film viewers live – or want to live. Earlier Indian films extolled rural values such as simplicity, honesty and family life, and although these are still seen in 1990s films such as *Raja Hindustani Indian King* (dir. Dharmesh Darshan, 1996) they have largely faded from the screen. The early 1990s had figures such as the actor Govinda, who were associated with non-urban life and its values, though often as poor people who came into conflict with the local rich. A popular genre until the mid-1990s was the 'Thakur' ('feudal landlord') film, which featured overbearing landowning castes ruling the decent poor with a heavy hand and cheating members of their own families, who then sought revenge. This was the motive behind films such as *Ram Lakhan* (dir. Subhash Ghai, 1980) or *Karan Arjun* (dir. Rakesh Roshan, 1995), which were sidelined by the rising diasporic romance and cinematic emphasis on consumerist culture.

Hill stations featured in earlier Indian cinema as tourist destinations, but by the 1990s only Ooty (Ootacamund) was still used. Even films which were shot in Ooty such as *Jab pyaar kisi se hota hai/When Someone Falls in Love* (dir. Deepak Sareen, 1998) featured Swiss landscapes, though these purported to be in India – unlike the scenes that were shot in the UK. *Ajab Prem ki ghazab kahani/ The Amazing Story of Wonderful Prem* (dir. Rajkumar Santoshi, 2009) included a composite of several hill stations, including Mahabaleshwar and Shimla.

Rural images were later reintroduced as they became part of the new culture of consumerism, with tourist destinations featuring heavily. One form in which rural places have survived in mainstream Indian films is as

The story of Prem (Ranbir) is set in a hill station in *APGK*.

a kind of tourism for the new consumer. Thus the Rajasthan seen in *Lamhe/ Moments* (dir. Yash Chopra, 1991) or *Bhool bhulaiya/The Labyrinth* (dir. Priyadarshan, 2007) is one of tourist destinations, although during this period more exotic overseas locations became popular. Yash Chopra continued to shoot in Switzerland, with his couple in *Darr/ Fear* (1993) finding that, in the song 'Darwaza band kar lo'/ 'Close the Door', the walls of their dream house could be pushed back to open into a Swiss meadow. Switzerland became an ever more popular shooting destination, with successful comedies such as *Haseena man jayegi/ The Beautiful Woman Will Consent* (dir. David Dhawan, 1999) filming there, but in recent years producers have sought out new cities such as Berlin in *Don 2* (dir. Farhan Akhtar, 2011), which was probably also intended to appeal to Shah Rukh Khan's famous German fans), or new countries such as Spain in *Zindagi na milegi dobara/You Only Live Once* (dir. Zoya Akhtar, 2011). Other parts of the world are shown more as backdrops or tourist or consumer destinations rather than as places which carry much meaning to Indians.

While the small town and the village became places that were barely part of the popular imaginary during this period, more realistic films began to use these locations. Prakash Jha's 'Bihar' films, which use small-town and village locations but not in Bihar, and the recent UP films (see below) evoke dystopias, while art cinema and non-Hindi cinema continue to use these locations as well as Mumbai. A satire on the media, *Peepli (Live!)*, was produced by Aamir Khan, whose endorsement helped it reach a wide audience. This concerned itself with the problems of village life, not least of which is the issue of farmer suicides, but had the protagonist migrate to the city to work as a labourer, as even urban poverty is better than life in the village.

## Caste

The couple dreams of their new house, whose wall will open onto a Swiss meadow, in *Darr*.

*ZNMD* – three heroes and their car in Spain.

It is often said that caste is not mentioned in Hindi cinema. However, caste names are often used as surnames and many characters have recognizable caste names, quite often the Punjabi Khatri or other north Indian upper-caste names such as Malhotra or Khanna, notably in Yash Raj Films. It would be more accurate to say that films rarely raise caste as a social issue. This is partly because the main characters are usually from the same or similar upper castes, but why this should be so and the accompanying silence on caste needs further examination in order to better understand popular imaginings of what caste means today.

Caste is a much-misunderstood category, variously viewed as religious, social or political or a combination of these. There is much controversy about whether caste is foundational to a hierarchical Indian civilization, whether it is concerned with traditional occupations or whether the 'caste system' was invented by the British as part of their taxonomy of India. Nationalist leaders debated the merits of caste, while others hoped it would wither away in the face of modernity. The debates continue as to its historical origins and it remains a fluid category which means different things to different people. However, caste is enshrined in the Indian Constitution and in Indian law, where its meanings are more precise, though still contested.

Although caste discrimination, especially the practice of 'untouchability', was outlawed in the Constitution of India (1950), the Indian government enshrines it in law for its policies of positive discrimination, known as 'reservations'. In 1935 the government used the categories of Scheduled Castes (SCs), formerly called 'Untouchables' and 'Harijans' or 'children of God' by Gandhi; now known as Dalits: 'The oppressed') and Scheduled Tribes (STs) for indigenous people. Other Backward Castes (OBCs) were acknowledged in the Constitution and are regarded as economically and socially disadvantaged. While the figures are not clear, approximate proportions are as follows: the upper castes, which include Brahmins, warriors and merchants, form around 15 per cent of the population;

roughly 15 per cent are other religions (many of which have some form of caste); the OBCs form what has been estimated at wildly differing figures between about 30 and 50 per cent of the population (mostly due to a problem of definition); 16 per cent are SCs; and 7 per cent STs. Twenty per cent reservations were first brought in for Dalits soon after Independence, but the major controversy during the period on which this book focuses is that, following the recommendations of the Mandal Commission in 1990, 27 per cent of reservations were allocated for OBCs, which means that in some states half the positions in certain government institutions are reserved for the lower castes, including in higher education.

Following the extension of reservations, amid other political and social changes, groups have sought to renegotiate their status. This is not the upward mobility of raising one's status (Sanskritization) but rather a downgrading of one's caste in order to access government reservations.

Minorities, that is religious minorities, do not have access to reservations. If Dalits convert to Islam or Christianity, they lose their eligibility for reservations, while Muslims, who often have some form of caste, do not have access, although the Mandal Commission declared a number of Muslim groups (totalling about half the Muslim population) to be Backward groups. However, this refers only to specific communities and some Muslim groups are pursuing this matter, with south Indian states – where some leading political groups are anti-Brahminical – being more active than the north.

Caste was often seen as disrupting democracy, but recent years have shown that political mobilization by lower castes can alter the balance of political power – as seen in UP and Bihar. Bihar and UP have highly caste-based politics which have been successful because of their sheer numbers, despite the rise of Hindu nationalism (Hindutva). The rise of the lower castes in north India, even though this is the area from which the 'normal' Indian comes, and he is high-caste, is noticeable by its absence, except in particular political films. Perhaps the political world impinges more on Delhi, while those in Mumbai are unconcerned as politics is not their most important means to an end.

Things are certainly changing for some lower-caste Indians, such as business people and entrepreneurs, for whom the caste system is becoming more flexible and is less important than money, class and other social categories. However, caste's operations are multitudinous and it operates at many levels, such as an extension of family and kin networks which are important for jobs and housing, and caste oppression remains a serious social issue for many.

There is no major Dalit or OBC star in the Hindi film industry. While Dalit writing has become prominent in many Indian languages, Dalits are not known at any level of film-making, though why this should be so is unclear. Perhaps elite caste networks are far more powerful than is usually recognized, and those in the film industry have not been studied, although the dominance of Punjabi Khatris and Bengali Brahmins – at least until recently – has been notable. Many film stars are Muslim (such as the Khans) and some Christian (Mala Sinha; John Abraham is Parsi-Christian), but the absence of Dalits remains striking.

There is no single reason why films do not specifically raise the issue of caste. Caste may be shown without being named (unless the film includes a caste-specific profession such as that of a priest, who would have to be Brahmin, or if wedding rituals shown involve high castes), and one can avoid using caste names and use 'Mr Raj', 'Miss Suneeta' instead, even though audiences would know that these were high-caste people. Generic middle- to high-caste names are generally used in films, mostly Brahmins, Khatris, Thakurs, Seths, Kayasths and so on, and these pass without mention. Films that have specifically mentioned caste stand apart, although they have been criticized for their plotlines: for example, the 'Untouchable' girl sacrificing her life in *Acchut Kanya/The Untouchable Girl* (dir. Franz Osten, 1936) or the character who is found to really be a Brahmin by birth in *Sujata/The High-born* (dir. Bimal Roy, 1959), or when India needs to pull together and to do this has to have a Dalit (Kachra) and a blacksmith, Arjan – in *Lagaan*. *DevD* (2009), the adaptation of the 2002 version of the classic cinematic story of Devdas, now plays down the difference in (sub-)caste between Devdas Mukherjee and Parvati Chakrabarty, while focusing on social class.

One of the few recent mainstream films that engage with caste is *Swades*. The film has very Gandhian overtones, even, as previously mentioned, in the name of its hero, Mohan (Mohandas K. Gandhi). Mohan, a NASA scientist, is a Brahmin (Bhargav), but he takes up cudgels on behalf of Dalits in the village to allow them access to the village school. The film is very much a mainstream Hindi film in its narrative, use of song and the presence of Shah Rukh Khan, but is one with a social message at the heart of its entertainment. This and the cinematic quality of the feature put Gowariker's work closer to the non-mainstream realist cinema, as is Vishal Bharadwaj's *Omkara* (2006), a reworking of Shakespeare's *Othello* story where Omkara Shukla (Othello) is the son of a Brahmin father and low-caste mother, while the other major figures are all Brahmins: Tiwari, Tyagi, Upadhyay, Mishra.

'Parallel' or 'middle' cinema, a more realist form, mentions caste overtly in films such as Shyam Benegal's *Ankur/The Seedling* (1974), whose heroine Lakshmi (Shabana Azmi) is a Dalit; Phoolan Devi in Shekhar Kapur's *Bandit Queen* (1994) was known to be a low-caste Mallah (boat-person). Jabbar Patel's Ambedkar biopic, *Dr Babasaheb Ambedkar* (2000), an English-language film about the writer of the Indian Constitution who was born a Dalit, is a robust attack on 'untouchability'.

Interestingly, some mainstream films have had characters whose caste has been clearly stated and which is sometimes important to their characters. Brahmins may be rogues, usually loveable ones, such as 'Munnabhai' (full name, Murali Prasad Sharma) and Chulbul Pandey of *Dabangg*. In *Rang de basanti/Colour it Saffron* (dir. Rakeysh Omprakasu Mehra, 2006), Laxman Pandey is involved in right-wing Hindutva politics, but is shown to know more about the revolutionary freedom fighters than his fellow students.

A big hit among young viewers was *Jaane tu . . . ya jaane na/Whether You Know or Not* (dir. Abbas Tyrewala, 2008), where much of the narrative is to do with caste. The hero is a 'non-violent Rajput [warrior]' with

The dead Rajput talks to his family from his portrait in *Jaane tu . . . ya jaane na*.

a very martial name, Jai Singh Rathore (played by Imran Khan), who eventually fights a man who hits the woman he loves. Jailed for the night, he meets two other Rathores who are related to him. They remind him that his caste duty is to beat someone up, get arrested, then ride a horse and that he ought do this, just as his late father, rather than his non-violent mother, would have wanted.

Films occasionally show caste mixing but it is not highlighted. In *Ram Lakhan*, Lakhan Pratap Singh, from a Thakur family, marries the daughter of Devdhar Shastri, who has a Brahmin name but who runs a grocery store as if he were a *baniya* (merchant). In *Dabangg*, the hero is a Brahmin who marries a potter, a Dalit caste.

Dalits usually feature only in 'political' films such as those of Prakash Jha. In Jha's *Raajneeti*, Ajay Devgan plays Suraj (a figure like the dispossessed brother, Karna, in the *Mahabharata*), while in *Aarakshan* (dir. Prakash Jha, 2011), Saif Ali Khan (whose father was a prince and whose mother is from an elite Bengali family) plays a Dalit who romances Dr Anand's daughter, who is presumably upper caste – one of the truly striking moments in Hindi film's depiction of caste.

Indigenous people in India are called 'tribals', whose depiction in films is usually embarrassing as they frequently wear ridiculous clothes, usually fairly skimpy costumes, with Himachal hats that often look more like something one would wear to a children's party. There is a parody of the set-piece tribal dance in *Chintuji* (dir. Ranjit Kapoor, 2009), a film in which Rishi 'Chintuji' Kapoor plays 'himself', spoofing the Hindi film star. The 'tribal dance' has the tribals singing names of iconic film directors in 'The Akira Kurosawa' song (the only Indian film-maker mentioned is Satyajit Ray). Should the hero romance a 'tribal' woman, she becomes a 'village belle' to avoid the mention of caste.

The silence on the caste issue could be to avoid controversies or censorship. When caste is mentioned, there may be objections to hurting the feelings of a community – hence the removal of the word *mochi*, 'cobbler', from a song in *Aaja nachle/Come Dancing* (dir. Anil Mehta, 2007), as it is a caste name rather than that of the profession *charmakar*, 'leather worker'. It is often held that the use of caste names is illegal, but this seems to be contested. The silence may be more to do with an imaginary of a modern casteless India that sees caste as an embarrassing pre-modern survivor.

Many urban, middle-class Indians say that caste is unimportant. This is because this group lives in modern cities that allow caste to be ignored, at least within their social group, where they are all likely to be upper-caste, coming from the three upper caste groups which make up a small proportion of the Indian population but which form almost all of the new middle classes. People are aware of their own caste group and traditions, although they may wish to confine them to their private, home lives. Broad alliances form in caste groups such as the *baniyas* and the Brahmins, which are vegetarian groups who prefer not to marry non-vegetarians. Often overheard is the phrase that it is easier to marry a non-Indian than someone from another caste.

The new middle classes may be silent about caste but they are fully aware of it, not least because they are the mainstay of anti-reservations supporters. For them, reservations are bitterly resented, combined with a distaste for the lower castes and a sense that they themselves are discriminated against. Reservations have changed their lives as they now have to bypass government institutions such as schools and colleges by going private or sending their children abroad; they now no longer seek government posts, in which they once formed an elite, turning instead to new professions such as information technology.

Caste remains hugely important in India today, especially in villages, where there are denser traditional occupations and networks which are at their thinnest in the city. While there are Dalit millionaires who prove to be exceptions to the rules, there are very few Dalits among the new middle classes. Arvind Adiga, in *White Tiger*, refers to these groups as those who live in 'the darkness', 'the vanished', as they are unimportant in the eyes of the successful because they are poor, low caste and barely touched by liberalization. They simply do not figure in the imagination of Bollywood.

This absence of the low castes means that Hindi cinema is caste-blind, rather than caste-neutral – providing that everyone who mixes socially is upper caste. This is their version of the caste-free society, while the lower castes perhaps dream of a caste-free society where everyone is so wealthy that caste no longer matters.

## Class

Films from the 1950s, trying to address the average Indian, frequently show the poor as noble and suffering, often possessing greater moral and ethical values than the rich, who are invariably seen as corrupt and amoral. A classic example is Raj Kapoor's *Shree 420*, where the wealthy Seth Sonachand Dharamanand is dishonest and evil while the poor Raj and Vidya are good. The two women, Vidya and Maya, are distinguished by a love of virtue and kindness in the former case and a love of money and lack of good qualities in the latter. Raj is torn between the two lifestyles, for he can transform himself and join the wealthy just by a change of clothes, while the film's bigger question is whether his goodness will be corrupted.

Older films show feudal riches and lifestyles, featuring Seths (merchants) and Thakurs (landlords), as well as the modern urban wealthy. In the 1950s, the wealthy were highly Anglicized, but during the 1960s a more modern styling began, seen best in Yash Chopra's *Waqt/Time* (1965). The good were now shown as being benevolent and respectful to the poor. A recurrent theme was rich-poor romance, so the rich boy falls for the poor girl in *Bobby* (dir. Raj Kapoor, 1973), or rich girl-poor boy in *Aan/Savage Princess* (dir. Mehboob Khan, 1952) and *Jab jab phool khile/Whenever Flowers Bloom* (dir. Suraj Prakash, 1965). The story often hinges on finding out that the poor partner's family was originally rich but deprived of its fortune for a range of complicated plot reasons, such as the suspicious father rejecting his child in *Awaara/The Tramp* (dir. Raj Kapoor, 1951), or illegitimacy, as in *Trishul/The Trident* (dir. Yash Chopra, 1978), while the swapping of babies has remained a frequent motif from earlier films such as *Munimji/The Clerk* (dir. Subodh Mukherjee, 1955).

Class in cinema spreads over a much wider range than just the very rich and the very poor. The films show interactions between many classes whose lifestyles and moral worlds are marked quite distinctly. Moreover, characters from these classes address audiences from other classes: because Amitabh Bachchan's Vijay movies seemed to address primarily the urban working classes, their appeal extended far beyond these classes, to anyone seeking an aesthetic of self-respect.

The Indian middle classes increased in number and in wealth after 1991, representing an enormous market primed for an influx of goods. However, while India is getting richer and income is rising overall, the distribution of income is getting more disparate. It is hard to define exactly what is meant by 'middle class' in any culture, let alone estimate its size, but around 250 million people seems to be a reasonable figure for India. This is about 20–25 per cent of India's population, a substantial increase on the 5 per cent of people defined as middle class at the time of Independence. While the economic divisions between classes may be absolute, the other features that define class, such as culture, education, lifestyle and consumerism patterns, show some overlaps, with many of the rich enjoying the culture of the new middle classes. The middle classes include a national bourgeoisie that created the postcolonial hegemonic version of Indian culture, perpetuated through government organizations (such as academies, universities and museums). This class enjoys India's classical traditions of music, dance and art, and reads literature in various languages, including English. They are largely secular and liberal in their views. Its older members would be likely to watch foreign cinema or the art or festival cinema, while the younger generation may well now enjoy mainstream cinema or at least the indie (*hatke* or multiplex) cinema.

It used to be said that Hindi cinema is the cinema of the working class and uneducated, seeking a few hours in aircon to escape the agonies of everyday life. In fact, although many of Hindi cinema's origins may be traced to the culture of the bazaar, in its early days it was also associated with traditional Brahminical elites, Parsi and Gujarati entrepreneurs and the products of the new colonial education. For example, the personnel of Bombay Talkies, a major studio of the 1930s, were foreign-educated and well travelled in Europe (and included several Germans), while Calcutta's New Theatre was staffed with lawyers, princes and other prestigious people. As the educated elites, or at least the male adults of those elites, turned their backs on this cinema in the 1980s – later it was often perceived to be a lower-class medium, although many film-makers were Anglophone and well educated, such as B. R. Chopra and the Anand brothers. Some of the others, however, were from shady worlds, and some of the female actors came from families whose low status was connected with working as performers; other female actors were from the upper classes, such as Durga Khote and Sharmila Tagore; male actors included members of elites – Amitabh Bachchan, for example.

In the 1950s, Hindi cinema tried to address all Indians, so while they often depicted elites, the films were peopled with a range of classes. In the period *before* the main focus of this book, that is, the 1980s, many of the films had strong working-class references, even if characters were socially mobile. They showed the urban working class particularly in action films, which usually had rape and revenge themes, as well as dramas heavily peopled with dacoits (bandits), smuggling, the underworld and the police.

The late 1970s and '80s, as well as witnessing the flourishing of the 'parallel' or 'middle' cinema, also saw mainstream film-makers such as Hrishikesh Mukherjee making films that appealed more to middle-class sensibilities. Domestic and light-hearted romances – often female-centred – portrayed modernizing Indians and their dilemmas, with characters who were often professionals – judges, doctors, teachers, journalists and so on. This period was when the middle classes were said to be reacting against the violence of the cinema and deserting it for television, which developed as a different imaginary located in the home. Television became particularly popular among women, many of whom could adapt their domestic schedule around the programmes. Domestic soap operas expanded rapidly from the 1990s onwards, with satellite and cable television bringing in a whole host of new viewing choices for the middle and upper classes.

These class differences were clearly marked in the cinema, but Hindi cinema has always been an entertainment arena, concerned not with presenting the realities of class issues but rather showing the way class is imagined. A popular theme is social mobility, very difficult to achieve in real life but easy in films, with their rags-to-riches stories as poor but clever men build business empires; or mobility can be achieved through marriage, where love conquers social divisions and a taxi driver can marry an upper-class girl (*Raja Hindustani*) or a street thug a doctor (*Munnabhai MBBS*).

The depictions of the wealthy in Hindi cinema are lower-class fantasies of the wealthy, which Ashis Nandy calls the slum's eye view. The characters are wealthy but they do not have the education and culture of an elite, being culturally lower class. These are not the upper classes' view of themselves but depictions of the nouveau riche. These class distinctions are seen best in comedy films. They depict the culture espoused by the new middle classes, which may be close to that of the lower middle classes but differs from it in that its consumerist lifestyle opportunities are those of the rich. This middle-class viewpoint filters not only the rich in Hindi films but also royalty, so the Great Mughal and his wife in *Jodhaa-Akbar* behave like a modern middle-class couple in a costume drama.

There are also comedies such as *No Entry* (dir. Anees Bazmee, 2005) which show the new middle classes' view of the rich. This film is a comedy about marital infidelity and suspicion set among the very wealthy, who are assumed to be preoccupied with such matters. The film abounds with jokes about money, suggesting that there is a price for everything and everyone: 'upgrading' women is compared to upgrading a car, and friends bet Rs 200,000 that they can arrange for a married man to be seduced. A Gujarati character swears on Reliance (the company owned by the business-tycoon family, the Ambanis) rather than God, and a fortune-teller declares that one gets the fortune one pays for.

The characters are not 'Westernized' in *No Entry*, at least as far as women's style of dress is concerned, even though the film was shot mostly in South Africa, despite containing references to Goa. The social embarrassment of the middle classes is typified by issues of not knowing how Western to be, so the wife jumps back when a journalist tries to hug her, but when the husband enters a club, he offers a *namaste*, which causes great hilarity; he is told that he is not in a temple. The family's idea of entertainment is to watch a Govinda film, *Sandwich* (dir. Anees Bazmee; made three years before it was released in 2006).

Govinda is one of the great heroes of the lower classes. Anil Kapoor, Akshay Kumar and Salman Khan are also popular in these comedies, but they are all all-rounders, who have played action or romantic heroes among other roles, while Govinda has been almost exclusively a one-man entertainer.

The actor Govinda (Ahuja) is known as the 'Virar ka chokra'/'the lad from Virar', after the downmarket suburb of Bombay where he grew up. Although he was a Congress MP for five years, his fame comes from the 120 plus films he has made over almost 30 years in the industry, the most popular of his many blockbuster hits being crazy comedies he made with the director David Dhawan, which are packed with doubles, twins, mistaken identities – even with two wives.

Govinda is one of the few stars who are proper entertainers, rather than heroes or simply stars. His ordinariness is part of what makes him so successful. Govinda is a highly talented dancer, but his appalling taste in clothes on- and off-screen has made him a figure of ridicule among the elites, while endearing him to his fans. Even if he plays a wealthy character, as in *Hero No. 1* (dir. David Dhawan, 1997), the point of view from which his role is presented is very much that of the poor person, a caricature of the rich. Govinda's films are not films of the people by the people, but they are one part of the mighty Hindi film industry, which realizes that there is money to be made at the lower end of the market

where 'the masses' understand the character, his anxieties and dreams. Govinda's films are also popular with 'the classes', or the more upmarket audiences, who, like 'the masses' appreciate his jokes – they understand the referents, the situations he finds himself in, his reactions and those of the other characters.

Govinda's films play on the fact that the poor can impersonate the rich and vice versa. In *Coolie no. 1* (dir. David Dhawan, 1995), he is a poor man, a porter, who is pretending to be rich as part of a revenge plot on a businessman who wants a wealthy husband for his daughter. Govinda swaps between his rich and poor acts while the rich man is shown to be a man of means by props such as bowls of fruit to denote luxury. In *Raja babu/His Lordship* (dir. David Dhawan, 1994), Govinda is a poor man adopted by a rich couple, so he again swaps identities, as he does in *Hero no. 1*, where he plays a rich man pretending to be a servant. The heroines are usually from wealthy homes and show all the bad traits of the rich, until the love of the poor man sets them straight.

Comedies of rags to riches and back again are also popular, as in *Hera pheri/Monkey Business* (dir. Priyadarshan, 2000) and *Phir hera pheri/ More Monkey Business* (dir. Neeraj Vora, 2006), which also play on stereotypes of rich and poor and people acting out of character in these roles. The character Munnabhai, a street thug, impersonates professionals – a doctor in *Munnabhai MBBS* and a history professor in *Lage raho Munnabhai* – and shows that his understanding of emotions and human nature are far more important than education. Again, it is his good nature that wins over the upper middle-class woman.

Karan Johar's *Kabhi khushi kabhie gham* of 2001 depicts a super-rich family, the Raichands, who are broken by the adopted son marrying a 'poor' woman, whose family owns a sweetshop. Her lower-class status is clear because she is a Hindi speaker and lives next to the Raichand nanny. The class background of the adopted son's biological family seems to come under suspicion from the Raichand patriarch, who disowns him for his disobedience over his choice of wife.

The poor's imagination of a rich man: Govinda in *Coolie no 1*.

Govinda working as a coolie in *Coolie no 1*.

The film moves between the old India, the holy city of Haridwar where the Raichand elders live, and the old Delhi of the poorer family to present-day India and Britain. The Raichands have magnificent houses, including a palatial home in India, near Delhi, although the exterior is clearly European, and the school that the boys attend is at the hill station of Mussoorie, though again it has been shot at a European location. The family's money is shown in their consumer purchases of cars, helicopters,

Raichand House
Diwali, 10 years ago

The Raichand house in *K3G*.

designer clothes and huge houses, the full extent of which can be seen in their lavish Diwali celebrations. The fashions and style of this film were much copied and perhaps are responsible for changing the style of men's wedding attire from Western suits to elaborate Indian outfits.

More recently, films have dealt with the disenchantment with wealth, or at least putting its acquisition second to self-fulfilment and other values. This is not connected with the moral glorification of poverty seen in earlier films, for these characters are free of any long-term anxieties about their financial security, as they mostly have wealthy parents. *Dil chahta hai*/ *The Heart Desires* (dir. Farhan Akhtar, 2001) and *Zindagi na milegi dobara*/You Only Live Once (dir. Zoya Akhtar, 2011) exemplify this trend. In the former, three male leads are trying to find new lives and loves after college, whereas in the latter, three male leads go on a road trip in Spain where they confront their pasts to understand their futures. *Wake Up Sid* is about a wealthy kid who did no work at college as he was expected to enter the family sanitary-ware business but later seeks personal fulfilment through photography. *3 Idiots* (dir. Rajkumar Hirani, 2009) shows college kids who discover that self-fulfilment and being true to oneself will lead to happiness.

## The Poor

The Gandhian adoption of poverty as a virtue, in an almost Christian sense, was taken further and more pragmatically by Congress after Independence. Nehru's policies of socialist planning – attention to the poor and to policies for promoting development, industrialization and modernization – were not successful, and India's economy fared badly, but the principle was established that poverty should be abolished (Indira Gandhi's *'garibi hatao'*/'remove poverty') and that the poor were both suffering and virtuous, although likely always to be with us.

The poor form around half of India's population, making India the nation with the largest proportion of poor people in the world. Even though definitions of poverty are disputed, one standard is the World

Bank's Extreme Poverty Line of US$1.25 a day. It is estimated that at least half of India's children under five are suffering from malnutrition.

The presentation of Indian poverty by the West in the mass media is invariably resented. Danny Boyle's *Slumdog Millionaire* (2008) is often singled out for perpetuating this view. Films made by foreigners about India seem to cause particular offence, and even Indian film-makers such as Satyajit Ray have famously been criticized for showing India's poverty. The host of international awards given to these film-makers is seen to uphold the view that this is how the rest of the world sees India.

For many of the middle classes today, writing about India's poor can be seen as anti-Indian, and scholars such as Ramchandra Guha, who has argued that India is not by any means a superpower, or Pankaj Misra, who has been critical of India's world role, have precipitated many ad hominem attacks on them, despite their national and international acclaim as writers. An exception is Katherine Boo's book *Behind the Beautiful Forevers*, a close description of a slum community, perhaps because of its narrow focus rather than a wider view of the nation's failure.

While older films showed the poor though usually well nourished, as in *Mother India* or Raj Kapoor's films, more recent ones rarely do so. This is not a trend that is unique to film as the poor are becoming increasingly invisible, and there are many people living in much of urban India who refuse to acknowledge their very existence. Excluding the poor has become easier for India's rich as they have often abandoned government services, such as schools, hospitals, transport and even power and water supplies, and have set themselves up in housing colonies ('gated communities') where they micromanage their own economies, allowing the poor in only as servants.

The Hindi films largely follow these patterns. In the 1950s, the noble poor who show dignity in their suffering were seen in a wide range of films by Raj Kapoor, Guru Dutt, Bimal Roy and Mehboob Khan. In these, the hero is usually a Nehruvian figure redeemed by development, or he rejects the world for another or is simply crushed by it. The poor are virtuous and their poverty adds to their virtue.

Hindi films have long played on the fear of being poor, with the hero's parents or children dying for want of money for medicine, for example. This is the imaginary of a very real abyss: the lack of any state support in the face of illness and death, where the family, who may be powerless or in conflict with the hero, is the only support he has.

Salim-Javed's hero Vijay, played by Amitabh Bachchan, embodied the struggle of the poor for their rightful place. Unlike earlier figures, Vijay was happy to break the law to achieve his goals, which usually included redeeming the honour of his mother. His moral right was never questioned but his means were challenged, and often resulted in his death.

On screen, poverty is located outside the city, in villages – hence the taxi driver, Raja, in *Raja Hindustani*, although it is rare now to see agricultural workers in Hindi films. *Swades* (see above) is one of the few big mainstream films to mention rural poverty, but it was not a big hit. *Peepli (Live!)*, a satire on the media set in the context of rural India, where characters are driven to despair by poverty, could not be regarded as a mainstream film – despite its promotion by Aamir Khan.

The city-based gangster films, while overtly crime thrillers, are often about a poor man who tries to get rich by illegal means. This genre can be traced through Raj Khosla's films of the 1950s and Vijay in the 1970s to the present, including Raj Khosla's son's film, *Once Upon a Time in Mumbai* (dir. Milan Luthria, 2010). These films are about style and cool as self-respect, although their younger protagonists are often interested less in codes of honour and more in ways of getting rich quick, of accessing wealth and power.

Shyam Benegal, who started making his many films about the poor and oppressed in the 1970s, has also shown them in his more recent commercial films, such as *Welcome to Sajjanpur* (dir. Shyam Benegal, 2008). The destitute are now seen only in art cinema. The situation is very different in regional cinemas, which are more socially engaged and show a wider range of social groups. Marathi cinema has produced popular films about serious topics, such as the farmer suicides in *Gabricha Paus* and social activism in *Mee Sindhutai Sapkal/I am Sindutai Sapkal* (dir. Ananth

Narayan Mahadevan, 2010), in what seems to be aimed at a middle- to upper middle-class audience.

While the very poor may not see Hindi films, many relatively poor people see mainstream Hindi cinema occasionally. Some can share its fantasies even if very distant from their world, but many of India's poor find that these films are too remote from their imagined worlds. In response to this, some local 'films' are now being made in digital format whether local remakes of hit films in Malegaon, Maharashtra (documented in *Supermen of Malegaon*) or in the Bhojpuri cinema (Bhojpuri is a language/dialect of Hindi spoken in Bihar and by migrant workers), which has grown enormously to become a real industry of its own. The worlds depicted in these films are quite different from that of Hindi cinema, which show poverty is now mostly excluded from the cinema favoured by the new middle classes.

## Back with *Dabangg*

However, one film, a mainstream entertainer, has challenged many of the divisions of region, caste and class discussed above – *Dabangg*. It made great waves at the awards, with critics and with the fans, breaking all records in its opening weekend. *Dabangg* picks up on earlier films and non-Bollywood films, in particular in its songs, which are huge set-pieces.

The hero, with the unlikely name of Chulbul Pandey, is a policeman played by the biggest box-office star of recent years, Salman Khan. Khan was originally a romantic hero in the family blockbusters directed by Sooraj Barjatya (*Maine pyar kiya/I've Fallen in Love*, 1989, and *Hum aapke hain koun . . .! (HAHK)/What Am I to You?*, 1994), but he has had enormously successful roles in many other types of film, including comedies (often directed by David Dhawan) and action films (his most recent, *Ek tha Tiger/Once Upon a Time There was a Tiger*, dir. Kabir Khan, 2012, seems to have broken all opening records).

*Dabangg* means 'fearless', but it is a word that the director said would be known only by north Indians, thereby giving the film an immediate

flavour of the north, where the film is set. Chulbul Pandey lives in Laalgunj, in Uttar Pradesh's sugar belt. Apart from the lush monsoon/post-monsoon opening, the town is shown as very dry and dusty, with a feel of the Wild West, often emphasized by the style of background music.

Laalgunj is a dystopia, of no interest to outsiders, but it is not somewhere that the inhabitants think of leaving. It is far from metropolitan India in every way and is such an awful place that it seems that all of India's problems have been dumped there, hidden safely away from the main cities.

Chulbul Pandey (Salman Khan) in uniform in *Dabangg*.

Honeymoon in the UAE in *Dabangg*.

The only time the hero leaves Laalgunj is for a honeymoon in the UAE (United Arab Emirates), which would be implausibly extravagant for even the most corrupt policeman. The issue of Indian bonded labour is avoided in favour of presenting the modern Arab dream: driving along dunes, flying falcons, staying in luxury hotel suites, taking the new metro and ogling belly dancers.

*Dabangg* includes some of the typical narrative features of a Hindi film – a love story, two step-brothers in conflict and a villain who kills the mother, nearly kills the father and then tries to kill the two sons. Yet it is all slightly distorted, as the love story concerns a Brahmin man and a potter woman; there is a step-brother, because the mother has married again after being widowed (which is unusual); and the hero seems little better than the villain. However, the film is a string of attractions, with its set-pieces and grand speeches – almost a pastiche of Bollywood (and other) films, though it explores acutely the very form of the Hindi film. Indeed *Dabangg* is almost nostalgic for 1970s Bollywood style, present-ing itself as a new exploration of the form although it has little sentiment for the dystopia in which it is set.

The changing imaginary of modern India is clear in the films of the last two decades. This new interiorized Indianness tries to ignore caste, though the silence speaks loudly. Regionality in Indian film is moving from humour to one that celebrates some regionalism but favours a loosely defined Indianness. Class, although still based on a lower-class perspective of class defined by wealth alone, has become one of the most significant and more complex social markers.

# THREE

# Religion: Myths, Beliefs and Practices

In the nineteenth century, Western orientalists held that India was the repository of great religiosity and spirituality – a rich heritage but one which was located firmly in the past, in contrast to the success of the rational, materialistic and scientific West. Although this view was upheld by many of India's nineteenth-century social reformers, such as Rammohan Roy (1774–1833), it also exoticized India and essentialized it as backward and non-modern. Modernity was expected to see religion and superstition fade, to be replaced by science and rationality. Yet it seems that, since the late twentieth century, the world has become more religious, with rising religious fundamentalism and religious nationalism. It may be that the category of 'the religious' has shifted, so while religion and politics are now closely entwined, caste is now seen less as a religious, and more of a political, category. India has also witnessed the formation, and later rise to power, of groups espousing Hindutva, Hinduness or Hindu nationalism, and in the years since Independence religion seems to have entered the public sphere, which was previously held to be secular.

Hindi films offer a revealing way of looking at how religion has been imagined in India and how it has changed over the last two decades. The post-1991 situation has been particularly interesting. Hindutva has played a more important role with the coming to power of the BJP (Bharatiya Janta Party) in national and state governments, while there have been several key political events with religious connotations, such as unrest and pogroms after the Ramjanmabhoomi-Babri Masjid events disputing the birthplace of Rama in 1992 and the Gujarat riots following the Godhra train fire in 2002. Worldwide attacks by Islamist groups such as Al Qaeda, notably 9/11, and many instances of terror attacks in India, notably those of Pakistani members of Lashkar-e Toiba in Mumbai (26/11), have increased Islamophobia within India. These events have affected the way religion and religious communities are imagined, so one would expect a major impact on the films made during the last twenty years, with a rising Hindutva movement reaching its height (with the election of the first Hindu nationalist government after Independence) in parallel with the rise of global Islamism.

India is not an unusually religious society but, like many others, its cinema depicts religious belief and practice as part of the everyday world of its contemporary life, considering religion as part of a wider culture though frequently touching on political and social issues.

## Religion in Hindi Films after Independence

The (Hindu) mythological and devotional genres which had been popular during the silent period and the 1930s had largely been relegated to B-movie status by the 1950s. They were replaced in Hindi cinema by the omnibus social genre, usually referred to as 'socials'. The Islamicate films – that is, movies concerned with the social and cultural, rather than religious, life of India's Muslims – also changed. Although the 'Arabian Nights-style' fantasy and the Muslim devotional were now also B-movies, some of the other Islamicate (sub-)genres, namely the historical (usually about the Mughals), the Muslim social (contemporary Islamicate society) and the courtesan film (about the *tawaifs* [courtesans] patronized by Muslim elites) had their greatest moments after Independence. Other films that featured Muslims were often grappling with the legacy of Partition, seeking to find a Muslim modernity whereby Muslims could be seen as suitable citizens of the new India.

It is striking how many social-genre, or 'social', films, especially those made after Independence by major directors such as Raj Kapoor, Bimal

Roy, Mehboob and Guru Dutt, avoid any mention of religion and how this trend continued for several decades. Film-makers usually eschewed issues such as caste, although *Devdas* (1955) mentions sub-caste as an obstacle to marriage. Religious intermarriage is another taboo theme, although Raj Kapoor's *Barsaat/The Rains* (1949), where the hero is clearly a Hindu, gives the heroine an ambiguous religious identity, as her name, Reshma, could be Hindu or Muslim and her father is a Kashmiri boatman, all of whom are Muslim, yet she addresses her family with Hindu kinship terms. Moreover, Hindu–Muslim relations were deemed to be too sensitive a topic in the context of the events around Partition, in particular the Tribal Raids in Kashmir in 1947, and films covering these relations risked being censored heavily or even banned. For example, *Nastik/The Atheist* (dir. I. S. Johar, 1954), whose hero becomes an atheist after seeing the Partition riots, and whose travels to seek vengeance become a pilgrimage of sorts, was banned in 1954, finally being shown in the 1960s. Even everyday religiosity was largely avoided, notably ritual practices and temple visits. There were few films showing gods being active in the physical world, whether incarnate or as efficacious images, though there were depictions of devotion, often female family members singing *bhajans* ('hymns') or praying for the recovery of loved ones, such as *Albela/Darling* (dir. Master Bhagwan, 1951) and even leftist films such as *Jagte raho/Stay Awake* (dir. Amit Mitra and Sombu Mitra, 1956). Hindi films were rarely as anti-religious as those made in the politicized context of the Tamil film industry, which was anti-Brahminical, as exemplified in *Parasakthi* (dir. R. Krishnan and S. Panju, 1952), a film that criticizes both the priesthood and the cult of the deity, Parasakthi.

The problem with looking at how religion is imagined is that it is not easy to identify where culture ends and religion starts. Hinduism is almost exclusively Indian, so which part is (Indian) culture and which is (Hindu) religion cannot be easily distinguished. Defining Hinduism's theology and belief is difficult, and its emphasis on ritual brings it even closer to culture and everyday practices – which also vary enormously from region to region and caste to caste. This lack of clear boundaries or thinking-through of categories is why it is often said that Hinduism is a way of life rather than a religion. Everyday culture in India contains many references to what may be regarded as the religious, marked in people's names, greetings, weddings, festivals and dress. While overtly religious practices may be sidelined, in India it is impossible to remove the all-pervasive effects of what is often thought to belong to the religious domain. These are not just beliefs in contingency and fate but also ideals of love, romance and happiness and notions of sacrifice and justice, which are steeped in traditions that blend religious and philosophical ideas about religion with cultural links, all of which form key elements of the social and underpin the Hindi melodrama (that is, the melodrama film form) with regard to ideas of love and devotion.

What the religious domain consists of has to be reconsidered, as many categories are constructed as religious which might be understood more accurately as political or social. The conflation of religion and culture in the face of globalization, multiculturalism and market forces has led to the rise of a fundamentalism that promotes values and ideas which are not essential to religion. Two striking examples in India would be the category of caste, often regarded as a religious rather than a social or political category, or the category of Muslims, who may be viewed as a political group rather than a religious one. These categories are not mutually exclusive. For example, Dr Ambedkar, the Dalit leader, used Buddhism, a religion, for political uplift – his aim was to become casteless by renouncing Hinduism.

All of the cultural forms mentioned are key elements of everyday culture and, as such, underpin the Hindi melodrama. In other words, in Hindi films it is hard to separate religion from culture and, as Hinduism is the largest religious grouping in India, it appears as the default option. However, the films do not show varieties of Hindu practices and beliefs but nearly always opt for a norm that is high-caste and north Indian, especially those belonging to the Arya Samaj, a conservative reformist group popular among Punjabis. Rituals that were mostly associated with certain communities, such as the Punjabi *karva chauth* ritual, where a wife fasts for her husband's welfare, have become popular in films and have spread to real life. In other words, films create a new way of imagining religious practice which often standardizes regional or caste practices as pan-Hindu.

Islam is a much more precisely defined religion than Hinduism, with a number of key beliefs, but in India some of its everyday practices have been shaped by the centuries of contact and dialogue with Indian culture, and the confusion of culture and Hinduism may lead to the wrong identification of these practices as Hindu. The Muslim community is addressed by the Indian state as a separate group, which does not give them access to the 'reservation' system even when they are socially disadvantaged, but does provide them with a different legal code, namely the Muslim Personal Law, which incorporates the Shariat.

## Religion in the Industry

Many practices of the Indian film industry are drawn from Hindu traditions such as *muhurats* (auspicious timings), for beginning work on new films, or numerology, which may influence the spellings of film titles and stars' names; films may show images of favoured gurus and gods before the opening credits or use Hindu prayers (Eros International uses the Gayatri Mantra). Yet this is unremarkable as it is no different from other cultural arenas in India where Hinduism is entwined with everyday culture – for example, the lighting of a lamp at an inauguration.

Islam is less overtly present in the practices of the industry, although many travel to the shrine of Garib Nawaz at Ajmer to seek blessings for new films just as others, Hindu and Muslim, may visit Sai Baba's shrine at Shirdi. There are many prominent Muslims at all levels in the industry, and a striking feature of the last two decades is that three of the major male stars are Muslims, namely the (unrelated) Khans: Shah Rukh, Aamir and Salman. All three are from mixed communities – Shah Rukh and Aamir are married to Hindus, while Salman's mother was born a Hindu. Salman is alleged to have received 'fatwas' for joining in Ganpati processions, part of the Ganesh festival, which are a major event in the Mumbai calendar, but is known to have a very large following among Muslims, so his producers release his films at Eid to catch the holiday audiences. Shah Rukh is known to observe Muslim practices as well as celebrating Hindu festivals at home and his films are often released at Diwali.

There were numerous Muslim stars in previous decades, although many have remarked that in the period that has seen the rise of Hindu nationalism, they have not adopted Hindu names as many did in the 1950s. These earlier names were used not to conceal identity but to have a name which sounded modern and pan-Indian – Yusuf Khan became Dilip Kumar, for example. But this renaming practice was also followed by Hindu stars who had old-fashioned or regional names, so Harikrishna Giri Goswami became Manoj Kumar and Kulbushan Pandit became Raaj Kumar. Women were also keen to be distanced from any association with *tawaif* or courtesan culture, hence Madhubala (originally Mumtaz Jahan Dehlavi) and Meena Kumari (Mahjabeen Bano), while Nargis dropped her Hindu (Tejeshwari) and Muslim (Fatima Rashid) names in favour of a secular but Islamicate name.

Film stars, while mostly the subject of sexually salacious gossip and rumour, are important figures for imagining lifestyles and fantasies. Rarely of interest as religious figures per se, they may be observed and imagined as successful figures who came originally from minorities in India, and who can be religious while also being syncretic in their family lives, where they observe religious pluralism. Hindu film-star families such as the Bachchans have had their religious activities closely monitored, whether visiting Tirupati, making a barefoot night walk to the Siddhivinayak shrine in Mumbai or the image of Lalbaugcha Raja, the most celebrated of Mumbai's statues, in the annual Ganpati festival. Religiosity, especially simple devotion, is highly esteemed and valued, although some have been criticized for engaging in superstitious or regressive practices.

# Hindu Nationalism and Cinema

It is difficult to distinguish signs of Hindutva from those of 'Indian values' or from a powerful set of Hindu beliefs and practices often referred to as 'Hindu Family Values' (HFV), which have been particularly celebrated in films featuring India's diasporic population. In the 1990s, the diasporas were shown endorsing 'Indian values' centred around the family, food, religion and nationalism, as in *Hum aapke hain kaun . . .!* A striking, if sometimes heavy-handed, approach to the diaspora or NRI-film can be seen in *Pardes*, which featured an Indian girl, Ganga (her name, the goddess of the River Ganges, implying her purity), whose family want her to marry the son of a wealthy family friend who lives in America but she still sings, 'I love my India'. The film's slogan is 'American dream: Indian soul'. From this time, HFV films became more popular, and perhaps it is not a coincidence that they rode the Hindu wave when the BJP (Bharatiya Janata Party, the political party of Hindutva) was in government: 1998–2004.

It seems a leap to connect these images to Hindutva politics, although an absence of Hindutva elements would constitute a notable lack of an expected feature in this period, whether positive or negative. It appears that this absence may be a deliberate decision by producers based on market forces and arising from the traditional secularism of industry personnel. It does raise the important issue of self-censorship in an industry operating against a backdrop where Partition produced potential issues of communal conflict and where there have been constant threats – such as the very real ones posed to theatre owners when the Shiv Sena threatened action over the screening of *My Name Is Khan* after the star, Shah Rukh Khan, said he would like Pakistani cricketers to play in the IPL. In order to reach the broadest possible audience, producers are often unwilling to risk raising issues that are too political or controversial. In other words, this may be a point at which the imaginary world of Hindi cinema excludes controversial or alienating ideologies by simply refusing to let them enter, as they would fragment the wider reach of the film.

However, some film viewers may interpret any feature of Hindu belief and practice as a sign of Hindutva, where others may not see them. The absence of explicit Hindutva in the films may be like that of caste – an absence which is known but whose divisiveness means it cannot be admitted.

While two major 'Hindu genres' of Indian cinema, the mythological and the devotional, are no longer made as mainstream Hindi films, the epics have remained important texts. The two great Indian epics, the *Mahabharata* and the *Ramayana*, have been retold many times in Indian culture over the last 2,000 years and more, as their stories become myths which imagine social worlds that are repeatedly interpreted as ways of imagining and understanding social relations, family and culture. They are not just religious texts, in that they are regarded as *itihasa* (history) in the case of the *Mahabharata* and as poetry – the original poem or *adikavya* (where *adi-* means original and *kayva* means poem) – in the case of the *Ramayana*. So they are seen as wider cultural texts but today are often regarded as primarily religious because each of them is the story of an avatar of Vishnu, Krishna and Rama, and these figures give a different moral and ethical dimension to the reading of these texts.

The BJP and its allies harnessed the media via popular visuals and cheap technology such as the music cassette to get their message across. One of the most important ways in which this was done was via the televised religious soap operas of the *Mahabharata* and the *Ramayana* from the 1980s. Indian cinema has made many versions of stories and episodes from the epics throughout its history, from the silent mythologicals to current animated films. Its earlier films, notably in the mythological genre, also drew on the epics for stories that evoked India's quest for nationhood and identity, and the industry has set the pattern of referring to the epics, whether their stories or characters, in easily recognizable ways, to underline and discuss problems in the family and other social issues.

The epics have remained vast resources, perhaps more so after the massive success of the television dramas. During the last twenty years they have remained key to ways of thinking about family relationships, with the ancient and already-known stories bringing their mythological resonances to contemporary cinema. In this two-decade period, the *Ramayana* has no longer been drawn on for stories about the restoration of the righteous king, as it was in earlier films such as *Ram Rajya/The Kingdom of God* (dir. Vijay Bhatt, 1943), nor for those about the ending of fighting and evil as in *Chhalia/The Cheat* (dir. Raj Kapoor, 1960) or virtuous women being 'Sita-Savitris' (Sita, the ideal woman in the *Ramayana*; Savitri being the epitome of the devoted wife in the *Mahabharata*). Instead, the *Ramayana* has been looked to for the tales of family relationships that underlie this epic, in particular those that involve remarriages and adopted children.

In Sooraj Barjatya's *Hum saath saath hain: We Stand United* (1999), the plot concerns the division of a joint family. The second wife starts to see the son from her husband's first marriage as an outsider, even though she formerly raised him as her own. In *Kabhi khushi kabhie gham*, the adopted son who breaks the family's patriarchy is sent into exile by his father despite the support of his mother, unlike the *Ramayana*, where the father is forced to exile Rama after being tricked by one of his wives. The love between the two brothers in *K3G* is very much that of Lakshman for Rama, total devotion and dedication to one another, an example seen clearly by name in Subhash Ghai's *Ram Lakhan* (1989), although the motif of older good brother as policeman and younger brother as rebel is not the story of the relationship of Rama and Lakshman.

A few films refer to Ravan, a character from the *Ramayana*, as a force for ill – this is a figure who is very much in the public imagination with the burning of his image at the annual Dussehra festival marking the end of evil and the restoration of good. In *Agneepath/The Path of Fire* (2012), Kancha Cheena lives on the island of Mandwa, a modern version of Lanka in the *Ramayana*. Vijay, however, has no brother, only a mother and a sister, so the reference is attenuated, and Vijay and Kaali are no Rama and Sita. At the death of Kancha, Vijay also has to die as he has no righteous rule to bring once he has avenged his family.

The *Mahabharata*'s numerous stories have featured throughout Indian cinema over the last twenty years, but often indirectly. For example, when the wives' brothers intervene in the affairs of their in-laws, in films such as *Beta/Son* (dir. Indra Kumar, 1992) and *Raja Hindustani*, the figure of Shakuni Mama comes to mind without there having to be an explicit reference. Using names from the *Mahabharata* also brings the associations of the epic's characters, so Arjun is always a hero. The two brothers in *Karan Arjun* take the names of cousins who fight each other, though for the film it seems more important that each of them represents the ideal hero.

Although the *Mahabharata* is often referred to as a text about moral dilemmas rather than about love and devotion, it is also discussed in the context of governance and politics. The film which has the closest links to the epic in recent years is *Raajneeti*, one of the biggest hit films of 2010. A drama about two sets of rival cousins, *Raajneeti* takes aspects of the *Mahabharata* and blends these with the modern American epic, Coppola's *The Godfather* (1972), as a way of understanding political dynasties and schisms in dysfunctional but powerful families.

*Raajneeti* reworks several key scenes from *The Godfather*, such as the fiancée killed in a car explosion meant to kill the fiancé, and two of the heroes, brothers Prithviraj Pratap (Arjun Rampal) and Samar Pratap (Ranbir Kapoor), are modelled on Sonny and Michael Corleone, but there are also scenes and characters taken from the *Mahabharata*. Samar Pratap is as much Arjuna as Michael Corleone (although reading for a PhD in Victorian literature), while Prithviraj is also Bheema. Their opponents are Veerendra, the Duryodhan figure (Manoj Bajpai) and Sooraj Kumar (Ajay Devgn), the Karna figure, an illegitimate half-brother of the Pratap brothers and adopted by Dalit parents, who becomes a Dalit leader. The Pratap brothers' mother, Bharti, has a son before marriage, like Kunti in the epic, but, instead of her affair being with the Sun himself, it with her political guru, who is called Bhaskar, or 'the Sun', and their son is called 'the Sun' – Sooraj. His adopted father is the Prataps' driver rather than the charioteer as he is in the epic.

There is no Yuddhisthira, King of Dharma, in *Raajneeti*, but Brij Gopal (Nana Patekar) is Krishna the statesman rather than the pastoral god. Brij

Gopal is Bharti's brother and hence *mama* (maternal uncle) to Prithviraj and Samar, drawing parallels with the wicked Shakuni (although he is on the wrong side of the family), while his name and skilful negotiations suggest Krishna.

Brij Gopal sets out to kill Sooraj but cannot when he finds that he is the son of Brij's sister, Bharti. Brij orders Samar to kill him, but at the moment when Samar is about to do the deed, he hesitates and Brij Gopal begins to speak almost as if he is Krishna on the battlefield of Kuruskhetra, advising Arjun on his duty in the *Bhagavad Gita*, while here advising Arjun on his duty and preaching a pragmatic morality.

Although the heroine is called Indu, recalling Indira Gandhi, she appears more like her daughter-in-law, Sonia Gandhi, not least because the star (Katrina Kaif) looks as (non-)Indian as Sonia. Indu is a quasi-Draupadi – she wants to marry Samar but marries Prithviraj despite still loving Samar. Sonia joins politics as a widow, with her first post being as Chief Minister, so the references to Sonia Gandhi are clear, but Samar goes to the USA, though says he will be back, and a sequel is expected.

The analogies to the *Mahabharata* are not heavy-handed in this film, which suits viewers who do not know the story. Today the epic remains a living story for many in India and its use here as a drama of family conflicts and of governance, linking the private and the public, underlines the imagining of the destructive nature of family politics that calls to mind the Nehru-Gandhi dynasty. India's modern myths are being built in the political sphere, yet no one dares to make a film about the Gandhis, although the *Mahabharata* can be retold endlessly.

The persistence of these epic myths, themselves the repositories of imagined worlds over centuries, is striking; their stories and characters are adapted, retold and reinvented to make them contemporary. They have shaped the way people have understood the world and interpreted it and have become part of the Hindi cinematic imagination, linking the cinema to the world of mythology. Other stories, including folk tales and novels, such as the story of Devdas, also play significant roles, but the great epics show their continued cultural influence as they continue to shape the ways in which powerful and political families are imagined.

## Reincarnation and Religion at the Heart of a Film

Farah Khan's superhit, *Om Shanti Om* (2007) – about a 1970s film extra, Om, who is murdered and then reincarnated as another Om to fight his battle once again for his love, Shanti – is such a spoof on the film industry that there is little conviction or religiosity in its reincarnation theme. Another hit film, which encapsulates much of the early 1990s imaginary, is *Karan Arjun*, boasting three major stars of the 1990s – Shah Rukh Khan, Salman Khan and Kajol – as well as a strong supporting team. The film picks up many of the themes from the 1980s which have faded out during the last twenty years, namely feudal families who rule localities without any intervention from the state, in particular from an ineffectual police force. They exist in a world which seems non-modern and that includes reincarnation and direct intervention by the Goddess in the world of humans. Two characters are named from the great warriors of the *Mahabharata*, although here they are real brothers who work as a team rather than half-brothers divided by circumstances and there is no Krishna to guide them.

*Karan Arjun* is a reincarnation and revenge drama. In it, a woman called Durga has two sons, Karan and Arjun. Labourers in a rural quarry, the sons learn that they are the grandsons of the dying Thakur (landlord), who apologizes for being misled by Durjan Singh, which led to the death

of their father. Durjan has the boys killed, but Durga prays to Kali for their reincarnation to avenge the family. They are born in the city, but throughout their lives the boys are shown having flashbacks to the murder of their previous incarnations, and when they meet they have a feeling of connection. They are the only people who do not accept unquestioningly that they are reincarnations of Karan and Arjun, as do those from their first lives, including their mother.

Although Kali does not become incarnate in the film, her temple is a major location for the action and she communicates through flashes of lightning and the ringing of the temple bells. Everyone prays to her, including the villains, but she is only on the side of good. Also, Durga is a name for the Goddess, and when she bangs her head on the sacrificial post until blood flows, she is clearly the *bali*, the sacrifice herself, a victim, with the priest standing as a silent witness.

*Karan Arjun* falls very much into the watershed of the pre-Bollywood movie (see chapter One), as it is a village drama with *thakurs* and shows popular religion. The heroes are very much located in this pre-liberalization space and have no luxury consumer goods. They travel by horse, train, camel cart and scooter, while the villains have the standard pre-liberalization indulgences of the white Mercedes and flights on Air India. The film shows advertising hoardings, suggesting possibilities of consumerism, even though poverty is still depicted as noble. The only person who speaks English is the villain's son, who has the most glamorous, and depraved, lifestyle.

This film shows Hindu beliefs and practices which are not connected with any form of political Hinduism or Hindutva, but uphold the law of *karma*, of reward for actions, with its unquestioned beliefs in reincarnation and the reward of the righteous alongside the active presence of the Goddess. It is one of the last major Bollywood movies to be set in this type of religious imaginary, which is now found only in the devotional films of the B-circuit. The mainstream has moved to a more 'modern' type of religion as a part of culture, where religious images do not perform overt miracles but do remain efficacious. So, a close-up of an image may be followed by a miracle which viewers may attribute to the image, such as in *Rab ne bana di jodi*, where the image seems to grant the husband's wish that his wife will not see through his disguise but take him for another.

In 2012, a film which might have been expected to spark controversy became a big hit. *OMG: Oh My God!* (dir. Umesh Shukla) satirizes self-appointed religious gurus, who in this film agree to appear in court on behalf of God when an atheist businessman tries to sue Him after his insurance claim is rejected as 'an act of God'. Krishna himself becomes manifest, converting the atheist by giving him holy books whose truth leads him to uncover religious charlatanism. The film's portrayal of a modern Krishna, present in the world (played by superstar Akshay Kumar in Western dress and performing motorbike stunts), along with the acknowledgement of the truths of the scriptures, found favour with audiences,

Krishna appears on earth in *OMG: Oh my God!*

who interpreted it as a tale about the cleansing power of religion rather than an attack on true belief and devotion.

## Popular Hinduism

The films of the 1990s mostly show popular beliefs rather than orthodox religion, and such beliefs are usually shown at moments in the film where they do not challenge religious belief but instead seem to be part of the wider world, rather than a central theme. Hinduism is not a faith and does not require belief, but it attaches great importance to ritual and practice. Presenting such rituals and practices in films shows how they should and could be done, and these filmic representations change their performance in everyday life through the adoption of rituals from other communities, the imitation of costumes and gestures and the use of film songs outside the films themselves.

With the rise of consumerism and the new middle classes, films have begun to show very elaborate versions of rituals and festivals. Diwali, 'the festival of lights', marks the beginning of the year in some parts of India. It is a major harvest festival when Lakshmi, the goddess of wealth, is worshipped and lights are lit to commemorate the establishment of Ram Rajya – the rule of Rama. Given the growing worship of wealth, this is a prime festival for elaborate consumerist events, which have largely replaced the new clothes and firecrackers shown in the old films and which are still key to the festival. The Diwali celebrations in *Kabhi khushi kabhie gham* have marble statues, silver ritual vessels, brocades and silks, a palatial house packed with celebrants and a family which commutes by private jet and helicopters. Rahul (Shah Rukh Khan), the adopted son, reaches home for this festival but is rejected for refusing to accept his father's plans for him. The younger brother dreams of reuniting the family, but it is a funeral that brings him home.

The celebrations in *Kabhi khushi kabhie gham* are much more elaborate than in *Hum aapke hain koun . . .!*, which was a loosely tied-together string of songs about life rituals, including engagements, weddings and a pregnancy ritual (*simant*). The latter film's plotline was thin but its strength was that it was a film celebrating the family as the centre of the characters'

Diwali celebrations at the Raichands' house in *K3G*.

The thali (tray) for worship at Diwali in *K3G*.

world, with the hero's jeep sporting a graffiti-style slogan – 'I love my
family' – and all members of the family having their roles to play. The
religious rituals of life bind the family together, with the joint family or
Hindu Undivided Family being the true unit of society, which demands
loyalty and sacrifice as well as providing love and support.

This importance given to the family as the major source of morality,
and the religious underpinnings of this belief, are manifested clearly in
the films. Hindi cinema does not show a post-Enlightenment universal
morality but a set of networks and duties which take priority over the outside world. The religious nature of these is clear in *HAHK* as, when all is
lost for the young couple who are being dutiful in following their family's
wishes, the dog, Tuffy, on a sign from a statue of Krishna, delivers a letter
which explains the romance and the family stops the wedding in progress
to unite the lovers. Sooraj Barjatya's *Vivaah: A Journey from Engagement
to Marriage* (2006) again explored the sanctity of the family and marriage
and the issues of an adopted child, though this time a daughter.

Weddings and other rituals feature in many films, although none is
so centred on them as *HAHK*. The Punjabi wedding features in many films
as a fantasy of romance, family unity and the display of wealth in costume
and dance, but it is underpinned by religious traditions and the use of
wealth indicators as signs of the bride being a Lakshmi (bringer of wealth)
to her new family, while dance is shown to denote both celebration and
the link between human and divine love that is also often elaborated in
song lyrics.

The world of festivals as shown in film enters real life as the famous *karva chauth*, which has spread from being a ritual practised only in certain parts of the country to a generalized festival. The fast builds on the idea of the devoted wife and has been adopted, thanks to its exposure via the film world, as an everyday norm. Some husbands have even started to fast on the day as a sign of devotion to their wives and to invent a new tradition to cancel out the gender imbalance.

*Holi* songs and ritual are very popular in films, but more as a carnival of colour, family mischief and possible romance than to suggest a serious time of misrule. In *Darr/Fear* (1993), Yash Chopra presents the festival in a big song sequence as a time when families dance and hug, but the confusion caused by colour and noise allows a stalker to enter the space of the family and to apply colour to the heroine, giving it a rather sinister feel.

The Karva Chauth
ritual in *K3G*.

Religion also runs through the ways in which cities are evoked in films by their major religious festivals. Calcutta is defined by the Durga Pooja festivities in *Devdas* (dir. Sanjay Leela Bhansali, 2002), *Parineeta* and *Kahaani*, while the regal statues of Ganpati mark Mumbai in films such as *Don* (dir. Farhan Akhtar, 2006) and *Agneepath*. The depiction of festivals is often for spectacle and to mark the hero and heroine as standing apart from the crowd while knowing the traditions, but it is often a point where the anonymity of the teeming crowds allows a specific action to occur that is usually critical to the plot. The idea of losing oneself in the festival – which is so powerful and beautiful but also frightening – is part of the event. If a song in a movie featuring a festival is a hit, then it is guaranteed play-time every year at that festival, bringing the film world and associations with the star into the city.

Religious behaviour is seen as a norm which binds people together as domestic rituals are part of everyday life. In *Jodhaa Akbar*, Jodhaa's worship of Krishna within the imperial palace is shown not only to demonstrate Akbar's tolerance and sympathy towards Hinduism but also to make the imperial couple seem more like a normal, modern, middle-class couple. Religiosity may be shown as part of a person's character, as devout and good people pray and fast and put their faith in God. Sometimes religious practice may show hypocrisy, as in *Khosla ka ghosla/Khosla's Nest* (dir. Dibakar Banerjee, 2006), where a businessman is an ardent devotee of Mataji, the

Goddess, and will follow all the ritual requirements of worship but be totally corrupt in his work. It is normal in films for prayers to be rewarded, often by efficacious images as with Krishna and Tuffy the dog above or the crystal Ganesh images in *Dil to pagal hai/This Crazy Heart* (dir. Yash Chopra, 1997).

Films are open to religious interpretations, so even a rare excursion into science fiction in Hindi cinema may evoke divine figures. In *Koi mil gaya/An Encounter* (dir. Rakesh Roshan, 2003), an extra-terrestrial called Jadoo ('Magic') befriends young Rohit (a name for Vishnu or a son of Krishna) and helps him overcome his learning disabilities. Rohit's son becomes a superhero and stars in *Krrish* (dir. Rakesh Roshan, 2006). To read *Krrish* as Krishna might be an exaggeration, but Jadoo is blue with a golden tilak on his forehead like Krishna and responds to the sound 'Om'.

The goddess at the pooja festival in Calcutta in *Devdas*.

Ganpati festival celebrated in the chawl (workers' housing) in *Agneepath* (2012).

Akbar is moved by Jodhaa's devotion to Krishna in *Jodhaa Akbar*.

Another superhero film, *Ra.One/The Demon* (dir. Anubhav Sinha, 2011), did not identify the hero with a deity as he is G.One (Jeevan, 'life') but his enemy is Ra.One, pronounced as Ravan, the enemy of Rama.

Gods themselves appear as superheroes in animated films which are made for children and provide them with new myths and images of the gods. Ganesh and Hanuman appear as children themselves and befriend children. In *My Friend Ganesha* (dir. Rajiv S. Ruia, 2007), a lonely boy being brought up in a Westernized family is told stories about Ganesha (or Ganesh) by his maid. The god appears and becomes his friend, giving him superhuman powers. The boy persuades his family to worship Ganesh at home and soon all their family problems are solved. In these films adults are creating children's imagination of religion, drawing on Western styles to make the gods live in the world, where they are modern, benevolent and more like friends than divine beings.

The massive hit film *Bhool bhulaiyaa/The Maze* (dir. Priyadarshan, 2007) is set in what seems to be a haunted house. The film mocks superstition but favours the oldest forms of Hindu belief – that is, Vedic Brahminism. It shows how the orthodox beliefs and ritual practices of a guru concur with the tenets of modern science, psychology and psychiatry as practised by an American-returned doctor. The medical diagnosis of dissociative personality disorder blends with Brahminical horoscopes and rituals, allowing the doctor and guru to cooperate in solving the mystery in order to cure the patient.

The problems in the film are to do with family squabbles. Although the mental health of the adopted daughter is questioned, it is the stranger who marries into the family who is the danger. She is cured by a religious ceremony, under the guidance of the doctor. When the doctor wants to marry, at the end of the film, he still waits until he asks his parents' permission, to underline the need to combine the old and the new. This simultaneous operation of seemingly incompatible beliefs is very much part of a worldview which does not seek to be exclusive but to incorporate views from other ideologies and religions.

## Pilgrimage and Religious Sites

Pilgrimage is important in India for all faiths and the sanctity of religious places is respected, with many people visiting holy sites of faiths other than their own. Popular sites such as Balaji at Tirupati get 23 million visitors a year and Vaishno Devi 17 million, while the twelve-yearly Kumbh Mela in 2013 was attended by around 30 million people. Pilgrimage films are a separate genre, belonging outside the world of mainstream films in specific markets of devotional and religious films and often made by the music company, T-Series, who put together *bhajans* – hymns – with visuals and descriptions of pilgrimages. The B-movie-style Muslim devotional films include long pilgrimages within India as well as the Hajj – the Islamic pilgrimage to Mecca; these also allow those who cannot make the pilgrimages to witness the sacred sites as well as recall or plan further visits. Sacred buildings are also sometimes shown in films to depict a transformative experience for the characters as well as to provide views of the buildings for the viewers. The Golden Temple in Amritsar is shown in films such as *Rang de basanti* and *Rab ne bana di jodi* to this effect, for example.

Non-Christian characters often visit churches and even pray in them, in order to show that they

*Rang de basanti*, a visit to the Golden Temple.

have religious sentiments and also to allow them to make a vow which they may fulfil or a wish which may later come true – such as the famous church scene in Interlaken in *Dilwale dulhania le jayenge*. Simran (Kajol) prays sincerely while Raj (Shah Rukh Khan) fools around. Although he looks at her praying with adoration, it is only when he wants her wish to come true that he returns to chat to God: 'Hi' and 'Bye'. Temples are often places where female characters demonstrate their religiosity while the male looks bored, or locations where the truth must emerge, as in *Saajan chale sasural*, where both of the hero's wives appear. Sometimes religious buildings are used for visual impact with no reference to the religious, as with the ghats in Varanasi in *Bunty aur Babli* or Badami in *Guru* (dir. Mani Ratnam, 2007).

Sometimes a pilgrimage is a plot device for a character to be absent, such as in *Aarakshan*, where the founder of an educational institution is away as the action unfolds but returns in time for the denouement. In *Tanu Weds Manu*, the families of the prospective bride and groom go on a pilgrimage where the behaviour of the bride is in sharp contrast to the requirements of pilgrims to be holy and pious, but it forms part of the film's travels across different parts of north India.

The many forms of Hindu and Sikh belief and practice are found across all types of Hindi films. They show religion as a part of culture as

Raj is moved by Simran's religiosity in a church in *DDLJ*.

well as depicting eruptions of divine action in the everyday and a popular belief in fate sitting alongside the more orthodox *karma*. Religiosity is valued highly and never mocked, while the 'Hindu' genres of the mythological and devotional film are no longer made for the mainstream cinema.

## The Islamicate Film

The one religious genre which has not only survived but is developing new forms is the Islamicate film. The sub-genres which were established in the early days of Indian cinema – the *Arabian Nights*-style fantasy, the historical, the courtesan film, the devotional, the Muslim social – have survived into the post-1991 era. While small in number, many of these are big-budget films which have been highly successful, offering striking ways of depicting Muslims and their culture.

The key elements of the Islamicate style, namely the language, the dress and the music, have been retained, at least as references, in these films. Formal, Persianate Urdu has faded, being replaced by a Hindi with a few Perso-Arabic words which evoke this style, largely because of the decline in the knowledge of Urdu. In *Jodhaa-Akbar*, where the grandeur of the Mughal court is depicted, the language moves from a form which can be followed by Hindi-speakers to one using less widely known words, for example in the song, 'Marhaba', a song of thanks to the Emperor for lifting the tax on non-Muslims, whose title alone is an Arabic greeting. Translations of the song, which has many Persian-derived Urdu words, soon appeared on the Internet to help those unfamiliar with the vocabulary. This reinforces the idea of the language of the Mughal court, which was Persian, without being incomprehensible to the audience.

The romantic, melancholic if not lachrymose *ghazal*, a song form which draws on an Urdu lyric style, is not hugely popular today, but the lively and rhythmic song, the *qawwali*, features in almost every film with an Islamicate reference, as indeed it does in many non-Islamicate films. Two Pakistani singers are particularly popular for singing *qawwalis*: Shafqat Amanat Ali, who sings in Karan Johar's films, namely 'Mitwa'/

'Friend' in *Kabhi alvida na kehna* (non-Islamicate) and 'Tere naina'/ 'Your Eyes' in MNIK (Islamicate); and Rahat Fateh Ali Khan, whose hit songs include 'Tere mast mast do nain'/'Your Intoxicating Eyes' in *Dabangg* (non-Islamicate). Kamaal Khan, a British Indian, sings 'Ishq sufiyana'/ 'Sufic Love' in *The Dirty Picture*. The *qawwali*, which has long been a popular form in Hindi films, became a feature of 'World Music', loved for its musical and vocal style, with the huge success of Nusrat Fateh Ali Khan, but in south Asia, its mystical devotional references, which blend idioms of divine and earthly love in Sufi terms, give it an added dimension. In *Rockstar*, the hero, Jordan, is not a Muslim but he finds his musical inspiration and his inner self in Sufism. The transformation starts when he spends time at the shrine of Nizamuddin, in Delhi, where he is discovered as a recording talent by Ustad Jameel Khan. Although Jordan follows the lifestyle of the archetypal rockstar, when his married lover returns to him to die, he enters a new world of spirituality, the film ending with a quote from Rumi – 'Out beyond ideas of wrongdoing and rightdoing, there is a field. I'll meet you there.' Sufism, as a mystical form of Islam, is often seen in India as similar to *bhakti*, or Hindu devotional religion, which appeals across religious divisions and marks an

The Emperor joins in the praise of Khwaja in *Jodhaa Akbar.*

aesthetically pleasing and accessible form of Islam which has a broad appeal to a wide audience.

While the veil is the garment most associated with Islam today, older Islamicate films employed it as a device for misrecognition leading to romantic complications and for a 'humorous' device – often involving men pretending to be women. It is used in some contemporary films, such as *Kurbaan/Sacrifice* (dir. Rensil D'Silva, 2009), to portray a sinister, oppressive Islam, while in others, such as *MNIK*, a woman gives up the veil in the post-9/11 era of Islamophobia but chooses to wear it again later as a mark of her religion and independence. In *Bombay*, the Muslim heroine, who has formerly worn a veil in public places, lets it fly off when she leaves home to run to her Hindu lover and does not wear it again once she moves to Bombay, where she wears clothes that do not distinguish her by her religion. While the historical Islamicate films and the courtesan films evoke a world of exquisite refinement in dress, as well as in other features, in more recent Islamicate films, modern Muslim women are associated predominantly with veils, rather than with fashionable clothing suitable for Muslim women, while beards and caps now mark men as fanatics, unlike in older films, where they simply meant 'Muslim'. This shift from

The town joins in Chulbul Pandey's dance in *Dabangg*.

beautiful and exotic, even erotic, dress to clothing marking religious extremism has to be viewed as part of the wider transformations within Islamicate cinema which in turn relate to changing views about religion and religious communities.

Although the last twenty years have included a revival of the historical film and its sub-genre the biopic, the only major Muslim historical is *Jodhaa Akbar*. The *Arabian Nights* sub-genre has almost vanished; the Muslim devotional film remains rooted in the B-movie circuit. Films featuring courtesans have always been rare, although several have been hugely acclaimed and successful, but they now seem anachronistic, and only a few films are made, such as the unsuccessful remake of *Umrao Jaan* and the hugely popular *Jeet/Victory* (dir. Raj Kanwar, 1996). In the latter, the dancer, Tulsibai, is a Hindu – not Muslim as in the older films – and she is no longer from the *nawabi* ('courtly') world of the Muslim elite but more like a Mumbai bar girl, a figure who is often romanticized as the beautiful 'tart with a heart' in, for example, *Chameli* (dir. Sudhir Misra, 2004), and exploited by men in *Chandni Bar* (dir. Madhur Bhandarkar, 2001).

The Muslim social (films set in contemporary Muslim society) from the period studied by this book are found within the more realist film tradition – notably in director Shyam Benegal's trilogy, which is based on the story of the film critic Khalid Mohamed's family: *Mammo* (1994), *Sardari Begum* (1996) and *Zubeidaa* (2001). The last of these moves more towards the mainstream Hindi film, with its style of music and the presence of the leading star, Karishma Kapoor, but is still outside the mainstream cinema, as was *Naseem* (dir. Saeed Akhtar Mirza, 1995). Muslims are shown as gang members in many films, with *Once Upon a Time in Mumbai* showing the rise of two leading 'Dons'.

In Manmohan Desai's crazy films about communal harmony, Hindu and Muslims mix as friends and family, but although a Muslim romances a Christian in *Coolie* (1982) there is no Hindu-Muslim romance. Even in *Amar Akbar Anthony* (1977), where the three brothers follow Hinduism, Islam and Christianity, each marries someone from his own community.

Interreligious marriages are often problematic with the communities and with the censors, unless one of the marriage partners is a Christian, in which case it is barely mentioned.

Irrespective of how much religious communities are in contact with each other, they also have clear boundaries, and cinema can pose only emotional solutions to the divide, where seemingly irreconcilable differences and prejudices are overcome by emotional outbursts. In everyday Indian life, much is made of the myth of communal harmony before 1947, whereas ways of living together separately were well entrenched in pre-Partition India. Festivals could be celebrated jointly but high castes were strict about observing dietary restrictions – a taboo that is still in place, with reports of Muslims being turned away from buying flats in some vegetarian-only housing societies.

The impact on a young Muslim man of the 1992/3 unrest in Bombay after the demolition of the Babri Masjid was shown in *Bombay* (dir. Mani Ratnam, 1995), but the film concentrates on romance in an interreligious marriage (between a Hindu and a Muslim) and combines realistic moments with elements of the Muslim social. No terrorists feature in this film, which attributes blame for the carnage to both communities. Seeking his lost children in the burning streets after the riots, the Hindu hero is asked his religion and declares that he is neither a Hindu nor a Muslim but just an Indian – that is, a secular Indian (a response that is usually required of Muslims) – and that the conflict is resolved, so restating the postcolonial supremacy of the nation over other identities.

*Veer Zaara* is a cross-border – that is, India-Pakistan – romance, where an Indian Air Force Officer falls in love with a Pakistani woman. Neither *Veer Zaara* nor *Bombay* has all the features of the older Muslim social genre, with exaggerated *adab*, or etiquette, and Indo-Islamicate features such as flowery language, locating Muslims in a largely pre-modern social world. *Bombay* shows how a Muslim woman and a Hindu man try to find a new life in a cosmopolitan city where new forms of religious politics threaten their existence as a modern couple, while *Veer Zaara* presents a modern, upper middle-class Punjabi world where the couple are divided by the political border but their Punjabiness is greater than the divide. The Pakistani woman's Sikh nanny plays a role in bridging the division between them. In these films, made by two of India's most important and successful directors, Mani Ratnam and Yash Chopra, the couples show that a difference of religion is not an absolute divide, and the identities of 'Indian' (*Bombay*) and 'Punjabi' (*Veer Zaara*) are shown to tie them closely together.

In *My Name Is Khan*/MNIK (see page 145), the intercommunal marriage takes place outside India. Although the hero's brother breaks his relationship with him because of this marriage, the problems between the couple are brought about by Americans, not Hindus or Muslims, as Islamophobia grows in the U.S. *Ek tha Tiger* has a Pakistani and an Indian secret service agent falling in love, after which they decide to abandon their patriotic duty and elope to Cuba.

During the last two decades, a new type of Islamicate film has emerged, showing Muslims as terrorists or enemies of the state. This new phase picked up on depictions of Muslims as terrorists in Kashmir – in films such as *Roja*, *Mission Kashmir* and *Fanaa*/*Destroyed in Love*. One of the earliest of these new 'terrorism' films was Khalid Mohamed's *Fiza* (2000), where the hero is inspired to join a terrorist group as Mumbai changes from a cosmopolitan city whose space is marked by the Muslim shrine of Haji Ali to a communally divided arena that is not safe for young Muslims.

In films drawing attention to communal issues, Muslims are shown as at least equal aggressors rather than as victims. The 2002 events at Godhra which led to massacres of Muslims in Gujarat feature only in non-mainstream films such as *Firaaq*. As mentioned above, it was 9/11 that brought the spectre of Islamist terrorism into major Hindi films. The impact on the lives of ordinary people of the Mumbai train bombings in 2006 was the central theme of *Mumbai meri jaan*, while *A Wednesday* presented an ordinary citizen claiming he had planted bombs in order to secure the release of suspects to draw attention to the public's weariness with regular terrorist threats. These movies appeared the same year as the attacks of 26/11, about which a film has been made by Ram Gopal Varma. There is a striking absence of films about non-Muslim terrorists, even though many terrorist attacks in India are carried out by these groups.

In 2009 and 2010, three big-budget films raised issues of terrorism: *Kurbaan*, *New York* (dir. Kabir Khan, 2009) and *My Name Is Khan*/MNIK. All three films were set mostly in the USA, placing Indians on the world stage of the War on Terror and highlighting an America allegedly under threat from Muslim terrorists.

*New York* shows that American brutality towards Muslims creates terrorists, as in this case their treatment as individuals motivates them to take action on behalf of their community, but it is somewhat ambivalent on the concept of the 'good Muslim', with the Hindu woman finding that her seemingly secular Muslim husband is an Islamist terrorist. This fear of a Hindu woman marrying a Muslim who is a ruthless terrorist is played out again in *Kurbaan*. Even the most seemingly sophisticated Muslim may well be a terrorist in disguise. Shot in the style of a horror film, the narrative shows the heroine bringing her husband to New York, only to find that he is part of an Islamist network where burqa-wearing women are confined to the house, with 'honour killings' of rebels and her own life spared only while she is pregnant. The hero seems outwardly reasonable, highly educated and able to lecture about Islamophobia but is, in fact, willing to kill Americans and his own wife. The discovery that the husband is not Indian but an Afghan, who has come to India via Pakistan after his own family was killed in the conflict, again creates the mythology that people become terrorists because of wrongs done to them. However, the evil behind his exterior charm, and the extent of his deception and desire for revenge, are underlined by the way in which the wife is shot, like the victim in a horror film in which he is the marauding monster.

The most successful of this group of films was Karan Johar's *My Name Is Khan*/MNIK). The plot of this film is described in chapter One, where Rizwan (Shah Rukh Khan), seeking to escape Hindu–Muslim troubles in Mumbai finds himself facing a new set of issues as a Muslim in post-9/11 times. Rizwan's life is filled with tragedies caused by Hindu–Muslim tensions and Islamophobia and despite informing on extremist Islamists

he still remains an object of hostility to Americans and other non-Muslims. All he wants to do is to get to the American President and say: 'My name is Khan and I'm not a terrorist.' Finally meeting the President and seeing that he does not believe that all Muslims are terrorists, Rizwan then reunites with the wife and brother who had spurned him.

The overseas locations are significant for these films as they raise the issue of global Islamophobia, which is very different from the anti-Muslim sentiments in India, where a substantial majority feel threatened by a minority. These films show Islam as a global force, a religion, often associated

The Islamicate world of Delhi as the setting for romance in *Kurbaan*.

The Afghan woman (Kirron Kher) turns on the Hindu wife (Kareena Kapoor) who tries to stop the bomb attack in *Kurbaan*.

with fanatics who form a community without a homeland. Perhaps it is felt that problems facing Indian Muslims cannot be discussed in the Indian context without inflaming communal sentiments so the films portray threats coming from Americans rather than other Indians.

The normative view of some vague Hindu culture in cinema means that Islam, which is different in many cultural terms, is always marked as Other and it is only in the last few years that we begin to see modern, non-religious characters who participate in a general Indian culture. These include Ali in *Dhoom/Blast* (dir. Sanjay Gadhvi, 2004), Farhan Qureshi in *3 Idiots* and Imraan Qureshi in *Zindagi na milegi dobara*.

Christians form a very small minority in India, at around 2 per cent of the population. In the years after Independence, Christianity was associated with the British and with Anglo-Indians, so had a very visible presence – especially in Presidency cities, cantonments and hill stations and missionary and other religious schools and hospitals, as well as in the shaping of the working week with a Sunday holiday. The film industry has had several reasons to give undue prominence to Christianity because of the influence of Hollywood, while the industry's centres in Bandra and Juhu are where many east Indian and Goan Christians live and there are many Goan personnel in the industry, mostly in the orchestras. Indian Christian girls wore Western clothes at a time when others in India rarely did, so miniskirts and hotpants, such as those seen on-screen in *Bobby* (dir. Raj Kapoor, 1973), while hardly likely to be encountered anywhere in India at the time, seemed less implausible if the character was a Christian. Vamps, too, often had Western names such as Lily and Mona, while the pre-eminent vamp and cabaret dancer, the Anglo-Burmese Christian actress Helen, lost her natural look to become a green-eyed blonde.

In Hindi cinema, Christians are seen as eccentric, often as drunks, but they are not alien to Hindus in the way that Muslims are. Despite the attacks on missionaries in several parts of India during recent decades, Christianity is imagined almost as a sub-sect of Hinduism – some Westernized form in other words. There are no objections to a Hindu marrying a Christian, while films often show non-Christians praying in

churches (a famous scene in *DDLJ*; Prem in *Ajab Prem ki ghazab kahani*)
and white weddings are depicted quite frequently, where they seem to
have a semi-secular effect. The heroine of *Ajab Prem* is a Christian, which
may be to do with the hill-station backdrop or perhaps an effort to explain
the actress's strongly accented Hindi. The same actress, Katrina Kaif, also
plays a London-based Christian in *Jab tak hai jaan*. Karan Johar features
a Christian schoolteacher in *Kuch kuch hota hai*, called Miss Braganza by
way of tribute to Bobby Braganza of *Bobby*, who might be an older version
of the 'twenty-first century girl'.

Karan Johar's production *Kal ho na ho* features a family which is
mixed Christian and Sikh, with religious difference forming little of the
conflict within the family, while the story shows a belief in angels in a
way which is part of American popular culture rather than Christianity.
In *Ajab Prem ki ghazab kahani*, Prem, even though a Hindu, prays to
Jesus in a church and then meets a Jesus lookalike who takes him back
to his beloved. He claims to be dressed as Jesus for a play but then seems
to be a vision. It is quite rare to see Christian imagery in films, although
*Khalnayak/Antihero* (dir. Subhash Ghai, 1993) portrays its hero, the 'villain'
of the title, as the man of sorrows.

It is hard to think of an instance of a representation of a Jain in Hindi
films in recent years, although Jains have played an important role in Hindi
cinema, not least the Barjatyas, long-established distributors with Sooraj
Barjatya – one of the most significant directors of the last twenty years.

Sikhs feature much more frequently in Hindi films than other religious minorities. There are many prominent Sikhs in the film industry, from Dharmendra and family, often called by their caste name, Jat, to the lyricist and director, Gulzar. Punjabis are seen as loud, fun, honest and brave; Sikhs are shown to have an intensified Punjabiness. Sikhs were once mocked as being heroic but shown to be a little dim, like the child in *KKHH* who tries to count stars, but this is fading as the foolish Sikh is the smart one in *Singh is Kinng* and *Love Aaj Kal*. The many films about Bhagat Singh celebrate this great Sikh freedom fighter, while in *Veer Zaara*, the Sikh woman, played by Zohra Sahgal, is the bridge between India and Pakistan. RDB shows the power of the Golden Temple in Amritsar to purify, while in *Rab ne bana di jodi*, the image of the Guru is efficacious in hiding the husband's double act from his wife.

Indian culture requires an Indian identity, which is often confused with one that is culturally and ritually Hindu. Yet Hindi cinema has remained popular with India's minorities, not least with Muslims, despite the orthodox Muslim view that film is *haraam*, or forbidden. In recordings made during the attacks on Mumbai on 26 November 2008, the young terrorists' conversations with their command in Pakistan reveal that they were stunned by the luxury and technology in the hotel, commenting on the television screens, which distracted them from their grisly

Guru Nanak's image helps Suri in *RNBDJ*.

objective. Their controllers also resorted to *filmi* dialogue when in touch with the Indian authorities, '*Picture abhi baaki hai*' – the words quoted after a trailer: 'The film is yet to come.'

The depictions of religion in Hindi cinema are diffuse and varied, often making generalizations in favour of an all-Indian morality and spirituality where forms of devotion such as Sufism or *bhakti* can override religious difference, allowing the presence of religion to help pave the way for tolerance and acceptance. The films show a religion as a mixture of beliefs and practices rather than dogmatic or exclusive, reinforcing popular discourse in India that all religions are equal and religiosity and spirituality are to be valued.

# FOUR

# Emotions: Sadness, Anger and Happiness

Superstar Amitabh Bachchan is often quoted as saying that one should leave the movie hall with a smile on one's lips and a tear drying on one's cheek. Although the pleasure of experiencing emotions in relation to texts has been discussed by India's theoreticians (including theories concerning *rasa* – 'flavour' or 'sentiment' – which deal with emotional responses to texts developed in the context of Sanskrit courtly literature over the last two millennia), the role they play in inviting people to enjoy films still needs to be explored fully.

Indians frequently say that they like to express their emotions openly and that they therefore want the characters in films to be very emotional; thus characters are seen to be behaving in ways that are believable ('emotional realism') even if everything is rather magnified by the melodrama. This supports the contention that an emotional response is a good one rather than a necessarily rational one; hence on-screen emotions may reveal what may be considered the right way to behave when responding to a threat or seeking revenge – and viewers may admire or even emulate this.

Many film scholars argue that audiences must be emotionally bound to films as readers are to texts. The audience relate to the emotions of the characters in many ways, not necessarily identifying with the emotions that the character feels. It seems that the charisma of film stars may be derived from the emotional relationships they create with their audiences, and certain Hindi film stars are associated with particular emotions.

This chapter is about feeling as a way of understanding people and how to exist in the world. It examines the emotions of film characters as well as the audiences' response to them, looking at the use of melodrama in the Hindi film as a type of emotional realism, as well as discussing the ways in which emotion plays a role in film viewing, keeping the audience's focus on all aspects of the film. This is connected to the self-perception of Indians as being very emotional and the value put on public emotionality and its display as a way of defining Indianness.

## Emotions and Film

The history of emotions is trending now in Western academia. The emotions, devalued by Kant as being in opposition to rationality, are now seen as foundational to rationality, while in everyday speech the phrase 'emotional intelligence' also marks this seismic change. The emotions are studied within various disciplines, and they have also been important in film studies, as a part of research on melodrama and more recently on the importance of the emotional response that focuses the attention of the audience. The charisma of the star, a major topic in film studies, may also be defined through the emotional response he or she generates in the audience, whether projected by the star or imagined by the audience.

The idea that audiences identify with screen characters is too simplistic a way to describe the emotional connection of audiences to films. Emotions in film have a cause, unlike in real life, where they can be objectless yet for the audience they have an object which they *know* is not real. The films may not evoke true emotion, or only temporarily: I may jump because I am scared but I am not so scared I want to run away, as I remember it is a film. A film may evoke empathy in me, the viewer, for the character experiencing the emotion rather than my feeling the same emotion. When someone is angry, I may or may not feel angry, too; or I may admire their anger; or I may be repulsed by it. I might cry and feel sad, but I am choosing to make myself feel sad or be sad for the character, rather than for myself.

In Indian films, the imaginary world of emotions does not present emotions as bad or negative, with even jealousy usually being just the trigger for a reunion between a couple (though it triggers self-destructive behaviour in *Aap ki kasam/My Promise to You,* dir. J. Om Prakash, 1974), but values and cherishes emotions such as sadness, rather than trying to exclude it in favour of happiness – and even happiness is presented as more than just a couple living happily ever after. The pleasure of heightened emotions and the emotions as a basis for living a good and considered life underlie the Hindi film imaginary.

Hindi films fulfil all the requirements of melodrama as they foreground emotions over all other issues, as characters are placed in situations where extreme emotions are called for, facing issues of desire and romance, the family, suffering and implausible plot twists of coincidence, chance and fate. A melodrama needs a wide range of emotions, and Hindi films include combinations in their *masala* or spicy mix, as even a dark melodrama contains comedy and a war film will usually centre on family drama.

Key features of the Hindi film lead to heightened emotions, notably the emphasis on exaggerated language, which uses rhetorical flourishes in often-stylized 'dialogues' that are quoted in other speeches and are also found on media ranging from the Internet to coasters and T-shirts. These dialogues whip up emotions with loaded words such as *Maa*, or 'Mum', used frequently in Hindi films. For example, in the Amitabh Bachchan film, *Deewaar/The Wall* (dir. Yash Chopra, 1975), his brother says his worldly goods are irrelevant because 'Mere paas maa hai'/'I have Mum'. In *Kuch kuch hota hai*, a school competition requires a girl to talk about a word. Hers is *Maa*, and as her mother has died, she is unable to speak, so her father steps in and explains the need for a mother. Finding a stepmother is the plot of the film and the sympathy of the audience for the girl's need is focused by this one word.

Songs and background music are also essential to this emotionality and they link to extra-musical cultural experiences such as memory, associations and connotation through their musical style. The lack of the explicitness provided by words creates mood and sentiment, or words in songs can add to its meanings. Also, meaning in music has its own system, such as the use of tempo, rhythm, pitch and volume, while emotions may be associated with particular musical instruments in specific musical cultures. For example, the *shehnai*, a wind instrument, may sound melancholy to a Westerner but is closely associated with weddings in India. The *sarangi*, a bowed instrument, and the piano are often associated with sorrow and death in Hindi movies. They provide affective triggers for the audience, so in *Kal ho na ho*, the piano theme of the title song begins with soft piano but builds up volume with crashing chords and orchestration as it introduces Shah Rukh Khan as the Angel of New York, with swooping camerawork giving a feeling of flight. Later in the film, as the Angel's death approaches, the theme is played in a sorrowful way, quieter and slower, moving the audience to tears as the song's words of living for today now seem full of regret rather than positive thinking.

Hindi cinema usually uses Western music for its background scores, drawing on meanings created in Hollywood and elsewhere. The songs are famously hybrid, creating a musical equivalence of multilingualism, many elements of which may even be present in one song. Songs also have a role outside the films, where they circulate for many reasons, adding to the referential frame as other meanings become associated with them beyond their use in the film itself.

Emotions affect the imaginary, augmenting and influencing rational thought as well as creating effects in lives and the world. From the range of available emotions and categories of emotions, the rest of this chapter discusses some of the key emotions for understanding Hindi films and how they see modern India. The focus remains on the last twenty years, beginning by looking at how genres have changed.

The categorization of emotions is far from fixed in everyday life. It is striking that many film genres in Hollywood are categorized by emotions, such as the comedy, the 'weepie' and the revenge drama. Very few films follow just one emotion, nor do they necessarily go through the whole gamut, but rather change emotions to create mood, delineate characters and develop stories. Hindi film's generic boundaries are notoriously fuzzy, and this use of a predominant emotion for categorizing films works well as a generic marker which is recognized by producers and audiences alike. The most striking emotions in the films are analysed below in the form of their on-screen depiction to suggest how these are experienced by audiences and what this says about shifting cultural imaginaries.

The 'weepie' remains a popular form, with sadness and melancholy being found throughout Hindi films rather than forming a generic category. One of the most important film-makers and producers during the period of this book, Karan Johar, is a master of melancholy, and his use of sad songs and tearful characters have proved massively successful with audiences. Anger and revenge, associated with Amitabh Bachchan's 'Vijay' films of the 1970s and 1980s, when he was labelled 'The Angry Young Man', remained popular themes, at least till the early 1990s, after which they became incorporated into other genres. The one genre which has become more popular than ever is the comedy, with its focus on happiness, but it is one which has perhaps received less critical and academic attention as these films are often described in the press as being fun if you 'leave your brains at home'.

One genre which might be expected to be more productive in this time of social change is the horror film, which may raise anxieties and fears. They have been relatively few and far between, however, apart from Vikram Bhatt's *Raaz/The Secret* (2002), which was inspired by *What Lies Beneath* (dir. Robert Zemeckis, 2000) and plays on anxieties about an affair which leads to the woman's suicide and her haunting of the husband and wife, as well as other deaths. Its huge success has led to the making of *Raaz 2* (2009) and *Raaz 3* (2012). Mahesh Bhatt's *Murder* (2004) draws on features of horror and suspense, with its suspected murders and kidnaps arising after a woman has an affair before finally reuniting with her husband. Although these films were big hits, they were not followed by more horror films, though there are often rumours of more being planned and the genre thrives on the B circuit.

A genre that is small in terms of numbers, largely because of expense, but hugely popular, is the action thriller. The success of the *Dhoom/Blast* franchise – *Dhoom* and *Dhoom 2* (2004 and 2006, dir. Sanjay Gadhvi) and *Dhoom 3* (dir. Vijay Krishna Acharya, 2013) – has been partly because it presents glamour and thrills in a new manner, the first *Dhoom* leading to a sudden upsurge in the popularity of motorbikes among the young. *Race* (dir. Abbas Mustan, 2008), about brothers double-crossing each other because of a woman, took up the theme of motor-racing just as F1 entered India, again associating speed, glamour and style in order to excite and dazzle the audience.

Emotions, or at least a spectrum of them, can be easy to identify in Hindi film, where symbolic and iconic representations are well established and underlined by music. Melodrama focuses on the exteriority of the emotions, so a passionate moment is often shown to occur in a thunderstorm with appropriately dramatic music or cuts to a fire, which may also be referenced in an accompanying song.

Certain Hindi film stars are associated with particular genres, which in turn are linked to specific emotions. For example, Shah Rukh Khan, who initially appeared as a villain ('negative hero') or in comic roles, is now most closely associated with the romance and in particular the diasporic romances, which include the blockbuster weepies of Karan Johar. Ranbir Kapoor is associated with melancholy, though often offset by comedy. Certain actors are known for their performances in comedies, notably Govinda, Salman Khan and Akshay Kumar, but the last two were originally less generically confined, both being action heroes, and Salman has played some of the widest varieties of roles, with his films having some of the biggest box-office returns in India. This chapter also explores how a star's charisma may be associated with an emotional communication with the audience, allowing the imagination and creation of certain emotions.

## The Pleasure of Tears and the Melodrama

The melodrama seeks to elicit an excess of emotional response from the audience. Sadness and tears lie at the heart of the melodrama and in the Hindi film there is no need to hold back. At the end of a Hindi film, eyes

Maya (Rani) weeps in *KANK*.

are wiped as the credits begin to roll and as the lights come up tears seem the surest guarantee that it was a really good film. Some deride Hindi films as escapist fantasies where the audience goes to be removed from life, but why would they want to escape to a world full of sorrow?

Sadness is a major feature of melodrama, and Hindi films often play on sorrowful aspects, where tears are an appropriate reaction. The pleasure of tears needs to be viewed in context, as it is triggered by many different factors. The characters in the film may cry to draw attention to their emotional states, further emphasized by the filmic features of the close-up. Tears of joy flow at happy reunions as well as tears of sadness at sorrowful partings. If characters are crying because they are sad, this is further intensified with sorrowful music or particularly sad songs, while if they are crying because they are overwhelmed by happiness, music may also come to a crescendo to underline this as the camera closes in on each character crying. (The denouements of film classics such as *Dilwale dulhania le jayenge* would be particularly good examples of the latter, leading the audience to a final happy resolution.)

The audience often cries when the characters cry. The audience is moved to empathize with the characters, perhaps because of concern for them or because they are emotionally overwhelmed, or perhaps an audience member is just unhappy. It seems strange that the audience enjoys seeing a film that makes them cry, so what explains this? Could it be that the audience enjoys the feeling of abandoning themselves to melancholy and reflection, whether it is because they are reminded of something they no longer have (such as lost love), or something that cannot happen to them, as it is too good to be true? Yet crying also shows a way of being happy, or perhaps the audience may feel happy as they admire themselves feeling sorrowful and sympathetic. It is even suggested that tears are physically calming, as they secrete hormones and so engender pleasure by relaxing tensions, in particular at the climax, when narrative tensions can produce 'nail-biting' moments. It is also unclear why not all sad films make the audience cry, even if they make them very sad.

The pleasure of crying may also be do to with feeling that one is experiencing the worst feelings imaginable – loss, fear – but that one is able to think about it and to deal with it, unlike in real life when one would be experiencing all sorts of reactions beyond just the emotion itself. Watching a film, one may feel sorrow without real loss, so one may think about the sadness of saying goodbye but not feel as though one has been abandoned and left alone. So one may experience the mood of sadness rather than feel 'objective' sadness or a recollection of loss, of what might have been, but one can have mastery over earlier feelings of fear and helplessness, unlike real sadness or depression where the individual feels both powerless and that he or she has lost something. There are none of the other symptoms of negative states of mind, such as loss of feelings, desires and appetite, disrupted sleep, disturbing thoughts or delusional beliefs. Moreover, while the viewer may feel a loss of control, of helplessness, he or she is also waiting to be reassured by the film's narrative resolution, plus in melodramas the sufferers – at least those who survive until the end – are normally comforted or rewarded. One can also narcissistically admire oneself being sorrowful and tragic as well as experience the pleasure of letting oneself feel sad in a world where one is meant to be happy and cheerful all the time.

While the modern hero is a young man in search of his place in the world or a happy family man, the superstar Shah Rukh Khan is the hero whose suffering is manifested in tears and long speeches in all his films. He usually plays a middle-/upper-class urban sort, often the trans-national, decent, modernizing, respectful Indian. When Shah Rukh Khan is a hero in a Yash Raj film, he suffers but the films are not 'weepies'. In his first for this studio, *Darr/Fear* (dir. Yash Chopra, 1993), he suffers for being in love with a woman who does not love him. Although he played a stalker, the audience saw him as the film's hero, and his passion was seen as being wonderful rather than sinister. In his other romantic Yash Raj films, there are sad, even sorrowful moments – for example when he suffers when his romance seems to have to end but he ends up finally getting the girl: in *DDLJ*, *Dil to pagal hai* and *Veer Zaara*. In *Rab ne bana di jodi*, he suffers as his wife does not fall in love with him after their marriage, but the film ends on a comic note; in *Jab tak hai jaan*, his suffering makes him careless of his life but the ending is a happy one. These films all take the familiar route of falling in love, separation and suffering and final reunion. The suffering is often silent and sad rather than dramatic and so may or may not evoke tears. In two Yash Raj films starring Shah Rukh Khan, there is a different story. In *Mohabbatein/Loves* (dir. Aditya Chopra, 2000), he learns from his beloved's suicide to express sorrow in his music then use it for education reform; in *Chak de! India*, there is no romance and sorrowful moments are about social ostracism.

Shah Rukh Khan's status as the most tearful hero in Hindi cinema derives from his massively successful films directed by Karan Johar or others for Dharma Productions. He is separated from his adoptive mother by her husband (*K3G*), gets divorced (*Kabhi alvida naa kehna*) and his stepson is murdered (*My Name Is Khan*). These films often co-star Kajol, who, like Shah Rukh Khan, weeps beautifully, the sorrow of the story being reinforced by dialogue, gesture, close-ups and searing music. Shah Rukh Khan is suffering for different kinds of love – romantic and familial – and

his sentiments are injured. His actions, which involve weeping rather than taking revenge, win others over to his cause when he is wronged.

Dev (Shah Rukh Khan) weeps in *KANK*.

While it sometimes seems that contemporary Indian society is focused on financial and other successes and consumerism, concerned about winners with no time for losers, Shah Rukh Khan – in real life an outstandingly successful person – can embody ideas about loss and sadness. In films, his character may be rich and attractive and in other ways successful, but even he has to undergo pain and suffering, creating a space for imagining grief and sorrow and acknowledging it. The film also contains these emotions, as the narrative, like life, will ensure that everything is all right in the end.

## Melancholy and the Artistic Temperament

While the 'weepie' wants the audience to respond physically by crying, melancholy, though often classed as an emotion, is also a mood. It is associated more with the creative person and also with nostalgia. It is a particular kind of reflective sorrow, often featuring the desire to remove oneself from company, to be alone and thoughtful and creative. Western literature, music and other arts share a long tradition of creative melancholy in individuals (Shakespeare and Keats) and movements (Gothic and Romanticism).

India has many traditions concerning the creative possibilities of sorrow, whether this be Sanskrit literature, where love – divine and human – is as much about separation (*viraha*) as union (*sambhoga*), or Buddhism, whose founding principles, the Four Noble Truths, are about sorrow. Hindi film drew on the Gothic with its dark and melancholy associations in the 1940s and 1950s, in films like *Mahal/The Mansion* (dir. Kamal Amrohi, 1949). These emotions have become part of the sensibility of many literary cultures – notably that of Urdu poetry, an important source for the Hindi film lyric, which is often deeply melancholic. The poet's complaints about unrequited love, the cruelty of the beloved, the loss of honour and faith, public disgrace and thoughts of death can often be read as those of the soul longing for God. It is mostly through these Urdu traditions that melancholy remains present in the Hindi film today, although largely in songs, such as 'Tanhai'/'Loneliness' in *Dil chahta hai*, 'Tadap tadap'/ 'Beating' in *Hum dil de chuke sanam* (HDDCS)/*I've Given My Heart, Beloved* (dir.

Aakash (Aamir Khan) visits Waverley cemetery near Sydney in a song about loneliness ('Tanhai') in *Dil chahta hai*.

Sanjay Leela Bhansali, 1999) or 'Aaoge jab tum'/'When You Arrive' in *Jab we met*.

Many Hindi films also play on the sorrow of nostalgia – a feeling that now is not the best time, and the past was richer and better, while the future means that even the present will be lost. Many films have looked back on recent decades to search for meaning there that perhaps evokes the India before all the recent changes began, with even gangsters being 'better' in the 1970s, when they were still ruled by a moral code, in films such as *Once Upon a Time in Mumbai*, while *Dabangg* is nostalgic for the old-style Hindi film, to which it adds many (post)modern twists. In *The Dirty Picture*, the heroine has a momentary break in her downward spiral of self-destruction when she becomes nostalgic about her past by looking at photographs, allowing her to finally open herself to love, depicted in the song 'Ishq sufiana'/'Sufic Love'.

Nostalgia is often part of the pleasure of the aesthetic of melancholy, which is a creative sadness, not a sadness that makes people weepy, passive and inactive. Melancholy can be a retreat from the demands to be a jolly, extroverted, socially engaged person who tries to avoid introspection. One of the most strikingly melancholic films is *Rockstar* (dir. Imtiaz Ali, 2011), where the lead character believes he needs to fall in love and experience loss in order to feel the pain necessary to create art. He ends up being angry, behaving badly and suffering, but he is not ultimately depressive as he manages to produce his music, which draws on the Sufi/Islamicate traditions of unrequited love, lost love and the cruelty of the beloved, where the artist is ready to give everything up for his passion. Ranbir Kapoor, one of the few new stars to emerge in recent years, seems to be finding his place as a melancholic, though interspersing this mood with comic moments to give an almost Chaplinesque effect in films such as *Burfi!* (dir. Anurag Basu, 2012), which was reminiscent of his grandfather, Raj Kapoor – one of the greatest figures in Hindi cinema.

The depressive hero differs from the melancholic hero in that he is doomed by his failure to act. One character who has mythical status in Hindi film is the gloomy Devdas, who first appears in a Bengali novel of

1917 by Saratchandra Chatterjee (1876–1938). This short novel concerns
the tragedy of a doomed young couple who are brought down in part by
a society that will not let them marry, but also through their own pride
and ineffectual behaviour. The film version made by Bimal Roy in 1955
became a classic, although not hugely successful in its day. A remake from
2002 was launched, as it were, to be the archetypal Bollywood production,
and its potpourri of film moments plus a play on star status, excess and
visual beauty and a strong musical score meant that the film did well at
the box office, even though it had a depressive, suicidal hero who seemed
out of step with contemporary heroes. Devdas was not only depressive
but also an alcoholic, though the film did not explore mental health in
the way that several recent films have (*Tere naam/In Your Name*, dir.
Satish Kaushik, 2003; *Woh Lamhe/Those Moments*, dir. Mohit Suri, 2006;
*Ghajini*, dir. A. R. Murugadoss, 2008; and *Kartik Calling Kartik*, dir.
Vijay Lalwani, 2010).

## Anger and the Desire for Justice

Anger is often seen today as a negative, destructive emotion which needs
to be managed. However, Plato, who famously claimed in his *Republic* that
poetry was bad for people as it stimulated emotion rather than reason,

argued that reasoned anger is necessary for us to pursue justice, while the desire to see it done is a virtue. In Indian culture, anger is often seen as a positive emotion in narratives of avenging gods and goddesses and heroes and heroines. For example, the *Mahabharata* features Draupadi's anger with Duryodhana as a major motivation for the story. Although anger is seen as a force which rights the moral order of the world, a concern that is central to the Hindi film melodrama, anger in the movies is often destructive – and usually self-destructive. Ashis Nandy calls the archetypal hero, Devdas, 'maudlin and effeminate', as his anger with his family, society and the women in his life leads him into ineffectual and impotent rage where he abandons his family, spurns the proposal of his childhood sweetheart, whom he loves, and later scars her face in anger, rejects another woman who loves him, ditches his friends and ultimately destroys himself through alcoholism and low living which have led to tuberculosis.

The most famous depiction of anger in Hindi cinema is Amitabh Bachchan's roles as Vijay, in films scripted by Salim-Javed. It is often suggested that his anger was an expression of the zeitgeist, as the 1970s was a particularly violent and troubled decade in India's history, whose nadir was the suspension of the Constitution during the State of Emergency (1975–7). This argument has been much refined by Madhava Prasad, who argues that the political upheavals and the breakdown of consensus between dominant power groups were particularly radical during this period. Yet other decades in postcolonial India have been as, if not more, troubled, while the 1970s began with India triumphant in its victory over Pakistan in 1971. It is striking, too, that other world cinemas also became more violent in the late 1960s and early 1970s, typified in the English-speaking world by films starring Clint Eastwood and Charles Bronson.

Vijay's anger was less a wider social message and more showing the suffering of the individual and how to return to a moral equilibrium by righting the wrong done to him. Vijay is not an angry loner, but he is enraged because of something that someone did to him or his family directly. He is not a rebel, but his anger is focused on one person and he will spend – and usually lose – his life in pursuit of revenge; he focuses on nothing else. Vijay's anger is brooding rather than impetuous. It is a purifying anger which seeks only its goal. This is not political anger, as it is never intended to bring about social change or global justice, but is about an individual showing up a generalized wrong and the focus is on setting that right. It is a moral issue, not a political one.

The morality of the source of the anger is not in dispute, but the action that Vijay pursues, in the cause of his *personal* morality, may be questionable and is usually contrasted with that of a second hero, a brother or a friend, who follows the *public* morality of the law. However, the audience is very much on the side of Vijay, whose values are based on those of older societies and moralities where family, loyalty, religion and self-respect are all-important. This morality cannot be sustained in a modern world and Vijay's values will conflict with the law. His vengeance or desire to punish wrongdoers shows how the emotion of anger can be a moral issue, about looking for retributive justice in the wake of humiliation. His anger takes many forms – indignation, hurt, contempt, vengeance and fortitude. In all forms, Vijay also displays something of the cult of the martyr; he is dispossessed and his father lets him and his family down; his mother is the one who binds the family together; girlfriends are often merely decorative.

Amitabh's striking physical features are used to great effect to create his screen dominance, notably his tall physique and remarkably deep voice. They enable him to communicate his emotions, particularly those around anger, portraying them in a manner that makes us focus on him and on his films. One of his strengths is his ability to display anger but controlled or expressed in dialogue, inviting the audience to respond with admiration and perhaps try to emulate his control, restraint, 'cool' and dignity, which are all acts of self-respect.

Following the success of these films, from the 1980s onwards another group of angry heroes arose, one of the most successful being Sunny Deol, whose muscled body suffered many torments in a series of vigilante films, where he struggled to put wrongs right. Sunny fought on bravely right up to one of the biggest hits in Indian box-office history – *Gadar*, where he took on the whole of Pakistan and its army on behalf of Indian honour. The trend was thus set for fight-ready muscled heroes, which continues up to the present, with Salman Khan perhaps the most popular of them all, taking the fighting to cartoonish and hugely entertaining levels – notably in *Dabangg/Fearless*, where he stops a fight to allow his adversary to take a phone call from his mother, after dancing to the ringtone.

Yet righteous anger did not go away. Vijay's moral authority, his reason and his passion for justice were harnessed in Amitabh's successful return to cinema playing patriarchal roles, beginning with Aditya Chopra's *Mohabbatein* and the following year with Karan Johar's *Kabhi khushi kabhie gham*. However, the patriarch can be emotionally unjust, especially to the young and to lovers, as he places justice even before himself and his own happiness, although he eventually comes round to reconnecting with the more emotional and less rational young.

Vijay's inheritor today may well be embodied by Aamir Khan. After successfully playing a wide variety of roles in the 1990s, including many where he was the wronged person who had to fight back, his first production, *Lagaan*, accelerated his career trajectory. In this and in the unsuccessful *The Rising: Ballad of Mangal Pandey* (dir. Ketan Mehta, 2005), he played the ordinary Indian, who fought against British injustice as a farmer then as a soldier. In *Rang de basanti* he played a young man who was inspired to adopt violence against the state by acting in a play about the freedom fighter Bhagat Singh.

Aamir Khan also starred in the biggest Hindi hit of 2009, *Ghajini* (dir. A. R. Murugdoss, 2008), a remake of *Memento* (dir. Christopher Nolan, 2000) and of a Telugu film, also called *Ghajini* (dir. A. R. Murugdoss, 2005). The 2008 version was said to be unnecessarily violent yet can be seen as a moral dialogue on mental disability and the limits of the human mind. The hero (if he can be called that), Sanjay Singhania (Aamir Khan), loses his memory after incurring a head injury when trying to protect his girlfriend, Kalpana Shetty (Asin), from Ghajini, who kills her for exposing his racket in selling female children into prostitution. Sanjay cannot remember anything for more than fifteen minutes and so writes notes to

Sanjay (Aamir Khan) writes on his body to help his memory loss in *Ghajini*.

himself, sometimes in the form of tattoos on his body, to remember who he is and where he lives, but most importantly so he can avenge the murder, mostly in a violent and bloody manner. Helped by a medical student, Sunita (Jiah Khan), he cannot ultimately be cured of the terrible injury he has suffered but at least he finds some sort of happiness and escapes punishment for crimes he had no knowledge of committing.

Starring in his own *Taare zameen par/Stars on Earth* (2007), Aamir Khan plays a teacher who champions the problems faced by dyslexic children and who argues against 'the system', as he did in one of his all-time biggest hits, *3 Idiots*. In the latter, he plays a student who encourages students to rebel against cramming and parental career choice in favour of self-fulfilment and personal growth, later emerging as some kind of Steve Jobs figure – that is, someone who is hugely successful in terms of the 'system' while being outside it.

Aamir Khan also produced a small-budget film, *Peepli (Live!)* – a satire on the media, who in this film prey on a farmer in the village of Peepli who is so desperate that he threatens to commit suicide in order for his family to win government compensation. The film would never have enjoyed the wide release it had were it not for Aamir Khan's backing. It perhaps also paved the way for Aamir Khan himself to become a major television star, with his series *Satyamev jayate*, which uses the Republic's motto 'Truth alone prevails' to investigate social issues ranging from female foeticide to domestic violence. The anger and passion Aamir Khan brings to this show builds on his star power and the righteous anger he displays in films to generate debate on an unprecedented scale about issues which have been widely discussed in the Indian media for many years. This show mobilizes the righteous anger felt by many Indians about how their society is changing (in their eyes for the worse) and also about what they perceive to be the failure of corrupt political elites in Delhi to deal with these issues. The rise and fall of Anna Hazare, a social activist, marked the hope that people put into individuals they saw could effect change outside government, with hopes for some of the Gandhian spirit of right and for 'truth alone prevails' bringing about social justice. Current anger about violence towards women, magnified in the mass response to the Delhi gang-rape of a student in December 2012, shows that the young are in an angry and rebellious mood, and astute observers like Aamir Khan can pick up on such sentiments and play an active role in forming the imagination of a righteous India, where young people are indeed interested in more than gloss, consumerism and glamour.

## Happiness

The Hindi film is thought to end with everyone, in particular the romantic couple, living 'happy ever after', with the suggestion of a fairy-tale ending. On closer inspection, however, a good number of classic Hindi films *do not* end happily: for example, the hero dies of unrequited love, ravaged by TB (*Devdas*, dir. P. C. Barua, 1935; dir. Bimal Roy, 1955; and dir. Sanjay Leela Bhansali, 2002) or without TB (*Mahal/The Mansion*, dir. Kamal Amrohi, 1949); the mother has to kill her son but is honoured by inaugurating a dam (*Mother India*); the hero is killed by the police

(*Deewaar*) or in a shoot-out (*Sholay*). Even in the romantic genre, the hero's first love often dies and the woman must marry someone else (*Kal ho na ho*), or the couple is reunited only in late middle age (*Veer Zaara*). It is only the type of romantic film where the ending requires a couple to be brought together within the embrace of the (extended) family so that they may live 'happily ever after', and also the comedy film, where all loose ends are tied up to restore the status quo ante. It is perhaps that there are two different kinds of happiness in question here: that of the screen characters and that of the audience.

## Happiness and Film Characters

For most people, although happiness is hard to quantify, and there is no objective proof for the statement, 'I am happy', most of us know when we are happy. Small things bring moments of happiness, but this is not the same as a broader happiness, which needs big things, including beliefs and values, a sense of achievement, love. There has to be a great engagement with the world and the idea of a greater version of happiness – an ethical life, a life worth living, a good life. This is not a perpetual state of bliss, nor is it something that can be quantified, despite the British philosopher Jeremy Bentham's attempts to construct a 'felicific calculus'.

The change in the West to the idea of feeling good rather than being good, being concerned with personal rights rather than duties, goes against the nature of humans as ethical animals. People constantly practise ethical behaviour as they evaluate, grade and compare behaviour. The recent interest in the study of happiness, and in particular the philosophy of happiness, suggests that it is time to consult great works of philosophy and religion again for ideas about how to live the good life – as suggested in the writing of Gurcharan Das and in popular religion.

Everyone is seeking to maximize their future happiness, weighing up things that make them unhappy and seeking to eliminate them from their lives. However, people are poor at predicting what will make them happy in the long run, and usually get this wrong. Many people think they could be made happy by feeling or being younger, whereas older, or at least middle-aged, people are usually more content; they would like to be wealthier, whereas lottery wins often make people unhappy, not happier. Most people believe they would be happier if they improved their looks, IQ or education, all of which are actually poor predictors of happiness. In fact, it is the commonsense view or homespun truths about what you need for happiness that seem to hold true: family, community and friends; money, though only enough rather than too much; work and status/ achievement; health; freedom; and to be able to uphold one's values.

Part of the recent study of happiness has been stimulated by the view that people nowadays are less happy than they were and that modern life makes it almost impossible to be happy. On the one hand this view makes sense, as social networks (real rather than virtual) are disintegrating, but on the other this may also be the influence of nostalgia, something many people indulge in, especially regarding Hindi movies, which are 'never as good as they once were'.

In melodramas such as the Hindi films, happiness can be more expressive and a particularly happy moment is usually marked with a joyful song and dance. This could be private – solo – in a couple, with a group or at a family event, usually an engagement or a wedding. Characters in Hindi films, whatever their social situation, are usually seen enjoying the pleasures of life (even if this is just in a classic dream sequence); this may be with family or friends, on holiday, at work or in seeking recognition (often as a creative person or perhaps receiving public acclaim from a crowd or people), consuming extravagant lifestyles, falling in love. Other emotions are also experienced in films, but happiness usually takes a share.

The characters who usually find happiness at the end of the film are the romantic heterosexual couple whose desire for one another is expressed in song and dance, usually against exotic backdrops as they travel the world, with the ending featuring a major event such as a wedding that allows a final burst of energy, colour, music and dance. This is the couple that should live 'happily ever after', finding fulfilment in their wealthy, consumerist lives, their unified family, their social standing or self-esteem, their freedom, their ability to live by their own values and, of course, their physical beauty and erotic desire.

The ending is also about narrative resolution, with tensions being relieved as situations are dealt with and stabilized. Displeasures and unhappiness caused by tension and sadness are resolved with a final major climax. (The Hindi film is meant to have a climax, or emotional high, at the end of every reel of the film.) It may be useful, therefore, to think beyond the pleasure of tears and the release of tensions to see if the ending of films such as *Devdas* may bring another kind of happiness, other than the emotional 'feeling happy' of the traditional happy ending.

Daniel Gilbert, one of the leading scholars of happiness, argues that there are three major kinds of happiness – emotional, moral and judgemental. The first is 'being happy', the second is 'happy because', while the third is 'happy about'. Emotional happiness is 'a feeling, an experience, a subjective state'; it's the usual kind of happiness meant, the kind discussed above. However, melodrama has clear links to what Gilbert calls 'moral happiness' or 'happy because . . .', which may arise from 'a life well lived'. This is what the Greek philosophers regarded as virtuous, or what Christians view as the reward for a life of virtue, even if not in this world.

In other words, the audience enjoys the film because they feel good about themselves, choosing the right things to do and experiencing good emotions on-screen. At the end of the Hindi film, the audience may be satisfied that justice is done, the law is observed, and the good are rewarded. This is a kind of happiness where the upholding of values adds to making one happy, along with the narrative resolution.

Gilbert's third kind of happiness, which he calls judgemental, or 'happy about' something, requires one to give approval, but one may well not be emotionally happy as such, even while understanding that one is satisfied with the outcome and sees the merits of the situation. An example would be: I am happy that the government is taking steps to reduce global warming, even though I am far from happy that petrol costs me more.

These three types are available to the audience in different types of film ending. As audiences feel compassion and other emotional relationships with the hero and heroine, there is always some relief at the end of the film as the suspense and tension of the narrative are resolved and one learns what has transpired for the characters. While they may or may not be happy, the audience, in a different mental state and position from them, may have a variety of responses to what happens to them.

The happy-ever-after ending is usually a wedding, often involving a family reconciliation, where the audience shares the happiness evident on screen and is maybe even moved to tears. The characters are happy and the audience is happy. This is the obvious happy ending, where there is emotional happiness for the characters and for the audience.

This kind of happy ending is most closely associated with the romantic genre of films starring actors such as Shammi Kapoor, Rishi Kapoor and Shah Rukh Khan or films associated with Yash Raj Films and Karan Johar's Dharma Productions. In many of these, the only narrative tension has been the romance, as the basics of life are already in place, so how does the film-maker create a narrative to sustain the audience's interest – or how does he distract them with attractions such as song, dance, comedy scenes and so on?

A good example is the second biggest hit of 2009, *Rab ne bana di jodi*. This is the story of an unhappy marriage where the heroine, Taani (Anoushka Sharma), feels compelled to marry a middle-aged dullard, Surinder/Suri (Shah Rukh Khan), and they settle into a life where he cares for her and she comes to care for him, though not love him. When he disguises himself as a cool dancer, and becomes her dance partner, she falls in love with him. This raises various dilemmas – is she in love with another man or with her husband? Does a woman love a stylish guy rather than a dork? Taani now realizes how much Surinder loves her and they finally go on their honeymoon, the film's idea that all couples have their own ways of falling in love reinforced in the tagline: 'There is an extraordinary love story in every ordinary *jodi* ("couple").'

Some Hindi films have happy endings grafted onto what would otherwise have been a tragic ending, so the 'Romeo and Juliet' story of *Bobby* has the couple saved by their fathers, who are then reconciled; or

*Pyaasa/The Desirous One* (dir. Guru Dutt, 1957) has the hero and heroine walk off into a new future together. Other films have had happy endings removed in favour of complex and unresolved endings, notably *Mahal*, where the original version had the two people who never became a couple coming back to the mansion (the *mahal*) together in another life, but in the censor-approved version, which is all that remains, the hero dies and the heroine and her husband Shrinath (Kanu Roy) walk apart on their wedding night.

Hindi films can even have two different endings, deploying the interval – which all Hindi films have – to offer a preliminary but unsatisfactory end which heightens the final resolution. In *Om Shanti Om*, the hero and heroine die before the interval due to the wicked scheming of the villain. However, they are reincarnated in the second part of the film, where they come to take revenge on the villain, who dies as they are reunited for a happy ending in the final reel. The hero and heroine have to be reborn to make sure that justice is done and that they find their own final happiness.

Gilbert's two more complicated forms of happiness, namely moral and judgemental happiness, seem to be productive ways of understanding the audience's emotions. There appears to be much overlap between these two forms, which are distinguished clearly from emotional happiness (the 'feeling' and usual meaning of happiness). Moral happiness is a more

*173*

stoical form of happiness – the life well led. The audience may also take pleasure in the morality of the melodrama as virtue is rewarded in the film. The key figure is often pious, good and kind and suffers before receiving recognition for their virtue in films, as in *Kal ho na ho*, where the hero seems to reject his lover so she can marry another as he knows he is going to die. Even if the goodness is too excessive to be believable, the audience would often like to believe that it is possible.

Judgemental happiness is more complex, as it is often far from being a state of emotional happiness, seeming to be a more rationalized, less emotional, type of happiness, which may involve no emotional happiness or feeling of being happy at all. It is hard to be entirely clear which form of happiness the audience might feel at the ending of films that involve some of the most important characters in Hindi film history.

Returning to *Devdas* (see page 171), the audience recognizes that his bad behaviour leads to his punishment and death but he is forgiven – and love is eternal. Devdas dies but he has fulfilled his promise to Paro, namely that he will return to her to die, and this is the fulfilment of his destiny. Paro knows Devdas truly loved her and will live the rest of her life in that knowledge (although there was not any possibility of a close relationship between the two after her earlier decision to marry another). Chandramukhi has given up her life as a courtesan and is on the road to reformed ways. By some standards, these two women could be said to be happy and the audience can share in the delight of this resolution of the narrative.

Is this just a sad ending for the audience because Devdas has died? The religious overtones of Devdas' death, notably the Sanskrit chants and Paro's worship of him, as well as the religious context of the childhood love of Devdas and Paro and the unnatural communication between the two of them, suggest clearly to the audience that they will come together in another life. So does this mean that, for the audience, this could also be a happy ending? Is the audience happy, knowing more about the characters than the characters do themselves? Are they happy that justice had been done, that no one has transgressed and that the reward will be in a future life?

In the last twenty years, Hindi films have tended to end with emotional happiness – the successful conclusion of a romance. Two of the most popular genres in Hindi cinema in recent years (see www.boxofficeindia.com) are comedies and romances, both of which are defined by emotional labels.

The social context of happiness in India also needs further examination. While more Indians are becoming richer, it is unclear whether the rapid changes in Indian society are making people happier. Some would argue that India's new social and economic opportunities would bring less happiness for the many who cannot access these, while others take a more extreme view that modernity is incompatible with happiness. Even once one has the opportunity to plan for happiness, people often pursue misguided ideas, notably working harder for more money at the expense of social networks and relationships. Has India abandoned the moral Gandhian ethos that might have led to more happiness through reforming oneself and one's society?

New, mediated discourses such as advertising or self-help products encourage people to think about lifestyle changes that may make them happier, although research suggests that these are hollow promises and the simple reality lies in common truths such as money cannot buy happiness and families and social contact bring happiness. Many Hindi films during the later part of our period, that is, from 2000, have raised issues of self-fulfilment bringing happiness, including *3 Idiots*, and show people struggling to find happiness, which they cannot define, as well as a place in the world that suits them rather than pursuing material dreams.

The happy-ever-after ending is also found in one of the most popular genres of Hindi cinema during the last decade, namely the comedy, a genre which raises many issues about entertainment as well as looking at the comedy itself to see what people find funny as part of the wider imaginary.

## Comedies

Happiness may be the goal of many genres, but the comic genre focuses on moments where the audience is meant to laugh at what is funny – that is, they are supposed to manifest happiness. Characters in the comic genres are often not happy as the story unfolds, but the films usually end with the characters living happily ever.

Hindi cinema has long had comic sequences as part of a mix of genres in the social film, so even the great melodramas of Guru Dutt featured Johnny Walker's antics among the tragic moments. Comic actors, male and female, took the roles of siblings and sidekicks – right up to recent decades, with Johnny Lever. However, comic films in which the hero played a comic role were rare. *Shree 420* has the hero, Raj Kapoor, as a comic for much of the film, but this was unusual, with only Kishore Kumar really playing the lead as a comic actor.

There was a brief flowering of the comedy of manners in the middle cinema of Hrishikesh Mukherjee – including *Bawarchi/The Cook* (1972), *Chupke chupke/Secretly* (1975), *Golmaal/Confusion* (1979) and *Khoobsurat/*

Prem (Ranbir Kapoor) as Chalu Chaplin in *APGK*.

*Beautiful* (1980) and others in the 1970s and '80s. These often featured misunderstandings arising as a result of a person being in the wrong place at the wrong time or from a small lie told to smooth a situation which then develops into a series of lies and deceptions. Amitabh Bachchan showed himself to be a fine comic actor in the 1970s, especially in the films of Manmohan Desai, such as *Amar Akbar Anthony* and *Coolie*.

Many of the major box-office successes of the last two decades have been comedies. These consist mostly of strung-together comic moments in often incoherent plots, where complicated narratives have to be tied up by the end. Like pre-novel narratives, they have no development of character or situation but present a sequence of events which could take place in any order. Even the category of comedy – farce, caper, slapstick – is not clear. They are often adapted from other cinemas – Hollywood or Malayalam or Telugu – and throw in anything they like, from a gag to a character. The genre requires a physical reaction: if you do not laugh, or at least smile, it is just not funny. (I must point out that these films, which seem so 'brainless', to use the term by which they are referred to in the press, are usually extremely funny.)

Just as the major directors and stars of the big romantic and 'serious' films are well known, so are those of the comedies. The major directors of the 'belly laugh' comedies are David Dhawan (especially for his films with Govinda), Priyadarshan (*Hera pheri*, where he cast two action stars, Sunil Shetty and Akshay Kumar, along with Paresh Rawal, is something of a classic), Anees Bazmi (*No Entry*, *Singh is Kinng*) and Sajid Khan (*Housefull*).

The greatest comic star of the 1990s and early 2000s was undoubtedly Govinda, an all-round entertainer and one of the best dancers in Hindi cinema, who was well matched by Karishma Kapoor in a series of comedies, mostly directed by David Dhawan. Govinda played a simple, good-hearted character, whose innocence leads him from one comical situation to another, digging himself deeper and deeper into misunderstandings, disguises and ludicrous situations. Kader Khan often supplemented Govinda's roles with his verbal humour, along with Shakti Kapoor's vulgarity, which drew on that of Dada Kondke.

Several action heroes turned successfully to comedy, including Akshay Kumar, who starred in blockbusters such as *Singh is Kinng*, *Housefull* and *Bhool bhulaiyaa*. In the last, he was joined by Rajpal Yadav, marking the trend for some of India's most highly skilled actors – Paresh Rawal, Anupam Kher, Boman Irani – to take to comedy.

Salman Khan was always thought of as an action hero, but his comic performance in *Andaz apna apna*/*To Each His Own Style* (dir. Rajkumar Santoshi, 1994), along with Aamir Khan, was noted, and he has become one of the top box-office stars in films which mix action and romance with comedy, including the brilliant *Dabangg* and *Chennai Express* (dir. Rohit Shetty, 2013), while Shah Rukh Khan's biggest hits are his romantic comedies. Perhaps today it is impossible to be a Hindi film star without a talent for comedy, on a scale not seen before.

Comedy in Hindi cinema, as in Hollywood, is male-centred, with few female comedians evident. The romantic comic heroines include Meena Shorey, Geeta Bali, Madhubala, Hema Malini and Sri Devi, whose comic talent, seen in films such as *Mr India* (dir. Shekhar Kapur, 1987), was revived in a gentle form in her 'comeback film', *English Vinglish*.

In India, as elsewhere, comedy is often about dealing with several distinctive things: people's fears, such as situations out of control, rules breaking down and people not knowing how to act appropriately; people who should be admirable being risible; and, of course, the plethora of comic situations revolving around sex. The audience can feel empowered by laughing at people in this state of confusion, as they know something the characters do not. Sometimes the joke turns on the audience, where viewers feel they know a character who then turns out to be someone quite different – so the foolish friend in *Bhool bhulaiyaa* is actually the cleverest person, who knows more than other characters or the audience.

Much comedy is about people behaving badly or oddly or out of character, for example, beautiful people played by glamorous stars acting as fools and bumpkins. While some of the 'character actors', such as Paresh Rawal or Johnny Lever, can skilfully transform themselves to look, sound and behave like comic characters, the stars are often funny because they

are handsome, boyish men with muscular bodies pretending to be fools.
The pratfalls and physical comedy are highlighted by the mismatch of their
spectacular bodies with the requirements of the comic role, which relies
mostly on physical comedy, so dance or action heroes are preferred as
comic heroes.

So, people who ought to have gravitas behave like children; family
men encounter seductive women; predatory women chase innocent men.
The characters in the comedies are often portrayed as being rich, but they
behave like poor people pretending to be rich. Cross-dressing allows men
and women to change ascribed gender roles, such as the effeminate male
and butch female servants in *Raja Hindustani*. Gay men used to be seen
as hilarious, so many people were amused by the story of the gay couple
meeting in Venice in *Dostana/Friendship* (dir. Taran Mansukhani, 2008),
which was also funny as a straight way of imagining gay romance. Comedy
is also created around people being in the wrong place at the wrong time,
especially when suspicious wives walk in on their husbands in situations
which look compromising. Slapstick, visual gags and pratfalls abound.

Language comedy is often quite basic and crude, concerned with
characters with strong accents (in films such as *Housefull*, for example),
whether these be foreigners such as the half-Italian Aakhri Pasta, Gujaratis
or even the British royal family. Parody and pastiche usually refer to older
Hindi films and can even extend to an entire film, as in *Om Shanti Om*.

These elements of comedy are about new social demands that people face about appropriate behaviour: how to dress and speak correctly, new expectations of sexuality and so on. It is not surprising that the biggest stars of comedy who guide the audience through these social minefields are among the best loved in India.

The other greatest comic star of the last two decades is Salman Khan. While the crowds have always loved him, he was often taken for granted by the elite audiences and journalists and academics writing on Indian cinema, as he was a good all-rounder in many hit films from the late 1980s onwards. It was the critical and commercial success of *Dabangg* in 2010 that meant that he could no longer be ignored. He brought the humour of the David Dhawan and Anees Bazmee films to a film which was simultaneously mainstream, cinephiliac and very funny indeed.

In some ways, Salman has stepped into the shoes of Govinda. Both are Mumbai boys, with a huge local fan following, mostly among men, and they have great appeal to the mass audience. Although Govinda romanced in his films, he played the innocent man/boy, caught up in situations beyond his control, usually involving multiple and mistaken identities; Salman also acted in films beyond the comic genre, such as family dramas about the Barjatyas and romances such as *Hum dil de chuke sanam*, as well as many action films. When the two came together in *Partner*

The innocent man on his wedding night: the song 'I Don't Know What to Do' from *Housefull*.

(dir. David Dhawan, 2007), Salman played the Love Guru, a savvy and
scheming rogue who is nevertheless brought down by his girlfriend's
son, who transforms him into a father figure, through which he finds
happiness. Govinda plays an innocent bumpkin who achieves his goal
of romancing a beautiful woman he first sees on television. These two
stars, whether playing innocents or rogues, have mass appeal, the fun and
capers enabling them to survive their clumsy crossing of a range of social
minefields.

It is not clear who the audience is for the comedies, but given the
content, the anxieties and amusement, it could reasonably be said to be
middle class and upwards, and non-intellectual. Comedy may also appeal
to the lower classes, who might also share these anxieties or have their
idea confirmed that rich people are ridiculous, and the young, who think
the same about older people.

Many films which are labelled comedies overlap with other genres,
or perhaps are interrupted by other genres, as the films have a proper story
arc, with development of the characters. Rajkumar Hirani created comedy

with an overt social purpose, with the advent of perhaps the greatest comic character in Hindi film, *Munnabhai* – again with action heroes turned comics: Sanjay Dutt as Munnabhai and Arshad Warsi as his sidekick, Circuit.

The emotions form bonds between films and their audiences, in sentimental attachments to the films, their songs and their stars, who express the films' emotions and values. Stars are associated with particular emotions – though not exclusively – and films play to this. In addition to the audience's emotional response to the character on-screen, the existing relationship that the audience has with the star is of great importance, because it affects our responses and evaluation of characters as these are framed and informed by the personae of the stars who perform them. It seems that charisma may be closely associated with the ability to communicate emotion.

Thinking about the feelings of characters in films, as well as experiencing emotions in films, is a way of understanding people, relating to them with non-rational reactions. The heightened forms of emotion seen in the

The fertility doctor has a sperm ornament on his car's mirror in *Vicky Donor*.

Hindi melodrama are not the everyday reality of the emotions but emotions in their purest forms. Tears are beautiful when shed by Shah Rukh or Kajol, and Shah Rukh and Amitabh approach death as one ought to, when one is prepared and is surrounded by loved ones. Anger is not petty but is sharp and focused on putting the world to rights. Happiness is not about personal comfort but seeing the world as it should be. Comedy is often subversive and may show how anxieties and worries are funny and should be put in their place. Emotional films are high-risk ventures for film-makers, as they have to be responded to immediately by the audience: if a comedy is not funny or a weepie is not sad, then the film is redundant.

In 2012, films such as *Kahaani* and *English Vinglish* had leading female stars, while *Vicky Donor* (dir. Shoojit Sarcar, 2012) raised issues of adoption in a comedy about sperm donation and Anurag Kashyap's epic, *Gangs of Wasseypur*, created waves among a younger audience as well as inspiring younger film-makers. Melodrama retains its hold, but a move to other forms of emotionalism in the Hindi film is taking place. The films are moving towards realism, although the melodrama still underpins them. This is part of the shifting understanding of emotion – an adaptation to wider changes in the world which require reworking ways of feeling and responding to such changes as well as ways of thinking about them.

# FIVE

# Home: Romance, Love and the Family

The joint family – one in which several generations or adult siblings live together – and the arranged marriage, where the partners are introduced with a view to marriage, are often regarded as defining features of Indian culture and society. These are institutions which are celebrated in many popular narratives across a range of media, from film to the baggy Indian English novel of recent years. Hindi films usually centre on the formation of a romantic couple outside the family in a 'love marriage', while family units are shown to be small, usually nuclear, and plots may revolve around escape from larger units, which often become oppressive or quarrelsome. Yet the ideal of the joint Indian family remains, with Hindi cinema covering a range of possibilities of romantic and family formations.

While smaller family units are increasing in India, the traditional closeness of family relationships is such that there are words for a host of relatives who would simply be called 'uncle' or 'aunt' in everyday English, to demonstrate different roles and responsibilities enshrined in the family. Even strangers and friends are addressed with familial terms, so older people in general are often called aunts, uncles, grandparents, brothers or sisters. Leaders of the new Indian nation were also called by family terms, hence *Chacha* ('Uncle') Nehru and *Bapu* ('Father') for Gandhi, and even now Mamta Banerjee, the Chief Minister of West Bengal at the time of writing, is called *Didi* or 'elder sister'.

The family romance remains a priority in Indian films as it does in other narratives, notably the *saas-bahu* ('mother- and daughter-in-law') television soap operas, which mushroomed from the 1990s onwards. Indeed, the two great epics, the *Mahabharata* and the *Ramayana*, are stories based around family relationships, as are many enduring narratives, such as Freud's complexes, based on characters from Greek literature and mythology.

Hindi films long had the theme of the hero falling in love and then having to bring the beloved into his natal family, who often resisted the couple getting together. These families might be nuclear families or the hero or heroine might have just one parent, but the early 1990s included films that present the joint family as the ideal Indian family. This reached its zenith in Sooraj Barjatya's *Hum aapke hain koun . . .!*, whose story revolved entirely around births, deaths and marriages, a celebration of the Hindu undivided family or Hindu family values. Other Hindi films explore the formation as well as the disintegration of these relationships, highlighting a range of desires and tensions, idealized and dreaded relationships, and archetypal figures, as well as looking at the role of gender, which is created and learned in these relationships.

## Gender

Hindi movies, like those of most other cinemas, are usually hero-centric, with films where a woman is the lead seen as belonging to a different category of 'women's films'. There are exceptions, notably from the days of the great female stars of the 1950s, such as Nargis in *Mother India*, and some of the Sri Devi or Madhuri Dixit films of the 1990s. In 2011/12, Vidya Balan (*Dirty Picture*, *Kahaani*) and Sri Devi in *English Vinglish* showed that a female star can open a film at the box office. Perhaps this is to do with increased female spending power, but it seems more likely to indicate the beginnings, at least, of a shift in the role of women in the imaginary, as family roles themselves are changing, along with ideas of romance. None of these is a major feminist film, but they prompt a reconsideration of the role of women romantically and sexually as well as within the family itself.

Gender roles are usually regarded as being regressive for women in Hindi movies, in that films show women's dreams of being beautiful, marrying a rich man and having a life as a wealthy homemaker in a consumerist fantasy. Yet alongside these there are often aspirations towards artistic success, a wish for family and work balance and mostly a desire to love and be loved. This means that heterosexual romance, marriage, parenthood and the fulfilment of other family roles underpin the melodrama, as it is at its core about the private world of the home and the family. The films may be conservative in this sense, although it will be seen that some of them push boundaries in quite surprising ways, but they rarely make a radical critique. They show the individual in fixed gender roles as part of the wider view of the family as the basic unit of society, and the entitlement to respect, happiness and fulfilment within it. Female characters who seek fulfilment outside the family, in particular in the films of Madhur Bhandarkar, such as *Page 3* (2005) and *Fashion* (2008), and also in *The Dirty Picture*, usually end up being punished by death, disgrace and other ignominies.

Nisha (Madhuri Dixit) in an image of fertility on a visit to the village in *HAHK*.

# The Couple

The key plotline of many films is the getting together of the romantic couple, which highlights gender roles, in particular male and female ideals as represented by the lovers, as well as setting a style of romantic behaviour mixed with consumerist fantasies. The romantic couple is usually the lead pair, and they are stars or, if they are newcomers, show star potential. This is because the Hindi film is star-driven, with each role connecting to earlier roles and to the off-screen persona of the star, usually known from the media and hence controlled or manufactured. The star is presented in the film *as a star*, rather than as a character, and as a maximized being – the most beautiful, desirable, talented and so on. The biggest star is the person who fulfils these criteria best. While in Hollywood the stars may have become more normal, in Hindi film the trend has been in the opposite direction, with the women becoming thinner and more glamorous, the men more muscled and the stunts less credible. Salman Khan, one of the biggest box-office stars, certainly proves this trend, while another more recently arrived but rapidly ascending star, Ranbir Kapoor, is much more ordinary. In their physique and personality, the star must conform to a set of norms about what is loveable and desirable, but they must not exceed them.

The male star is usually paid more than the female star, indicating his dominance – already mentioned above. He is meant to have a natural attractiveness based on charm and beauty. Much of the star's look is constructed, fashioned through exercise, surgical and cosmetic intervention, prosthetics, hair dye and wigs and a great deal of grooming. While the female star is young, usually in her twenties, several of the major male stars have been acting for the last two decades, but the age difference is barely noted, not least because they are well preserved. The growth of an extreme, muscled physique has developed during the period looked at by this book, with very few male stars not developing this body ideal and instead keeping a slighter, wiry appearance. The origins of the muscled body may lie in working-class wrestling traditions, supplemented by the

World Wrestling Foundation television shows, but its genealogy remains unclear, and the rise of the shaven-bodied male is very much more recent. The ideal of men being larger than women is reinforced by this while women, already usually slight, have been getting thinner during these decades, influenced by modelling and Western ideals, although the myth that female stars used to be fat is not true, with the occasional exception.

The Hindi male star is rarely blandly handsome but has a distinctive face with a striking smile or other feature. The female star is usually of an internationally accepted norm of beauty, though Indian in having long hair, big eyes and a round face, and has a small, slim but curvaceous body, an

aesthetic seen in the images made by Ravi Varma rather than the tradition
of miniature painting. The stars who define Indian beauty rarely look
Indian since they are usually particularly light-skinned and often light-
eyed or with light hair, as beauty, in India, is associated with fairness.

The muscled body of the male star may represent control and auton-
omy over one's body, commodifying and shaping it, supported by the
huge male fandom of Salman Khan, one of the leaders in the world of
the body-builder physique. Salman's shirt-removal has become a 'meme',
with online videos collating examples of this, while a highly anticipated
moment of his new films is the tongue-in-cheek occasion on which this
now occurs. This male body is more suited to action heroes but is now
becoming a norm for all heroes. Shah Rukh Khan famously displayed his
'six pack' for *Om Shanti Om*, but he is the only star who rarely shows his
muscles. Similarly, the female body is disciplined through diet and exercise and is often enhanced by surgery but has been an object of the gaze
for much longer than the male. The idea that this beauty is normal and
is to be striven for by those who wish to be loved is a familiar consumerist
ideal and one that seems to be spreading from the cinema into real life,
while the aesthetic ideal is one that is more familiar from porn movies
than from romances.

Masculinity as embodied in the Indian male star differs from the Western model. The hero is rarely the patriarch but is usually a more junior member of a family, and pet names for him and his parents may remain. He may be outside the family, looking to establish himself, but he is rarely outside society in the way Amitabh Bachchan was in the 1970s as the quest is now normally not for revenge for the sake of the family but for a way of finding one's position in the family and in the wider world. The star may be young, as Imran Khan or Ranbir Kapoor are now, but several of the current leading stars are now in their mid- to late forties, for example Shah Rukh Khan and Aamir Khan. Yet none of these figures represents the patriarchal male. Even in films where Amitabh Bachchan plays such a role (*Mohabbatein* and *Kabhi khushi kabhie gham*), his values are defeated by the younger male. The ideal man is perhaps not what might be expected: he is loving, gentle and kind, unless his family or certain women are under threat.

The mature, contemplative type able to control his emotions – as Amitabh Bachchan was in the 1970s, at least until he vented them verbally and physically at his own volition – is now rare. Some of the thrillers show this type of hero, a kind of James Bond, in films such as *Ek tha Tiger*, Shah Rukh Khan in Farhan Akhtar's *Don* (2006) and *Don 2* (2011) and Hrithik Roshan in *Dhoom 2/Blast 2* (dir. Sanjay Gadhvi, 2006) or as Akbar in *Jodhaa Akbar*.

The new hero is expressive, loquacious and often vulnerable, emoting and weeping openly, the prime example being Shah Rukh Khan. His behaviour verges on what would be seen as feminine in some Western societies but is very much masculine within his own terms. At some extremes, the emotional hero may not have any objective assessment of his own behaviour, being focused only on his goal, his passion being strong enough to blind him to rejection. He may thus effectively stalk the woman he desires, a role which audiences accept in the case of Shah Rukh Khan in *Darr*, for example, where the man the heroine loves is eclipsed by the rejected lover. The important thing is the depth of his devotion rather than its mistaken goal or its obsessive manner.

The innocent, or boy-man, is a frequent figure in Hindi film, dating back to the earliest days. He is a boy not so much because of his age, but because, even when he is older, a certain immaturity sticks. This figure is partly located in comedy – the innocent abroad – and was seen clearly in the earlier films of Raj Kapoor. Recently it has been embodied in Govinda as a fool who gets into implausible situations where he is redeemed by his good heart, a role also taken up by Akshay Kumar. Variants include loveable rogues, typified by Salman Khan, on- and off-screen. The latter two often take macho roles, typified by Sunny Deol, which played on power, control and domination, but are also now established as comedy heroes.

Women in Hindi films may be interested mostly in their private world of romance and family or venture outside only to retreat again. Within these confines, they are not usually passive, silent types but are spirited and vivacious. Their work can be their major focus although it is subordinated to romance, so in *Dil to pagal hai*, dance is a path to romance but not the heroine's main focus. Women are usually shown to be excessively feminine, but when they are not, such as Anjali (Kajol) in *Kuch kuch hota hai*, the hero does not even notice them until they adopt traditional gender roles.

Hindi films also play with gender alignment, so characters can be transvestite, as is Kiran (Suresh Menon) in *Partner* or the servants in *Raja Hindustani*, where the male and female adopt each other's genders but the butch woman marries a man. The housemaid's understanding that two characters are gay in *Kal ho na ho* was seen as so funny that it became a skit at a Bollywood awards ceremony, while *Dostana*, which has two characters pretending to be gay in order to share a woman's flat, has a kiss between male stars (Abhishek Bachchan and John Abraham) and, if certain moments in the film are taken out of context, can be viewed as a gay film, or rather as near as Bollywood dares to go at present.

## Romance and Becoming a Couple

The 'formation', or getting together, of the couple lies at the heart of most Hindi films, with romance an essential part of the movies. It is rare that the lead character is not in a romance, such as *Chak de! India*, where the superstar Shah Rukh Khan plays out of character as a realistic, non-romantic hero. The formation of the heteronormative couple – young, beautiful and ideal – is found in nearly every Hindi film.

Hindi film has a whole language of love and romance which has set the model for ways in which romance is imagined and emulated in real life. While the beauty of the stars may not be achievable and travel to the exotic locations may be beyond most people's budgets, elements such as the poetry, songs and language, and the film's style and manner, can be copied and referenced. The films' ideals of romance skilfully draw on existing traditions and social customs as well as adding a new twist to create a fantasy of who should be romancing whom, where and how; what to do and what to say.

As mentioned above, while Indian marriages are mostly 'arranged' – that is, the couple is introduced by their parents or other elders – Hindi films usually show 'love marriages', in which the couple find one another. Whether one has an arranged, love, 'love-cum-arranged' or forced marriage

Romance in the snow in *DDLJ*.

and whether marriage is seen to be about families and property or about finding a life companion, romance is still part of people's lives and dreams. For some, the ideal is the arranged marriage with romantic love growing after marriage, while even the most romantic expect a different type of love to develop in later years, and films show all these types of romance or marriage, enabling thought and discussion and stimulating the imagination. Hindi films are one of the best sources of ideas about romance and how it should be. Of course, not all romance ends in marriage. Films fetishize '*pahela pyaar*'/'first love' and the idea of romance, even if it was never more than an exchange of looks many years ago, or if it was someone too young to have experienced it; they also show the ideal way for romance to happen as well as ways of remembering old loves, which are always something to be cherished.

Love-cum-arranged marriage is frequent, as films show couples that fall in love to find that they were once childhood sweethearts, or the couple falls in love then finds this was the person their parents were planning for them in any case, as for one of the three couples in *Dil chahta hai*. Or it may be that the parents introduce the couple, who fall in love before marriage, as in Sooraj Barjatya's *Vivaah: A Journey from Engagement to Marriage* (2006) or his *Hum aapke hain koun . . .!*

In romantic films such as *Dilwale dulhania le jayenge*, or DDLJ (dir. Aditya Chopra, 1995), the first half of the film sets up the characters and the hero and heroine establish their relationship just before the interval, with the romance unfolding across Europe against a backdrop of tourism and nightlife. The first half ends when the girl's father decides it is time to take her to India to marry the son of his friend. The second half of the film, set in a village in Punjab, is concerned with problems the couple face as regards winning over the joint family by persuading them to understand true love: the love-cum-arranged marriage.

The meeting of the lovers is one of the major features of the first half of the film. It is a major node in the narrative and the film presents this in a new and exciting way with regard to circumstance and place which often involves the couple literally falling into each other's arms. The audience knows that the hero and heroine are going to fall in love but the couple themselves may or may not be aware of it. Love may be immediate, but usually there is initial hostility (*DDLJ*), misunderstandings and near misses, so they keep walking past one another (*KHNH*), or the couple does not realize that they have feelings greater than friendship. This idea of the meeting – the look, the eyes, the innocence and the instant connection (even if not realized) – remains central to the films. Sexual attraction is usually secondary to this idea of love and the look, with the focus on the face and the eyes rather than the body and the couple sometimes seeming blind to the other's physical beauty and skimpy clothing, although the heroine may even imagine her beloved without his shirt if he is Salman Khan in *Ready* (dir. Anees Bazmee, 2011).

The next stage is the point at which the couple realizes that they have fallen in love. While the meeting of eyes (whose literal meaning, *aankh milana*, also means 'to fall in love') is one of the big moments, sometimes the first glimpse leading to love, there may be meeting and disliking one another (*DDLJ*). Quite often, one may fall in love while the other does not notice as s/he is in love with someone else. The audience notices and, given that they know the star couple is going to be united, the tension lies in waiting to see how this is going to happen. The audience can then watch how the disappointed lover behaves in a loving way while never quite giving up hope, even if seeking to help unite his beloved with her former lover to show the selflessness of his love (*Jab we met*; *Hum dil de chuke sanam*). This then leads up to the necessary declaration of love, usually in English, which seals the romance rather than sealing it with a kiss.

Along the way the songs have important roles to play, not usually so much for the first meeting but to establish the characters of the hero and heroine, then to deal with the realization and developing of love, and also the song may or may not be part of the declaration of love. Songs are also consumed outside the films as part of love in the outside world and, like saying 'I love you', are pre-packaged ways of experiencing romance.

The locations and the *mise en scène* create the space that is appropriate for romance. Privacy and the pastoral idyll of the garden and the

Nisha (Karisma Kapoor) and Shiamak Davar's dancers in *DTPH*.

mountains – and, in the 1990s, Switzerland in particular – have now been replaced with the city, often London (*Jab tak hai jaan*) or New York (*KHNH*), which offers opportunities for chance meetings, glimpses, anonymity and spectacular backdrops. The many costumes, hairstyles and gestures are copied; holidays and honeymoons aspire to these locations. Yash Chopra's aesthetic of 'glamorous realism', as he called it, dominated this period in his own films and their emulation by others.

The sequences of music, song and dance, loved by audiences but denigrated as 'running around trees', are a key feature of Hindi cinema, where they are used to focus attention – usually on the romance, with music, lyrics and particular attention lent to the presentation of the couple (or one of them). Song and dance are consumed not only in the cinema but also beyond it in other media and forms, at weddings and informal performances. The song is the moment of pure romance, the perfection of its expression and depiction, linking the characters in the film to romance in the world outside and forming a popular language of love.

While music, song and dance as elements of romance are found in many cinemas, Hindi film has a variety of love songs to suit every occasion, and several are often featured in one film. They are usually an integral part of the movie, if not always of the narrative, and establish the characters, the nature of their love, their range of emotions and their verbal and visual expression. This romance fits in between the ideals of the family and of romance and sexuality; it sets ideals as well as inviting imitation and becomes normative as the way in which romance is portrayed.

Dance songs are popular for flirting and the display of the body

The kiss in *Raja Hindustani*.

and its movements, entwining the romantic and the sexual in dancing and movement, helped by skilful camerawork and editing. Some of these sequences, like Western music videos, are shot in an aggressively erotic semi-porn style, but in Hindi cinema erotic dances are motivated by stories – 'Choli ke peeche'/'In My Blouse' being performed by a police officer to trap the criminal (*Khalnayak*) – or item numbers (spectacular and sexy songs usually occurring when a star makes a guest appearance, such as 'Munni', a comedy-erotic song in *Dabangg*). Slow songs, often dream sequences, are often the most romantic and tenderly erotic. Love, romance and eroticism are tightly bound together in these songs and form a composite.

Kissing has been absent for much of Hindi cinema, although present in the earlier cinema, but returns during our period after the much-discussed kiss between Karisma Kapoor and Aamir Khan in *Raja Hindustani*. Emraan Hashmi became known as 'the kissing star' for the scenes from his movies, but Shah Rukh Khan has never kissed in any of his. Hindi cinema's famous 'codes', such as reflections of the couple in water beginning to ripple as they move nearer to one another, or a flower coming in between them and the camera or a bee drinking nectar, are now used only as parodies. The wet sari sequence, however, has survived, having one of its great moments in the song 'Kate nahin katate'/'Day and Night Are the Same' in *Mr India*, while the male hero now also enjoys a good soaking to songs of love, longing and desire. The erotic continues its popularity but in a form which can be viewed by a universal audience, allowing the imagination of further erotic images in addition to the overt suggestions of the movies.

The lyrics and the dialogues, usually written by different authors, add the idioms of Urdu poetry, Hindi poetry and popular verse as well as folk-song lyrics and Western songs, to create a language of love. While Hindi and Urdu are the main languages for love, English seeps through many films and Punjabi often appears. Different words for love – *mohabbat* and *ishq* from Urdu; *prem*, *pyar*, *sneh* and *chahat* from Hindi – all have their own meanings, while the English 'love' is now almost a Hindi word, not least because the films mix languages, whether Hindi syntax with English words or English syntax with Hindi words, as seen in film titles (*Jab we met*) and songs 'It's the Time to Disco' (*KHNH*), 'Dhoom' and so on. The songs draw on the various worlds of these languages and poetry, setting them side by side, in dialogue with each other, rather than letting any one eclipse another. Poetry from films reaches a wider audience than most other poetry, such as the poem that Aditya Chopra wrote for his father's film of 2012 with the same title – 'Jab tak hai jaan'.

The Hindi film song allows things which cannot be said to be expressed. Even the most inarticulate, illiterate character can become expressive in a song, finding the right language for emotions and expressions. Song lyrics can be analysed as poetry or literature, but they also create their own symbolic meaning in a powerful imaginary that is shared and understood but not always accessible to articulation.

Songs are given particular 'song situations' in a film to heighten particular types of romance or moments in the romantic story. Some of the most memorably romantic songs, out of tens of thousands over the last two decades, describe the heady joy of first love, which has the hero literally dancing with joy in 'Pehla nasha'/'The First Intoxication'. In *Jo jeeta wohi Sikandar/The Winner Is the Hero* (dir. Mansoor Khan, 1992); or the songs make a declaration of true love, as in 'Tujhe dekha to yeh jaane sanam'/'When I Saw You, I Knew This, My Love' (*DDLJ*); or a dedication to the beloved, as in 'Tere liye'/'For Your Sake' (*Veer Zaara*); and they mark the sorrows of absence in 'Tere bin'/'Without You' (*Guru*).

The idea of dancing and romance are inseparable in Hindi films, with the body adding to the expressiveness of language in what is called the 'picturization' of the song.

During the last twenty years, features of the romance have changed, with earlier films often raising the problems of the couple fitting in as part of the larger family, whereas more recent films are about the hero's uncertainty in making decisions about his life. The idea of love as friendship, which flourished during the heyday of the diaspora film in the middle of our period, especially in the films of Karan Johar, seems to have reverted to great passion in films such as *Jab tak hai jaan*, whose title (*As Long as I Live* in English) immediately suggests the association of such passion with death and which is underlined by the song 'Heer'. Recent hit films have shown romance in so many different ways that it is hard to find a coherent theme.

The film which set the romantic agenda for the 1990s was *HAHK*, where the younger couple meets when their siblings marry, with everything happening within the family, although the elders do not notice the romance unfolding before them. An arranged marriage within the family is stopped after divine intervention and the love marriage goes ahead; thus the film condones arranged and love marriage, albeit with parental guidance, suggesting that trusting in one's family and in God secures a good marriage based on love.

*Dhadkan/Heartbeat* (dir. Dharmesh Darshan, 2000) has a young woman breaking off her romance to have an arranged marriage. Although she suffers in the marriage due to her mother-in-law and her husband's step-siblings, she knows she has to reject advances from her former lover and a timely pregnancy ensures her status in the family as a mother. The return of the lover suggests a fear of former romance coming back to haunt a married woman, which is confirmed by the hysterical declaration of devotion to the saintly husband, suggesting that this is the critical issue in the film, and the arranged marriage is ultimately the happy one. This theme is shown somewhat differently in *HDDCS*, where, after an arranged marriage, the husband helps the wife in her search for her former lover, but she realizes that it is her husband that she truly loves.

One of the biggest hits of our period, indeed of all time, is *DDLJ*, which garnered much attention for being about romance in the diaspora but which is also important for presenting marriage as needing understanding between parents and children, as well as the acknowledgement of tradition and the imperative of parental consent for a love marriage. The girl's father harbours old-fashioned ideas of arranged marriage with a boy he himself has never met, but the film sidelines the old codes of honour, helped by the unpleasantness of the fiancé and the goodness of the lover, until even he is won over by his daughter's pleas.

Saratchandra's ever-popular stories, *Devdas* and *Parineeta*, written in the early twentieth century and made into films many times since, were reworked during this period (*Devdas*; *Parineeta*), both of these films showing that one should give up one's pride to marry the person one loves. In the former, this does not happen and everyone's lives are ruined while in the latter, there is a happy ending.

One of the films that define the romance in the last twenty years is *Dil chahta hai*, which follows three affluent male characters who are grappling with decisions about their futures after college. While part of their dilemma is about work, torn between their creative and vocational ambitions and their parents' wishes and financial realities, the major part of the film is about their romances. Akash (Aamir Khan) is too irresponsible to realize that Shalini (Preity Zinta) is in love with him, and it is only when she is about to marry someone else that he finally takes action; Siddharth (Akshaye Khanna) falls in love with an older woman (Dimple Kapadia) who has been left by her husband but who dies of alcoholism; Sameer (Saif Ali Khan) agrees to an arranged marriage. While the first romance is the most typically cinematic, the other love stories are in no way diminished by their transgression or their conventionalism, and the three friends grow up during these romances and learn much more about love and the world.

*Zindagi na milegi dobara* in some ways updates this film: a glamorous road trip around Spain during which three men once again struggle with their relationships while paying more overt attention to overcoming a phobia. Kabir's (Abhay Deol) story is about an unwillingness to make a romance into a lifelong commitment; Imraan's (Farhan Akhtar) is about dealing with his mother's former relationship with a father he has never met and the responsibilities of fathers and sons; the third story, Arjun's (Hrithik Roshan), is about life-work balance and finding the meaning of life. The film eschews a conventional happy ending for two of the characters, but again shows their growth in achieving understanding of themselves, others and the path to mature and responsible relationships.

Many films also deal with romance that goes wrong. In the early 1990s, several featured stalkers – *Dhadkan*, *Anjaam* and *Darr* being notable examples. In the last, the sympathy for the stalker engendered in the film was quite shocking, but the woman is usually protected from her stalker by the 'right kind of man', although in *Anjaam*, she defends herself and finally kills her tormentor. The haunting by a former lover, mentioned above for *Dhadkan*, becomes a ghostly haunting in the hit *Raaz*, where the spirit of a postmarital lover that the husband has murdered comes back from the dead, until his wife saves her husband by burning the dead body.

Duty and love are also linked inextricably. In Yash Chopra's *Kabhi kabhie/Sometimes* (1976), the hero feels that his first duty is to his parents rather than his lover. In *Dabangg*, the father realizes his daughter will not marry while he is alive so he kills himself. The hero who has earlier romanced her in 'Tere mast mast do nain'/'Your Pair of Intoxicating Eyes' then makes a blunt proposal, stating that his duty is to look after her.

Love is put before other kinds of duty in *Ek tha Tiger*, where romantic love is greater than love for one's country and prompts the Indian and Pakistani agents to betray everything they have sworn to protect. Earlier in the film, Agent Tiger has dinner with his boss, where they both complain that they have put work before marriage. Tiger's boss seems to regard his desertion as a personal, rather than a national, betrayal. Perhaps Tiger has left it too late for youthful romance for, as Zoya says: '*Ab tumhari umr shaadi ki ho gayi hai*'/'You've passed your marriageable age.'

The quest for the self is often realized by falling in love. Munnabhai falls in love by hearing Jhanvi's voice and then seeing his beloved (though no song) but has to find himself before they can be together; in *3 Idiots*, 'Ranchod' (Aamir Khan) has to walk away from his love because of his concealed identity but seems to find it inevitable that his lover will travel miles across the mountains to meet him.

Not all couples are of this 'ideal' type and indeed many of the films are about transgressive and different types of couples. One of the reform movements of nineteenth-century India sought to allow widows to remarry, something that is mostly a taboo even today. While Raj Kapoor's *Prem rog* (1982) sidestepped the issue somewhat by having the husband die on the wedding day, *Mohabbatein* and *Hum tum/Me and You* (dir. Kunal Kohli, 2004) argue that a young widow should remarry. In *Partner*, the heroine has a child but his father is not discussed; and in *Dabangg*, the hero's mother has remarried after she is widowed and again no comment is made.

Intercaste and intercommunal marriages have already been mentioned in previous chapters and age differences were mentioned above when discussing *Dil chahta hai*. As for gay films, there is not yet a mainstream gay Hindi film, as Onir's films, *My Brother Nikhil* (2005) and *I Am* (2010), which feature gay heroes, are more 'realist' in genre, found in the independent cinema multiplexes, despite the former being distributed by Yash Raj Films. This lack of public discourse and 'out' figures, despite much LGBT activism, is not surprising given that Article 377 of the Indian Penal Code, which criminalized homosexual acts, is still in force.

While Karan Johar's *Student of the Year* has the superstar of the 1970s and '80s, Rishi Kapoor, playing a gay dean at a college, two hit Hindi films produced by Johar's Dharma Productions raise gay issues, even if the characters themselves are not gay. *KHNH* has a comedy motif where a Gujarati servant walks in on situations where Shah Rukh Khan and Saif seem to be in a gay relationship, a joke extended by the two actors when presenting the 49th Filmfare awards in 2004. Gay audiences create their own readings of this and other films, often imagining the heroines changing gender or strict fathers rejecting their sons when they come out before finally forgiving them.

*Dostana* picks up on the theme of friendships from earlier films in a way which has a distinctly homosocial air to it, especially to Westerners and, it seems, the south Asian diaspora, who love these moments and the high camp of Bollywood. Abhishek and John pretend to be gay and make up a story about how they met in Venice, which sends up the way straights imagine gays, while Kirron Kher performs a parody of a gay man's mother. The film is not homophobic but sends up homophobia, despite having stereotyped images of gays. The famous gay kiss in the film was a great shock to many in the audience, not least because it was performed by two leading stars. In 2013, Johar's section of *Bombay Talkies* featured a gay love story – with no excuses.

These films were quite a risk, even for a major figure such as Karan Johar, and are very much a sign of the times. Shah Rukh Khan, who laughs off rumours about his sexuality, is having a very positive effect in general on the industry and his adoption of a 'gay' style (analogous to David Beckham's 'black' style) is an important symbolic step.

There is another kind of romance in Hindi film, as mentioned previously, where the 'falling in love' takes place after marriage and the film traces the growing romance between the married couple. The idea that romance takes place after marriage, or at least after the engagement and introduction with a view to marriage, is seen in conservative films like

*Vivaah*, which was a blockbuster hit. It tells of an arranged meeting, falling in love under family supervision and the solidarity of the whole family – at least by the end – in support of the relationship. In addition to DCH and HDDCS, discussed above, other films have developed this theme, such as *Namastey London/Hello London* (dir. Vipul Amrutlal Shah, 2007), where the heroine goes through a series of parodies of 'family introductions' and has a sham marriage with the intention of divorcing straight after the wedding. Ultimately, the Indian man loves his wife; he sticks to his traditional ways and values and eventually wins her over.

In *Rab ne bana di Jodi*, the hero steps in to marry his teacher's daughter. His wife is in love with her former lover and rejects her husband. The hero fails to make her notice him until, with the Guru's blessing, he changes his appearance to that of a reality-show contestant and becomes her dance partner. The film promotes several ideas: seeing God within the beloved; how appearance may cause initial attraction, but ultimately it is a person's qualities that matter; and how a simple life may be the good one.

## The Wedding

Romance in Hindi films leads to marriage. Sex before marriage is not seen as wrong, though there may be contrition, as in *Hum tum*, while 'live-in' relationships, as they are called, are seen as temporary in films like *Bachna*

*Vicky Donor.* Punjabis look horrified at Bengali wedding ceremonies.

*ae haseeno/Run, My Beauties* (dir. Siddharth Anand, 2008), and marriage is ultimately the goal. Films do not always end with a wedding and 'living happily ever after', but the wedding is usually a spectacular moment in the film, where consumption, romance, sexuality and the family all unite in a spectacle involving song and dance.

Whatever relationships one has before getting married, marriage is seen as a major turning point in one's life. Heer in *Rockstar* accepts she is going to have an arranged marriage but has a list of things she wants to do before it, such as see a sleazy movie. Yet her relationship with Jordan after marriage is on a completely different footing, although he seems blithely unaware of it. As with KANK, which shows adulterous sex romantically, the repercussions are grim and make the couple look bad.

The wedding itself is a moment of total fantasy, because the Hindi film allows the viewer to have a dream wedding beyond the means of all but the very wealthy. The screenings of HAHK were attended by women in their wedding finery, a new invention of traditions which exported new wedding practices to other areas of India. The defining *filmi* wedding was *Kabhi kabhie*, which set a standard for weddings which was picked up by Karan Johar and followed in real life, while many weddings are seen in *Band baaja baarat*.

Films used to show the '*suhaag raat*'/'wedding night' as a moment of sexual tension between an unknown couple – Raj Kapoor's *Aag/Fire* (1948) and Yash Chopra's *Kabhi kabhie* being among the most celebrated examples. The wedding night is the moment when the couple are first alone in a bedroom – or at least were traditionally – and ostensibly embodies the idea of bliss rather than awkwardness and fear. Now it is often assumed that this is not the first time the couple has met or seen each other's face and the occasion engenders much less anxiety. However, in films on-screen sex is still mostly off limits. The idea of the innocent boy and the knowing woman who knows exactly what she wants is seen to be hilarious, as in the song 'I Don't Know What to Do' in *Housefull*, where the bride, dressed in skimpy nightwear and brandishing a whip, tells her husband she is going to show him 'heaven'.

In the films of the late 1980s and much of the 1990s, there were plots that concerned bringing the couple into the family and the tension that that creates, particularly between the son and his mother. The son is often seen to ally with his mother and the bride has to find her own place in the family. In films like *Dhadkan* and *Beta*, the conflict escalates as the husband refuses to acknowledge that the problem even exists. The fear is often that the bride will split the family by demanding to set up her own home, and this can be exacerbated where the woman has financial independence and may go to work. The arrival of children often changes the equation as it diffuses much of the tension, the bride rises in status and the mother has a new role in childcare.

There is considerable anxiety on the woman's side that the bride will become a slave to the husband's family or even suffer a 'dowry death' – not a moment which has featured in mainstream movies. Such family negotiations have increasingly moved to television, focusing on tensions within a family and particularly between the mother-in-law and her daughter-in-law, as celebrated in television '*saas–bahu*'/'mother-in-law–daughter-in-law' soap operas – most famously *Kyunki saas bhi kabhi bahu thi*/*Because the Saas Was Once a Bahu*. Yet this perennial source of anxiety for protagonists and the wider family features relatively infrequently in film; this seems surprising, though perhaps there is an avoidance of this difficult situation. Many films show the happiness of the joint family or have stories about resolving conflict, where women may be dealing with childcare and housework but are not enslaved by them. Sacrifice is an expected part of this relationship but the rewards are considerable, too.

The in-laws are usually important only for the girl, as it is she who moves in with the husband's family, although her family occasionally re-appears in a film. In the big family drama *HAHK*, there is even a song between the two sets of parents-in-law: 'Aaj hamaare dil mein'/'In Our Hearts Today'. Aside from the relationship between mothers- and daughters-in-law, other relationships within the family are not seen as so problematic. The wife of the oldest brother is called the *bhabhi*, and she takes on a maternal role for all the younger brothers in the family, especially in *HAHK* and *Vivaah*. Conflict with the whole family does arise and in *Damini/Lightning* (dir. Rajkumar Santoshi, 1993), when the bride acts as a witness to the rape of a servant girl by her brother-in-law, the family has her declared insane and sent to prison, until her lawyer and husband intervene.

In most north Indian communities, it is usual for the woman to join the husband's family after marriage, so the situation in *Coolie no. 1*, when the husband joins the bride's family, is automatically funny. The hero seeks to prove, while pretending to lead a double life as a rich man though he is really a porter ('coolie'), that it is wrong to judge people by their wealth. The film also takes the lower-class view by following the required pattern of the woman adjusting to the man – but with the comedy lying in the rich girl having to live like a poor woman, eventually humbled and totally devoted to her poor husband so that her rich father has to accept them as a couple.

Conflict in the marital family has long led to separation, a reliable theme in Hindi films – perhaps most famously in Guru Dutt's *Kaagaz ke phool* (1959) – but while non-mainstream films have been more open on the breakdown of marriages, few Hindi films have grappled with this theme, an exception being *Aap ki kasam/My Promise to You* (dir. J. Om Prakash, 1974), in which a jealous husband divorces his blameless wife and realizes his mistake too late. Perhaps divorce remains too much of a taboo for many cinemagoers. It was widely held that *KANK* was filmed overseas as Indians would shun adultery and divorce in an Indian context – as they had with Yash Chopra's *Silsila* (1981), which tried to justify the relationship as one existing before the protagonists had to sacrifice their plans when his brother died leaving his girlfriend pregnant. *KANK* makes no excuses for the breakdown of the marriage; in fact, the partners of the adulterous couple are shown to be entirely blameless. Later, the couples stop being angry and become civil. The characters either find new partners, turning their back on a marriage where the couple are just friends, or stay in a tolerably happy marriage, as they all simply want to find soulmates and fulfilment.

Many films are marital comedies. In *No Entry*, a jealous wife is obsessive about her faithful husband being unfaithful. However, he is being led into temptation by a flirtatious husband whose wife thinks he is faithful. In *Saajan chale saasural*, the husband thinks the first wife is dead and so remarries, but his first wife returns, so he has to keep the two apart. In *Biwi no. 1/Wife No. 1* (dir. David Dhawan, 1999), the husband leaves his frumpy wife for a glamorous girlfriend, then his wife decides to have a makeover and becomes a model herself, sending the kids and her mother to live with her husband. In *Judaai/Separation* (dir. Raj Kanwar, 1997), the wife (Sri Devi) sells her husband (Anil Kapoor) to a rich woman (Urmila Matondkar) but later realizes the error of her ways. All these films take elements of marital problems – infidelity, boredom within marriage and the desire for money – and spin off a series of comic capers until finally the marriage is happily restored.

## The Family

While *DDLJ* is often celebrated as the first Bollywood film, Sooraj Barjatya's *HAHK* was a watershed release in bringing the audience back to the cinema halls. *DDLJ* celebrated the family by having the boy refuse to elope with the girl, despite her and her mother's agreement, because he wanted her father's agreement for a traditional *kanyadaan* ('gift of a daughter'). *HAHK* was about the joint family, about two sets of parents, two brothers, two sisters and a host of friends and relatives, and their everyday lives. Its celebration of the family – the hero's jeep even bears the graffiti declaration, 'I love my family' – shows all the life rituals and celebrations from birth through marriage to death, with its songs and costumes imitated in real life, establishing the film's depictions as definitive. This celebration of the family has remained a theme in Sooraj Barjatya's other films up to his *Vivaah*, which have mostly been huge hits, perhaps because of their romantic and familial conservatism.

The Hindi film has long upheld the ideal of the joint family, where several generations of a family or adult siblings live and eat together.

Sexuality is controlled by the family, with a bride leaving her parents' house to move in with her husband's family, at least in north India. The family is important for practical purposes in a country with no welfare state and where public institutions, such as the police force, are seen to be shaky, as it organizes food, education and medical care, allocating these according to its own principles. However, the joint family is not the norm but an ideal in India, as most people live in smaller units, often as nuclear families or with one elderly parent, or even alone. The family may be divided for reasons of employment, space, individual desires or disputes which resist resolution. Changes during the last decade have occurred not least because of new opportunities for the new middle classes, especially for women, who may still be wives and mothers but can earn more money outside and who, with their husbands, can access more recently available home loans to buy their own places rather than having to share with their relatives.

Before the 1990s, the family was the key unit and individual identity was less important than a man or woman's family role. Characters who did not have a family were usually wanderers or sad characters who spent the film trying to form a new family of their own. Films held on to the ideal of the joint family, and kept the dream alive, but a massive shift in the depiction of the individual, the couple and the family has taken place over the last twenty years as films have moved from issues to do with couples and families to couples who are very much on their own and make their own decisions.

While tensions between natal families and spouses are probably universal, there is a striking number of family feuds, usually over property. Yet despite this, there remains nostalgia, a longing for completeness and an entire family. While the films might remind one not to take one's own family for granted, they also create ideal families which may be more desirable than one's own. Films may show families breaking up and then being reunited through arguments, as in *K3G*, while death features in most of Karan Johar's films as the characters struggle to deal with bereavement: a wife and mother in *KKHH*, a father and a grandmother in *K3G*, a father in *KANK* and a son in *My Name Is Khan*.

It is still unusual to see an unpleasant, dysfunctional and abusive family on-screen. The emergence of tales of child abuse over the last two decades and serious criticism of the family has perhaps lain behind the appearance of family conflicts for which there can be no forgiveness. While *Devdas* has conflicts with his father, films now show parents who do not care for their children and are even violent towards them – for example in *Udaan/Flight* (dir. Vikramaditya Motwane, 2010).

Perhaps the strangest family of all is that in *Dabangg*. The mother (Dimple Kapadia) is not unkind to the son but is by no means the typical Hindi film mother, not least in having taken a second husband when she found life as a widow very difficult. Her relationship with her two sons is also quite strange, with Chulbul (Salman Khan) being more like the usual hero, wanting to look after his mother and becoming energized to attack the villain when he realizes his role in her death. On the other hand, she views her other son, Makhi (Arbaaz Khan), as weak, and he weeps until she gives him some of her money. Chulbul asks his mother to leave her husband and younger son to live with him but she refuses. The stepfather (Vinod Khanna) tells Chulbul that he simply does not like him so throws him out of the house after his mother's death. He also takes money as a dowry from Makhi's future wife and refuses to return it. It is unusual to see parents who do not care about their children, at least certainly not as much as they care about money. Chulbul takes money from a gang; Makhi steals it from him to give to his beloved's father; he in turn gives it to his stepfather, Mr Pandey; and Chedi Singh's gang then burns down the building in which it is kept. Some reconciliation is offered later in the film, when the father is in the ICU (Intensive Care Unit) in hospital. Chulbul's beloved's father is an alcoholic, who commits suicide in order to leave his daughter alone so Chulbul will have to marry her. She begins as a typical heroine – pretty and a bit feisty as she walks down the street swinging her money in the end of her sari. After their romantic honeymoon in the UAE, however, she becomes an ordinary housewife as they live in their dystopic small town, Lalgunj, in Uttar Pradesh.

## The Nuclear Family and Singletons

Hindi films have often showed fractured and incomplete families, often missing a parent. It is usual that the heroine's mother has died or the hero has lost his father, perhaps making them more innocent or more vulnerable. It is only in recent years that heroes and heroines have been shown to have no immediate family – that is, no parents or siblings. This does not seem to determine their character or status, by inviting pity, for example, but it highlights their status as individuals – something quite rare in Indian society, where the self is rarely alone but is usually part of some sort of broader community; Indian Law speaks to communities, who are defined by religion and caste, as well as to the individual citizen.

When Yash Chopra's *Dil to pagal hai* was released in 1997, many thought that the story made little sense, as they did not understand who the lead characters were in the absence of their families. The lead heroine was orphaned and so brought up by relatives, and the second heroine had family off-screen in London. Yet the film was a huge hit and trend-setter, suggesting that the audience now saw characters beyond their role in their family.

Films are usually about a couple getting together and creating a new family, with the films rarely ending with one of the leads living singly, unless the partner has died. The option of choosing to live alone is not one which is usually taken, and the formation of the couple and kin substitutes is the norm.

The nuclear family of two parents and unmarried children has been rising and is now the norm in films, as it is in other media such as advertising. While husband and wife may be part of a larger family and in frequent contact with them, they may not live together, suggesting that an ideal situation is that which young people now often dream of – living separately though remaining in close touch with their parents. This ideal may also be linked to the fact that educated children are settling in metropolises and moving between them for work, or that many of the younger educated class is moving overseas after education.

## Parents

Non-conjugal family relationships often seem to take a back seat to the romantic narrative in the story, but they are often critical to the main narrative. Those with parents are among the most important, as the hero may come into conflict with them as he seeks to find himself, before a final reconciliation, whereas the heroine's conflicts with her parents are usually due to her romance and choice of partner.

The Hindi film mother is usually a fount of love who is willing to sacrifice everything for her children, a stereotypical image being the woman in a white sari who dies for lack of medicine which her son is struggling to pay for. Following the model of Nirupa Roy, who had played goddesses in 'mythologicals' and then was such an iconic mother to Amitabh Bachchan as Vijay, the mother who loved and sacrificed for her son, most star mothers of the last two decades are former film heroines. Raakhee, a major 1970s heroine, played mother to a host of heroes in the 1990s, including Jackie Shroff and Anil Kapoor in *Ram Lakhan*, Sanjay Dutt in *Khalnayak* and Shah Rukh Khan in *Baazigar/The Gambler* (dir. Abbas Mustan, 1993) and *Karan Arjun* (and also to Salman in the latter). Jaya Bachchan plays Shah Rukh Khan's adopted mother in *K3G* and Preity

Zinta's mother in *KHNH*, while Kirron Kher has played mother, often a Punjabi mother, to a whole range of stars, from Shah Rukh Khan in *KANK* and Aishwarya Rai in *Devdas* to Katrina Kaif in *Singh Is Kingg*, Abhishek Bachchan in *Dostana* and a host of others.

Older Hindi films divided women into conjugal and maternal women. These categories are now changing as mothers remain maternal but are also conjugal – that is, have romantic interests. Perhaps the frequency with which widows were seen in the older films helped to deny many women's conjugal role and make them just maternal figures, but now Kirron Kher and others play attractive, glamorous mothers who can still be devoted to their children but in a role that is more as a friend and mature advisor. (It is now such a requirement that mothers be glamorous that, in *Mission Kashmir*, Sonali Kulkarni played Hrithik Roshan's adoptive mother even though they were born the same year.)

The son's devotion to his mother remains, and in *Border* the soldiers' back stories are appropriate to their age groups; so, one is married with children, one just married and one engaged but very close to his mother, widowed in an earlier war, to offer viewers the supreme tragedy of a woman who has lost both her husband and her son for the sake of the nation.

The father in Hindi films is often the link between the family and the outside world, and he frequently comes into conflict with his son, not usually as a Freudian conflict over the mother, but as the agent who takes the boy into the outside adult world, away from the home and the mother's domain into the public realm. A film's theme can often be about this transition, and the father is not usually seen as hostile or unkind but as someone who is trying to guide the boy, often hampered by his outdated views. Often, communication breaks down between the two until a final reconciliation occurs on-screen. Hindu tradition has the father taking a back seat in the family once the son marries and has his own children, but movies usually concentrate on the son's attempts to find his role in the world of men, or, if at a later stage of life, his father is rarely present.

The father's wishes for stability and security come into conflict with their children's hopes for self-awareness and self-fulfilment in many recent films, including *3 Idiots* and *Ajab Prem ki ghazab kahani*, even when their relationship is affectionate, as they have to negotiate and take into account changing values. Although such a film usually focuses on the sons, and the mothers typically act as a go-between in the crisis, the fathers are seen as well meaning but have to learn to accept that duty is less important to the young than finding themselves, as in *K3G*. Fatherless sons have to learn duty early, as in *Soldier* (dir. Abbas Mustan, 1998), where the son seeks to restore his father's tarnished name.

Fathers who behave like their sons are shown to be great fun, although they often seem more childish than the sons and rather foolish. They are over-affectionate, if not doting, and they encourage their sons to chase their beloved, clowning around in the process in films such as *Hero No. 1* and *DDLJ*, where they are usually insulated from the world by their wealth.

In *Jaane tu . . . ya jaane na*, Jai (Imran Khan) is guided by a photograph of his dead father on the wall to espouse a non-violent, non-Rajput lifestyle. However, he later finds out that this was his mother's story, and when he has a fight, his father, from the memorial picture, signals his approval of his son's true nature. There are other strange fathers, too, such as Sexy Sam (Amitabh Bachchan) in *KANK*, who gets up to bedroom capers with blondes, after which he forgets to remove his furry handcuffs (although we find out later he is lonely after his wife's death); but he seems to make a better father-in-law than a father.

Fathers and daughters have a more loving on-screen relationship, whose poignancy is emphasized by the father's duty to give his daughter away in marriage, after which she leaves her home to join her husband's family. This cherished relationship is seen in many films, including *Vivaah*, where the adopted daughter is treated more affectionately than the natural daughter, causing tension between the father and mother; in *RNBDJ*, the father is concerned about his daughter's future and it is his last wish that she be married; in *Housefull*, Boman Irani is totally wrapped around his daughter's finger, while his own mother looks like an elderly widow but is not beyond thrashing him with a stick and constantly reprimanding him.

Fathers can be over-strict with their daughters, so Amrish Puri in *DDLJ*, who is an old-fashioned father, holds his values above the wishes of the rest of the family but finally realizes that he should be more flexible. In *Mohabbatein*, the father chooses values over love and loses his daughter, and only at the end does he resign his position in favour of his dead daughter's lover.

One of the major shifts in the depiction of parents of grown-up children in recent years in Hindi films is that, not only is the mother seen as more attractive than was once the case, even when she has grown-up children, but also that parents continue to be romantic and sexual after parenthood rather than becoming asexual beings. A striking example is where, even as grandparents, the relationship between the couple is primary and remains romantic (*Baghban/The Gardener*, dir. Ravi Chopra, 2003). Other instances include the *mehndi* (henna engagement ceremony) song in *DDLJ*, 'Ae mere zohrazabeen'/'O My Beauty' (which quotes Yash Chopra's film, *Waqt*), as well as the Sexy Sam character mentioned above. Veer and Zaara meet after seventeen years but there is no doubt that their romance and physical attraction remains (*Veer Zaara*).

Lead characters, even romantic leads, are now often parents to young children, so the hero has a daughter in *KKHH*, the heroine in *MNIK*, the lead couple are parents in *Ta ra rum pum* (dir. Siddharth Anand, 2007) and one of the heroines in *Partner* (dir. David Dhawan, 2007) also has a child. Imagining middle age in India, let alone the question of when it begins, are tricky themes for film-makers. The problem has been faced by cinema stars who, as they approach 50, may be too old to play heroes, yet none of them is ready to leave. Amitabh Bachchan found a new place for himself in cinema in the new millenium after his success chairing the television quiz show *Koun banega crorepati?/Who Wants to Be a Millionaire?* He is now the offscreen national patriarch although he still also occasionally takes more unconventional roles in films. The problem with seeing middle-aged people as more than just parents, as romantic, creative, active members of society, seems to be an issue that regional cinemas, such as the Marathi cinema, are dealing with in a more creative manner than Hindi cinema.

Although the legal marriage of a Hindu male to more than one wife was abolished in 1955, it is still found occasionally in the film industry and in other parts of society, so the term *souten*, or 'co-wife', is still commonly used for a rival. Remarriages by widowers are not frowned upon, but the *souteli maa* '(wicked) stepmother' is very much a frequent figure, along with idioms of 'stepmotherly' – that is, unfavourable – treatment. Stepmothers are usually wicked and scheming, often aligned with another figure of mythical malevolence – the *mama*, or mother's or stepmother's brother. From the *Mahabharata*'s Shakuni Mama to his modern-day counterpart in *Raja Hindustani* and *Beta*, the *mama* represents a widely held fear, in north India at least, of the maternal family interfering in the woman's life after marriage to siphon off her husband's and his children's wealth. There is also a suggestion that the stepmother is a vamp and it is sexual desire on the part of the father that is allowing him to be deceived. Remarriage is usually encouraged only when there are young children to be cared for, as intended in *HAHK*. Stepfathers are very rare – *Dabangg* one of the few – and the term *soutela baap* is not in common currency.

*Guru* is one of the few films where the hero, in this case Guru, has a close relationship with his stepmother but not with his father. He later has a very complicated relationship with his adopted father, or rather grandfather, Dasgupta, where the two are at loggerheads over business though still very attached to each other in private, showing the endless mutability of family relationships.

Adoption has long been a theme in Hindi cinema's family dramas. Although adoption is not usually formalized, it is quite usual for a child to be brought up by another family member, either because the child's parents are dead or absent or because the adopters are childless. In *Golmaal 3/Confusion 3* (dir. Rohit Shetty, 2010), the couple adopts children because they married too late to have their own and childfree families are not normal in Hindi films, or outside small sections of metropolitan India.

In a joint family system, closeness to aunts and uncles is also regarded as normal. However, when a child is adopted from outside the family, questions are often raised about the wisdom of bringing an unknown person into the heart of the family. There is often anxiety that the person is only masquerading as blood and his or her loyalty is always questioned, although the resolution of the film always supports the child's inherent good nature and devotion to the family. This is seen in many films, such as *Bhool bhulaiyaa*, and those which draw on the *Ramayana*. In *K3G*, the mother accepts the adopted child fully (he and the biological child have a running gag about which one of them she loves more), but he comes into conflict with his father, who never fully accepts the son, although why he agreed to adoption in the first place is never explained. In *Ajab Prem ki ghazab kahani*, the heroine's (adopted) parents are cruel to her while the hero's father gets angry with him but, like his mother, adores him; the second hero's parents are seen as being obsessed with money and far too lenient in bringing up their son.

## Grandparents

Children may be brought up with in the same house as their paternal grandparents (Dada and Dadi) but may also be close to their maternal grandparents (Nana and Nani), and *K3G* features both grandmothers as part of its idea of a complete family. Grandparents are often firmly supportive of the younger generation and have a strong personal relationship with their grandchildren. In *Rocket Singh*, the grandfather brings his religious background as a Sikh and solid Punjabi attitude to the young man, while in *Dor/The Thread* (dir. Nagesh Kukunoor, 2006), the grandmother supports the young girl's questioning of her role in life. In *Mujhse shaadi karogi/Will You Marry Me?* (dir. David Dhawan, 2004), the hero (Salman Khan) has a dadi whom he respects and adores. Zohra Sehgal is a favourite grandmother, a role she has taken in many films, such as *Devdas* and *HDDCS*, and she plays Amitabh's mother in *Cheeni kum/Less Sugar* (dir. Balki, 2007).

Respect for the elderly is taken as a given, although films such as *LRMB* have highlighted an anxiety about them being seen as burdens on the young who need to be put into homes when they are physically and mentally fit and able to contribute to the family. The film that created a furore in India and overseas was *Baghban*. The slogan was: 'Can you depend on your family?', as the retired couple (Amitabh Bachchan and Hema Malini) find that their four sons are too busy to look after their parents but agree to take one parent each for a few months a year, thus separating the happy couple. The father writes a prize-winning story about their terrible treatment at the hands of their children and how much he loves his wife. Their adopted son, Alok (Salman Khan), is the one who steps in to look after them. When the book makes money and the parents can afford to live together again, their children come back but the father disowns them and they settle in their own house near Alok and his family. Apart from the intervention by the adopted son, the big shock for the audience was that the couple were still in love and lived for each other and were prepared to disown their unkind children and refuse to forgive their appalling behaviour. The view of the old as a nuisance and an inability to see them as people were among the questions that this film raised, and the answers it came up with surprised many.


## Siblings

While aunts and uncles feature rarely in Hindi film, siblings are found frequently. The love Bharat and Lakshman have for Rama in the *Ramayana* sets the standards for fraternal love at a high level, and it is one that the movies have upheld with devoted brothers such as those in *Gunga Jumna* (dir. Nitin Bose, 1961) and the many roles played by Amitabh Bachchan, even if his brother has to kill him to uphold the law (for example in *Deewaar/The Wall*, dir. Yash Chopra, 1975). In the last two decades of Indian cinema, stories of brothers have continued to draw on these mythological resonances (see chapter Three), although the popular thriller *Race* (dir. Abbas Mustan, 2008) has two half-brothers double-crossing each other and even one sleeping with his half-brother's wife, before one kills the other in a race over money. Sisters share a close and innocent relationship, and stories of two brothers and two sisters marrying each other remain popular (*HAHK*, *K3G*).

The melodrama of good and bad brothers has continued, while stories of twins and doubles (*Aankhen/Eyes*, dir. David Dhawan, 1993), especially of identical twins, one good and one bad – popular themes of melodrama – are less common now. There were such films in the early 1990s, to allow double roles for the lead, thus Shah Rukh Khan in *Duplicate* (dir. Mahesh Bhatt, 1998) and Salman Khan in *Judwaa/Twin* (dir. David Dhawan, 1997). *Kaho na pyaar hai/Tell Me It's Love* (dir. Rakesh Roshan, 2000) was strange in that it presented the hero in a double role, looking identical but with no hint of there being any connection between the two.

## Children

Films do feature babies, although the melodrama of the unwanted pregnancy has largely faded, with unmarried parenthood being shown as manageable in *Kya kehna/What Can I Say?* (dir. Kundan Shah, 2000) or even acceptable, at least in Australia – *Salaam namaste* (dir. Siddharth Anand, 2005). However, pregnancy and motherhood is still seen to give women a special status, so in *Kurbaan*, the terrorist husband would kill his wife if not for her child, which he thinks will replace his deceased one. A few films have raised the issue of infertility and surrogate parenthood, such as *Chori chori chupke chupke/Stealthily, Secretly* (dir. Abbas Mustan, 2001) and *Vicky Donor*.

Although few films were made for children until recently, now children are playing major roles beyond being just a cute kid or sibling or the hero and heroine's child, but these are mostly in non-mainstream films such as *Stanley ka dabba/Stanley's Lunchbox* (dir. Amole Gupte, 2011) and *I Am Kalam* (dir. Nila Madhab Panda, 2010). There are films about a child rather than being children's films – *Taare zameen par* – and a number of cartoon films aimed at children.

Karan Johar's films very much centre on childhood, especially the traumatized or disabled child. In *KKHH*, the child is entrusted by her mother, who dies in childbirth, to reintroduce her father to his lost love. In *K3G*, the younger son is fat and greedy, as well as being a snob; in *KHNH*, a disabled child is adopted by the mother but revealed to be the father's child from an affair; in *MNIK*, the wife's child from her first marriage is killed in a racist attack while the hero Rizwan is autistic, and shown to have suffered as a child.

## Friends

Friendship, or *dosti*, was the theme of many films in the earlier days – the creation of brothers outside blood relations. Now boys and girls can be friends, and the '*Mujhse dosti karoge?*'/'Will you be my friend?' of *Bobby* has become central to the Bollywood film. Male friendship still features regularly, though the relationship is less intense than in the older films, and the hero and sidekick, a role taken often by Johnny Lever, faded in the late 1990s, though is celebrated in Munnabhai's films. Also fading are the famous love triangles where two male friends are in love with one woman – or vice versa – and one has to sacrifice love for friendship, parodied in *Dostana*. Instead, we now see more casual friendships, often three or more friends who hang around together without necessarily being intimate.

Servants, who used to be framed as poor relations, are rarely seen these days, with a few notable exceptions, usually in comic roles, as in *HAHK* and *Raja Hindustani*, where they bring in a different social perspective, whether loyal and devoted or untrustworthy.

Pets, who show understanding and loyalty exceeding that of humans, are also becoming rarer, although notable 'anipals' included dogs (Tuffy in *HAHK* and Brownie in *Taal*, dir. Subhash Ghai, 1999), the pigeon in *MPK* (1989) and the monkey in *Aankhen*.

## The Changing Family Unit

Although the ideal Indian family remains the joint family, there has been a shift in Hindi cinema to showing the couple as an independent family unit, though parents still frequently appear. Children are also playing a bigger role, with the hero and heroine being shown as parents – the shift being to the idea of romance and love within marriage rather than romance leading to marriage.

The exception to the above is Karan Johar's *K3G*, a groundbreaking film which was marketed as a multigenerational film, with parents, children and a grandchild. Yet Johar also made films which show the breakdown of the family: in *KHNH* it is threatened by the actions of an adulterous father but saved by his wife, who is harassed by her mother-in-law, while the heroine marries her friend rather than her lover, who dies before the end of the film. *KANK* was about the breakdown of two middle-generation marriages, both ending in divorce. One marriage ends because the disabled husband is angry with his wife for not giving him and their son time and also angry with his son for not being a sportsman like he was. The other couple is infertile, but she does not love him. The older generation in the film knows how to handle its relationships, loving each other as friends and looking back on their old loves as part of their youth. But Sexy Sam has kept his son close and also his daughter-in-law. In *MNIK*, the heroine is divorced and she rejects her second husband after the death of her child until he makes his trans-American pilgrimage.

The film *K3G* is about love across the family and a demand for new values of understanding and forgiveness. Although the film's slogan is 'It's all about loving your parents', this is the one element that is never in doubt in the film, whereas the father's love for his family is subordinated to his love of duty to tradition. Amitabh reprises his role of the angry and unforgiving patriarch which he played in Yash Chopra's *Kabhi kabhie* and Aditya Chopra's *Mohabbatein*. His word is final in the family ('*Maine keh diya*'/'I said so') and his wife has to obey and serve him. His values are based on tradition (*parampara*) and honour (*izzat*) and notions that their wealth makes them more important than ordinary (*mamuli*) people. This sense of observing traditional forms, which leads to his break with his adopted son (although it seems unlikely someone so obsessed with tradition would have adopted a stranger) appears as outright unpleasant and the audience would lose sympathy for the character were it not played with restraint by Amitabh Bachchan.

The other great theme in *K3G* is forgiveness (*maafi*). From the beginning of the film, the younger generation is forever apologizing: Rahul for calling the young Rohan 'Fatty'; Rohan for calling Pooja a 'vern' ('vernacular', that is, non-English speaker) and lower class; Anjali for breaking vases at the Raichand house; and Rahul for not loving Naina. The father is the one who has to apologize at the end after his wife points out he is not a *patiparameshwar*/'husband-god' but one who makes mistakes (*galat*).

The film's plot is the construction of the complete family, mentioned at the beginning as having two children. The film follows the break-up of the family following a Diwali celebration, through a fantasy reunion

The family reunited in *K3G*.

in the major song 'Bole kangana'/'My Bracelet Speaks', to end with the two younger couples brought into the joint family, the final reunion being at a Hindu wedding.

In many ways, this film marked the zenith of the big family films of the 1990s, and after this the joint family plays a smaller role in the big hit films, with the focus now on the couple, and perhaps on their life after marriage and children, and parents and grandparents taking something of a back seat within this process of constructing the 'new' family.

SIX

# The World: Education, Work and Lifestyle

Education and work are imagined in Hindi cinema as means in themselves and as ways of participating in the wealth and prosperity of the new India. Films rarely show the reality of education and the workplace but there has been a change over the last twenty years to present school as more than a duty and work as more than simply a way of earning money or running a family business. Education and work may allow for social mobility and enhanced status and respect and for some may provide a way around the restrictions of caste, age and gender.

## Education

It is widely acknowledged that one of the major problems facing India is the lack of universal education, which is key to the country's development and to increasing its skilled workforce. Free compulsory education for all children under fourteen is meant to be a right under the Indian Constitution, but many children, especially girls, do not attend school. Standards vary widely across India's schools, 18,000 colleges and 335 universities, with the high end producing some of the world's best students, while hundreds of thousands of young Indians study overseas, especially in the USA (where Indians now form the largest overseas student body), the UK, Germany and Australia.

While *Devdas* (1955) showed the tedium of school with its bullying and incompetent teacher, *Mother India*, a film which contrasted the old village life with new Nehruvian development, has many references to the need for literacy, in particular for the protagonists to avoid the lure of becoming indebted to money-lenders. One of the major signs of hope in the film is a young woman teaching children to read and write. The desire for education was seen in other films where an indication that a family had hit rock bottom was when it could no longer afford school fees. The sacrifice of the older son who works to pay for his younger brothers' education was often seen, in *Deewaar*, for example.

In mainstream Hindi cinema, schools are usually a location for stories about defining social status, notably in Karan Johar's films. When Anjali (Kajol) appears as the maternal teacher of small children at an American-style summer camp in *Kuch kuch hota hai*, her transformation from tomboy to woman is confirmed. The summer camp looks like a child's dream vacation destination, though it is not dissimilar from the college where Anjali herself studies earlier in the film. In *Kabhi khushi kabhie gham*, the wealthy Raichand boys study in a British-style boarding school in Mussoorie, while the poorer Sharmas are classed as 'verns' or vernaculars, HMT or 'Hindi-medium' types who studied in non-English schools. Later, the younger siblings from the two families meet at college in the UK, where she is now designer-dressed and he drives a Ferrari.

Hindi films often feature boarding schools, which are partly relics of the elite British educational system where many people in the film industry have studied but whose place in the imagination is bolstered by English-language fiction, mostly the novels of Enid Blyton and J. K. Rowling. Such schools are usually portrayed as enjoyable spaces and are shot overseas, mostly in English stately homes. Themes do not focus on separation from the family but on these schools being fun places to play games and make friends.

Female teachers may be portrayed as frumps or glamorous types, perhaps in the way that they are remembered by their grown-up pupils, rather than for their transmission of knowledge. In *Main hoon naa*, a comedy in which Shah Rukh Khan goes back to school as an older pupil and romances the glamorous chemistry teacher, the Hindi teacher is an

old blue-stocking whose classes are dreaded. *Mohabbatein* contrasts two
types of male teacher – the old patriarchal head (Amitabh Bachchan) and
the young, caring music teacher (Shah Rukh Khan), who believes in
love; the setting is a Gurukul, a type of traditional educational institution,
perhaps more of a college than a school. This film reinforces the idea that
one learns more outside schools than in them, as seen in Aditya Chopra's
earlier film, *Dilwale dulhania le jayenge*, where the hero succeeds at sports
but his academic failures are presented as comedy.

Many Hindi films are set in colleges where the students are in their
later teenage years – roughly equivalent to the last years of Western (high)
school and the beginning of university – or in universities, with a lack of
clear distinction between the two. The focus in both settings is often on
romance and relationships. Social issues, or at least that of wealth, may
be raised when rich and poor students come into contact. *Jo jeeta wohi
Sikandar*, set in several rival colleges in the foothills of the Himalayas,
shows poorer students in conflict with spoilt rich kids, and how the poor
but deserving student wins a bike race and the girl.

In more realistic Hindi films, universities are places where the middle
and upper classes get caught up in politics, such as *Hazaaron khwaishen
aisi*, where students at Hindu College, Delhi University, are drawn into
the (Naxalite [Maoist insurgent] and Gandhian) political world of the
1970s or the caste-based sexual politics of Allahabad University. Mainstream
films often make fun of university. Thus Munna Bhai the thug, in his two
outings, *Munna Bhai MBBS* and *Lage raho Munna Bhai*, goes to medical

school in the first but then has to take a history degree in the second in order to keep face, please his parents and win the girl. In both films, his non-academic instincts are of more value than his education, so his magic hug (*jadu ki jhappi*) is better for patients while his inner conscience makes him a true follower of Gandhi.

Many films include mention of study overseas but it is unusual to show an actual university on-screen, except for the memorable casting of Manoj Kumar as a student at Magdalen College, Oxford, in *Purab aur Pachhim/East and West* (dir. Manoj Kumar, 1970). 'Oxford University, London' is mentioned in KKHH, while *Paa/Dad* (dir. R. Balki, 2009) is partly set in Cambridge University but includes shots of Oxford. Oxford also features in several films as a backdrop for songs but not as an integral part of the film. Many of India's elite studied at Oxbridge, which is still mentioned in many films, as in *Kuch kuch hota hai*, or shown, as in *Kabhi khushi kabhie gham*. However, now that many Indians study at American colleges they feature more frequently in today's films: perhaps just mentioned, as in *Raajneeti*, where Samar Pratap (Ranbir Kapoor) is studying for a PhD in the USA; some films are set in various (fictional) New York colleges, such as in *New York*; in *Kurbaan*, the heroine teaches at a New York university, where she finds work for her husband (a professor from Mumbai) teaching Islamic Studies.

The imagining of college and university as places for growing up and forming relationships, especially romantic ones, seems unremarkable. What is striking is the growth in the number of films which show life at university and just after graduation, including perhaps a spell doing vocational work, as a space for examining ideas about finding oneself, rather than moving into the career and marriage planned by one's parents. The film which seemed to begin this trend was *Dil chahta hai*, in which three men seek their vocation and romance after college. The conflicts were different but the principle the same in many films over the last decade. In *Wake Up Sid*, the hero fails at college, struggles with his parents over his desire to be a photographer rather than enter the family business and does not recognize love when he finds it. In *Rang de basanti*, the students discover themselves as activists; in *Band baaja baaraat*, the hero refuses to return to Haryana to work on the farm and instead becomes a wedding planner, while his co-worker sees her job as something to do until marriage. The hero of *Rockstar* finds his family will not accept him as a musician and he is unclear what being a musician really involves beyond the moment of performance. *3 Idiots* shows students struggling to negotiate their parents' plans for them versus their real desires.

This move to exploring ways of finding oneself and making a vocational choice is a very strong theme in big-budget films from the later 2000s. These films query the traditional pattern of children following well-worn paths into the family business, the cramming at school and obsession with grades which, rather than interest or aptitude, determine degree choice – medicine and engineering (science for the top achievers), then commerce, then the arts. The films may or may not be rebellious, with some depicting negotiation and reconciliation with parents while in others the hero makes a clean break. There also seems to be a move away from the dream of the school loser becoming successful in modelling, acting and other professions which are presented as effortless and glamorous; newer films show the need for considerable hard work, talent and mental stamina in the pursuit of ambition.

The students are overwhelmed in *3 Idiots*.

# Work

Work has had its own value systems in India, which may include the traditional or religious: *dharma* ('law' and 'virtue' among many meanings) represents what one ought to do, according to one's caste or parents' wishes; *artha* ('wealth') represents the acquisition of money and possessions. Some occupations also bring considerable social status and define class, but in recent years, as noted above, films have looked at new objectives in work as well as education – such as self-fulfilment, identity or self-definition. Work as self-fulfilment is part of the dream of self-help and an option only for the more affluent – not for those whose primary need is a basic income. Yet, growth of the private sector in India has offered some young people – mostly working in IT, insurance, banking, telecoms, retail and media – salaries beyond those of their parents, making these jobs attractive and glamorous on account of the financial benefits. A young, glamorous workforce in open-plan offices is replacing the old image of cabins organized hierarchically, ending with the boss's.

Films are usually vague about what people actually do for a living, but they do show how people imagine work, how they want it to be, how they understand it and how they fear it, misunderstand it and make their plans. In the old films, work was something that happened off-screen, unless the person had a creative job in art, music, writing and so on, where the boundary between work and leisure seemed more porous.

Hindi films have shown women in traditionally glamorous jobs – models, singers and performers – but also in more 'serious' professions, whether as journalists (Konkona Sen Sharma in many films), politicians (Katrina Kaif in *Raajneeti*), doctors (*Munnabhai MBBS*) or sportspeople (*Chak de! India*). Some women are shown as expecting to give up work after marriage, such as Shruti (Anushka Sharma) in *Band Baajaa Baaraat*, while others try to reconcile work and relationships as in *Love aaj kal*, where the heroine restores buildings. Some women prefer to work – Babli, in *Bunty aur Babli*, would rather be a con artist than die of boredom as a small-town housewife making pickles. Madhur Bhandarkar's films all show women who pursue their ambitions, whether these are in journalism, modelling or the corporate world, but their work causes them great suffering, which leads to them abandoning their careers.

## The Dream of Riches

A striking feature of Hindi films is the massive wealth of many of the characters. These are not just people who do not have to worry about money – these are *fantastically rich* people. Wealth is no sin in Hinduism. Kubera, the god of wealth, may not be a major deity today but Laksmi is ever popular, with a day set aside for the worship of wealth (formerly expressed as gold but now in other forms, too) on the festival of Dhanteras at Diwali. The tradition of the householder whose goal is to acquire wealth (*artha*), and to use that wealth in worship, is as much a part of Hindu thought as traditions of renunciation. Religious considerations aside, wealth also has many worldly benefits beyond opening up consumerist possibilities, notably acquiring status and prestige. In India, the desire to be acknowledged and recognized as an individual, and indeed to avoid humiliation, is seem as one of the major benefits that wealth brings. One of the sources of Amitabh's massive star popularity in the 1970s was the way he demanded respect even when poor, notably in *Deewaar*'s famous dialogue – '*Main phenke hue paise nahin uthata*'/ 'I don't pick up money that's thrown at me.' The emergence of Indians among the world's richest people is also celebrated, showing that India is becoming an equal of the developed countries and is thus avoiding national humiliation. Dhirubhai Ambani's 'rags-to-riches' story makes him a major hero while his wealth, even after being divided between his sons, Mukesh and Anil Ambani, is seen as a source of pride to many Indians. Antilla, a building belonging to Mukesh Ambani's family, is the world's most expensive private house and, although much ink was spilled expressing outrage over its luxury, others are proud that this house belongs to Indians and that they chose to build it in the heart of Mumbai.

Wealth in the earlier Hindi films was shown as that of landlords – *thakurs* and *zamindars* – and of the professionals, usually the old Anglophone middle classes, while the Seths, the merchant princes, mostly *baniyas* (merchant castes) and Parsis, began to be replaced by the new rich, whose wealth was based on vague 'business', as in *Waqt*. The old business communities were interested in accumulating wealth, which they spent on property, but otherwise many of them had fairly austere lifestyles with simple dress and food, distinguishing them from the new rich, who were overtly consumerist, spending freely on cars, fashion, entertainment and travel.

By the 1970s, films showed professionals who were also wealthy enough, though few films showed the service classes who dominated much of India at the time – the Civil Service, Foreign Service and the Military, in the clubs that were their enclaves – while *Kabhi kabhie* presented Delhi's well-off middle classes as architects, TV presenters, doctors and members of the armed forces.

Since the early 1990s, the rich have been shown almost exclusively as business people, involved in some undefined business activity or having inherited money (*HAHK* and *Vivah*). Yash Raj Films and Dharma Productions defined the lifestyles of the new wealthy in their films from the late 1990s, with the ultimate depiction of wealthy lifestyles being *K3G*, where the businessman Yashvardhan Raichand has fabulous wealth, allowing him to live in palaces and make tongue-in-cheek jokes about acquiring more helicopters for his fleet. His wealth brings no benefit without having a happy family, however. Yash Raj Films sometimes present more ordinary lifestyles in their movies, although retaining a large quotient of glamour, while other films have become almost pastiches in their depiction of the enormously wealthy. Yet the imagination of the wealth that business can generate remains a powerful fantasy.

Money often creates family problems, with a rich boy falling in love with a poor girl or vice versa (*Dil/Heart*, dir. Indra Kumar, 1990), which was often turned into comedy, especially in Govinda's films, where he plays with the identities of the rich and the poor in movies such as *Coolie no. 1* and *Hero no. 1*, both directed by David Dhawan. Many films showed attempts to deprive rich children of their inheritance, usually by scheming relatives and wicked stepmothers abetted by their brothers (*Beta/Son*, dir. Indra Kumar, 1992). New wealth has also emerged in rural India, which was earlier a byword for poverty apart from the wealthy landowners. Some farmers and other rural people have amassed considerable wealth, seen in Punjab in *Jab we met* or in Haryana in *Band baaja baaraat*.

The jobs of the rich are often those of the older generation in a film, while the younger generation – that is, the leading roles – are in the early years of their career where they are finding their feet. If they are in business, it is usually in the family company, though Rahul in *K3G* shows that he is able to set up his own company in London when he is estranged from his father. It is quite unusual to have a hero in *naukri*: 'service or paid employment'. Surinder (Shah Rukh Khan), in *Rab ne bana di jodi*, works for Punjab Power, an electricity company, in a numbingly boring job which emphasizes his unromantic and unglamorous character. His wife, Taani (Anushka Sharma), finds him utterly dreary and is only able to fall in love with him in his glamorous disguise as her dance partner, Suri. The film argues in favour of love as part of the everyday and mundane world but it would not have entertained the audience had it not contained the dance sequences from Surinder's alter ego.

In a film culture brimming with wealth, the working classes are now barely seen in contemporary films, nor are servants. In the 1990s, there were films where the poor were heroes, such as *Raja Hindustani*, where Raja (Aamir Khan) is a taxi driver/tour guide who falls in love with a rich girl. He refuses to accept her family's wealth, be educated or be gifted a house but prefers to carry on as

Shah Rukh Khan as the don in *Don* (2006).

before, embodying the dignity of labour. His first attempt to dress as a wealthy man ends in laughter; the second in a drunken brawl. *Karan Arjun* shows one of its heroes, Karan/Ajay (Salman Khan), playing a prizefighter, and its other, Arjun/Vijay (Shah Rukh Khan), as a stablehand, though both are restored to their feudal status by the end of the film. Sunny Deol played a boxer and a wrestler in his films, where he embarks on a physical contest as he fights to right the wrongs done to his family – *Ghayal/Wounded* (1990) and *Ghatak/Lethal* (1996, both dir. Rajkumar Santoshi).

Gangsters and smugglers have been popular subjects throughout our period as they offer audiences and film-makers ways of being both working class and vastly wealthy, derived of course from the proceeds of a glamorous life of crime, and they feature in a whole host of films, with some of Hindi cinema's biggest stars taking leading roles. Mafia dons and assorted criminals were also prevalent in the early 1990s, in films such as *Hum/Us* (dir. Mukul Anand, 1991) *Khalnayak* or *Satya* (dir. Ram Gopal Varma, 1998).

Films whose characters have close links to real figures (though by no means biopics) show the lasting role that many of these figures play in the Indian imaginary. Many people saw close links in Milan Luthria's depiction of the 1970s underworld in *Once Upon a Time in Mumbai* to the figures of Haji Mastan and Dawood Ibrahim, while the central characters of Ram Gopal Varma's *Company* were thought to be the notorious hood-lums Dawood Ibrahim and his one-time henchman Chota Rajan. Gangster films have become more sophisticated and glamorous, with the Bachchan family reprising the Corleones' role in Coppola's *Godfather* films in Ram Gopal Varma's *Sarkar* and *Sarkar Raj*, which were also said to have been partly based on the life of Bal Thackeray – the late leader of the Shiv Sena, an unelected political leader granted a state funeral in 2012.

Farhan Akhtar's *Don* was a remake of a film of the same name starring Amitabh Bachchan (dir. Chandra Barot, 1978), but he replaced the Bombay smuggler with an international criminal, based in Malaysia. Don's adventures became increasingly hi-tech in *Don 2* (2011), shot in many overseas locations, including Europe. A James Bond figure who is a RAW agent (the Research and Analysis Wing, equivalent to the UK's SIS) has also appeared to keep these new international criminals under control: *Agent Vinod* (dir. Sriram Raghavan, 2012) and Tiger in *Ek tha Tiger*.

The 'comedy gangster' is a new figure who first appears in Rajkumar Hirani's *Munna Bhai MBBS* and *Lage raho Munna Bhai* as a thug with a heart of gold whose romances lead him to mend his ways, while being caught up in many capers along the way. *Welcome* (dir. Anees Bazmee, 2007) has a family of gangsters presented as comical figures living in Dubai, while in Bazmee's *Singh is Kinng*, another such gangster family lives in Australia.

Samar (Shah Rukh Khan) as a sapper in *JTHJ*.

Policemen feature in many films where they are heroic in their relentless pursuit of their enemies, though struggling with internal corruption (*Sarfarosh/The Willing Martyr*, dir. John Matthews Matthan, 1998; *Gangaajal*; and *Khakee/The Uniform*, dir. Rajkumar Santoshi, 2004). The police were given a much more glamorous twist in *Dhoom/Blast* (dir. Sanjay Gadhvi, 2004) and *Dhoom 2/Blast 2* (2006) and with Salman Khan as the policeman, Chulbul Pandey (*Dabangg* and *Dabangg 2*). The armed forces are seen much more rarely, although *Border* was a great hit and the early 1990s saw a spate of army-themed films around the time of the Kargil conflict with Pakistan. Yash Chopra continued to make films with a hero from the armed forces – from his earlier films, such as *Kabhi kabhie*, to his recent *Veer Zaara* and *Jab tak hai jaan*.

## Lifestyles and Consumption

Economic liberalization has allowed many, but by no means all, Indians to become consumers in a way that was previously unthinkable. This is not to suggest that they once shunned goods as ways of understanding the world and themselves, of expressing identity and displaying their status, but merely that the options before liberalization were far more limited, whereas now they seem infinite. For example, at the beginning of this period the range of cars was entirely Indian and comprised very few models, notably the Ambassador, the Fiat-Padmini, the Contessa and the Maruti 800. By 2012, a whole new range of Indian brands of cars was being built by firms such as Tata; Mercedes are now manufactured in India and showrooms have opened in the 'metros' for ultra-luxury brands such as Bentley, Porsche and Aston Martin. The hiccups in the rise of consumerism noted in my book *All You Want Is Money* have long been forgotten and the rise of consumer spending seems relentless. Even those who cannot afford to participate in branded goods on a large scale may buy Rs-1 shampoo sachets and single cigarettes and sweets, while Coke and Pepsi are near-ubiquitous through myriad forms of advertising from product placement in films to star endorsements on shop signs.

Conspicuous consumption abounded before liberalization but was largely confined to the rich, mostly upper-caste groups, such as merchants, industrialists, the landed wealthy (*zamindars*) and India's princely families. The last were famous for their wealth and its display in every manner from palaces designed by Western architects and the keeping of elephants to fabulous jewellery and imported goods ranging from luxury cars to everyday items. They travelled the world and were dressed by couturiers and Savile Row tailors. However, their wealth was so extreme that they were entirely remote from the rest of the population, much like the early film stars.

The old middle classes were not rich by these standards but formed an educated service elite of (mostly) Brahmins and other upper castes. They defined themselves partly by their educational capital, but also by their cultural capital, for example appreciating Indian and/or Western classical music and, not least, speaking English and reading literature in English and often in another Indian language. They also owned goods from abroad that few could obtain – a showcase of souvenirs from all too rare foreign travel or from overseas visitors, for instance, as well as jeans and other desirable items. Today, their distinction in consumerism lies in having goods which are no longer available (such as shahtoosh shawls now that the antelope is a protected species), inherited saris, old jewellery, carved furniture and so on. Their lives had some elements of Nehruvian austerity, in part framed by living in a protected economy, but also of culture and restraint associated with the upper castes, with their taste being simple but refined as exemplified by Indira Gandhi's, notably her style in handloom saris. They valued education highly, sending their children to elite schools and often educating them in the English language and a European sensibility.

The new middle classes who have risen to dominance had a different group of leisure activities which were less art-oriented and more inclined towards mass culture – cinema, film songs and pop, television and the new media, which are also part of a wider youth culture. The Hindi cinema, which in earlier days – at least according to popular perception – had been for the urban working class, youth and the less educated, emerged as one of the primary entertainment forms for this group and increased its reach

through the new media. From the 1990s onwards, this group became the major target audience for cinema since they now had more leisure, more money, more enthusiasm for consuming and more opportunities to do so. They embrace consumption and are irritated with the state, which they regard as putting obstacles in their way.

The divisions between the old and new middle classes are familiar and often based around consumerist choices, with the old middle classes looking down on what they regard as vulgar and tasteless while the new regard the old middle classes as having boring and joyless lifestyles. The newly rich have also had to learn how to define themselves through consumption. The films picked up on the lower-class view of the wealthy. Films that show attempts to pass as a member of another social group by trying to share their taste can cause hilarity when it goes wrong. Raja, the taxi driver in *Raja Hindustani*, tries to dress like a *saheb*, or wealthy person, to suit his beloved. He sings a comic song, 'Saala main to saheb ban gaya'/ 'I've Become a Gentleman', but wearing a comically loud version of Western clothes and clownish make-up. The song, taken from *Sagina* (dir. Tapan Sinha, 1974), says that the suit and boots do not make him a gentleman but that he looks like a crow wearing a tail of peacock feathers. The heroine finds this hilarious because Raja looks like a clown, but this no doubt is partly comical because it raises the issue of embarrassment as a result of misinterpreting the social rules of another, higher-status group. This comedy is very different from the taunting of the heroine's step-family when Raja wears the correct upper-class clothes – his in-laws point out that he still does not know how to behave like one of them. The film argues that the taxi driver should not seek to act like the rich but rather the upper classes need to learn about relationships and dignity from the lower classes. Even the hero's style becomes something to which one can aspire, given the star persona of Aamir Khan and the film's positioning of the character in a way that aligns the audience with the lower classes.

However, films are also a guide to consumption and what one could and should do if one had the opportunities. The films' depictions of the glamour of consumption are part of wider media networks also seen in advertising, television, gossip and the writings of lifestyle gurus, as well as magazines and television programmes which have constant references to the films, their stars and their images of consumption. Consumerism has its own lessons and one of the places to learn them is the cinema. This is not just about crass product placement but rather presenting an image of a lifestyle, the issues around it and more besides in order to feed and stimulate the fantasy.

Chandramukhi (Madhuri Dixit) dances for Devdas in *Devdas*.

While the films are fantasy for most, India's super-rich, many of whom are avid Bollywood fans, really do live the lifestyles seen in the films,

though it is unclear to what degree the films influence their lives versus their lives influencing the films. It is probably a two-way dynamic. Film-makers such as Yash Chopra show the lifestyles of the super-rich in order to bring up topics encountered in life that are divorced from everyday economic and other realities, highlighting emotional and other relation-ship issues, but these lifestyle movies also create a desire to see how the rich live, to understand consumption and the ways in which taste may be shaped.

For the vast majority, however, consumerism on film belongs to the realm of fantasy as it shows what very few can afford: luxury housing, yachts, five-star travel and designer fashions. While the middle-class films of the 1970s and '80s, such as those of Hrishikesh Mukherjee, showed fairly realistic images and affordable consumerist goods such as handloom saris and domestic furnishing, the styling budgets continue to rise in their quest to depict an increasingly consumerist lifestyle. This is because the new India believes mobility is now possible and film-viewers enjoy these lifestyles vicariously in the hope that they too will have them one day. Meanwhile, they take pride in the fact that other Indians do indeed live like this.

The celebration of wealth in the films builds on delight in the growing consumerist culture that the middle classes can now afford. The former extension of life granted to consumer goods that was once

The handbag – Bag-wati – in *ZNMD*.

so common in India, from clothing alterations such as replacing worn collars to recycling, is now rejected by much of the rising middle class while it has become fashionable among more ecologically conscious groups, perhaps emerging as another definer of social status.

The depiction of excessive wealth in the films is also intended to allay anxieties about the loss of wealth, just as 1930s Hollywood depicted a world of excessive luxury at a time of widespread economic depression. In India, the long-term lack of financial opportunity for the majority and the constant anxiety about falling into the abyss, as well as loss of wealth in events such as the Partition and the problems faced by urban migrants, no doubt make the desire for wealth even greater in this first generation.

## A World of Leisure

Cinema is intimately connected with a range of leisure activities, from actually viewing the film to a host of associated pastimes such as viewing songs online, downloading ringtones, reading reviews and gossip and watching how characters enjoy their leisure time within the films themselves.

Leisure is one of the many opportunities afforded by wealth but one needs to have time free from work – whether that be employment or housework, childcare and other chores. For middle-class Indians, time is provided by servants and paid help taking over most of their 'menial' chores, leaving more time for work or leisure. For some, idleness is an easy option and the concept of the 'timepass' – something to do to waste time – arises, so a 'timepass film' is a dull one which killed a few hours.

Many people still cannot watch films in India – perhaps because it is too expensive, the cinema is too far away, they cannot access home-viewing screens, they have no leisure time or simply because their family prohibits its members from viewing films. However, many are simply not interested in films. Television is becoming a more popular medium in terms of viewership and the industry itself is now bigger than the film industry, but the latter is still pre-eminent in terms of impact, budgets, visibility and so on.

The cinema halls themselves have changed. The old Art Deco single-screens have often been allowed to go to seed or have been converted to multiplexes, while only a few (such as Liberty Cinema in Mumbai) have been maintained and restored. The new multiplexes are located in shopping malls and allow for the extension of consumerist opportunities as they are surrounded by food halls and shops, based on the model of Dubai, Malaysia, Hong Kong and Singapore.

Consumerist culture is very much about acquiring goods, but also about the activity of shopping. The old *kirana* (mom-and-pop) shops, local tailors and markets and bazaars still exist, while shops in the five-star hotels have long been popular with tourists – Indian and foreign – as well as with locals. Running a boutique was seen as a good job for wealthy women, as in *Jab pyaar kisi se hota hai* – a role now replaced by being a personal shopper or interior designer.

New Western and Indian brands and designers are found mostly in the malls that have been built since the late 1990s, where the new cinemas are located. Malls are used as locations in cinema, offering referents for new codes involving the newly very rich and their love of designer brands. Malls are used as locations in cinema, often mixing new middle class codes of shopping with those of the newly very rich who would actually prefer the designer brands. Malls provide a public space, albeit one that is privatized and cut off from undesirable parts of India such as the street and beggars. One can drive into a car park, shop, eat and watch a film, all in an air-conditioned environment protected from the heat or rain and in a location from which the poor are excluded. In Nishikant Kamath's *Mumbai meri jaan*, part of the anger of the poor coffee seller, played by Irrfan Khan, is because he is humiliated by being thrown out of a mall, not for trying the perfume samples, which he thinks are an amazing luxury, but for being the wrong kind of person to be in the shop.

Travel and tourism are very much part of the world of the Indian film, with the consumerist pleasures of travel itself featuring increasingly now that flying is becoming more accessible to the middle classes. Some films show train travel, though often in Switzerland, with Indian train travel tending to show only trendy young types (*Jab we met*) 'roughing it'. The desire of a scooter-owning family for a car, an emblem of full middle-class status, is portrayed in *Do dhooni char*/'*Two Twos Are Four*' (dir. Habib Faisal, 2010).

The films have long offered vicarious travel, showing pretty locations, hotels, clubs and restaurants, although the older films usually contained hill-station holidays in places such as Darjeeling and Simla, as overseas travel was reserved for the super-elite. These rarely feature now as the use of foreign locations in films has become so widespread that it is becoming unusual to have a top-budget film shot entirely in India. Sometimes the story depicts characters travelling overseas on holiday to show tourist possibilities, or for education or medical treatment, while others concerned diasporic Indians. Audiences certainly appreciate the use of glamorous locations and many countries now promote visits to Bollywood locations as well as providing tax-free benefits for shooting to encourage further Indian tourist travel. The perennial favourite location of London remains but has been joined by New York (*Kal ho na ho* and many other films), Australia (Sydney in *Dil chahta hai*; Brisbane and the Gold Coast in *Singh is Kingg*), South Africa (*No Entry*), Spain (*ZNMD*), Egypt (*K3G*), Italy (*Housefull*) and the UAE (*Dabangg*).

Indian locations are used to give some local colour so Goa, a popular tourist destination for Indians as well as foreigners, is featured in a road trip in *Dil chahta hai*, while in *Mujhse shaadi karogi* the film is meant to be set in Goa but a combination of studio sequences and Mauritius are used.

Romance in films involves a whole range of consumerist activities. Courtship requires going out dancing, drinking, eating and seeing concerts and films, all of which are consumerist activities and which often provide song opportunities, hence the cabaret visit shown in 'Ruk jaa'/'Stop!' in *DDLJ* or going to the cinema and seeing one's own romance unfold on the screen in *Dil chahta hai*. Weddings are major expenses and, like many festivals, are now massive consumerist opportunities, with big budgets needing wedding planners, as seen in *Band baaja baaraat*.

## In the Home

One of the greatest expenses for anyone is housing and India's cities have a housing crisis. However, the liberalized economy makes it easier for middle-class people to get home loans, allowing younger people to buy their own places, after which they have to furnish their homes. The housing seen in the films of the early 1990s was beyond most people's budgets as they showed palatial buildings, often furnished in 'Dallas Palace' style. Some elements could prove aspirational, so in *Dil to pagal hai* the loft-living lifestyles, complete with Pepsi machines, were too expensive to be copied, but the simple style of furnishing was not. Karan Johar's use of European palaces for houses in *K3G* was very different from the designer housing he opted for in New York and Philadelphia in *Kabhi alvida naa kehna*, but elements of both could be copied, even if just as colour schemes. Some other films of the 1990s had houses inspired by international hotel styles and indeed hotels were often used as sets pretending to be houses, sometimes with the lobby key-drop still showing.

The use of domestic space in the films has also changed with changing lifestyles. In *HAHK* (1994), the kitchen shows women at work as well as coveted electrical appliances; today, interior decor magazines suggest extravagant styles using imported fittings, especially for kitchens and bathrooms, and this is reflected in films – all part of showing the aspiration to make one's home into a private space that reflects the taste – as well as the status – of its owners. Sometimes space is used in a very non-Indian way, so in *Raajneeti* the family gathers around the kitchen table, which would mark a new trend for the very rich who would use the sitting room or have private rooms upstairs in the house.

## The Star Look, Consumerism and Fashion

One of the most imitated features of films is the style of the stars, whether that be hairstyles, clothing or even gestures and ways of speaking. As mentioned in other chapters, film stars are now brand ambassadors, beacons of advertising inside and outside the films. Stars promote unglamorous products such as anti-dandruff shampoo and cement or makes of cars that they would never dream of driving themselves. Product placement is frequent in films and is part of the consumerist world of cinema.

Films have created a look, a way in which beauty is defined and generated. It is a beauty that is fashioned, not born, as stars transform themselves in gyms, beauty parlours and operating theatres into groomed, thinner, toned or muscular, paler forms. The new muscular look began in the late 1980s with stars such as Sanjay Dutt and Sunny Deol, was then taken up by Salman Khan and is now almost mandatory for male stars. This can be connected to Western fashion but is also part of the Indian working-class male dream of the muscular body, linked to Indian ideas of fitness and health and other traditional role models such as wrestlers. It is also part of consumerist culture – you can even buy your body. Once, other than sportsmen or wrestlers, it was only the working class who were muscled as they performed physical labour and had to walk long distances but were often malnourished. The new muscled look needs healthy eating plans, or even bodybuilding plans (and steroids), while the middle class is now beginning to discover the need for exercise. The upper classes have dieticians, with Kareena Kapoor becoming a celebrity columnist after her famous size zero appearance. Men and women are emulating the modelling look, which may not be about health but may involve too much caffeine, drugs and cigarettes instead of nourishment.

Female stars have given up on the perms and 'big hair' of the early 1990s, typified by Madhuri Dixit. Despite the occasional crop or bob, long hair remains the fashion for women, though no longer the poker-straight styles of the 2000s but blow-dried bounce, coupled with colouring and various styles, as seen on Priyanka Chopra and Katrina Kaif. For men, conservative Western hairstyles are usual, with the *filmi* fashions no longer a marker of style, whether that was Amitabh Bachchan's stiff hair of the 1970s or the 'mullet' made popular by Sanjay Dutt and others in the 1990s.

Some male stars sport moustaches, such as Anil Kapoor and Jackie Shroff, while most other stars are clean-shaven, and when they wear

moustaches it is much discussed in the press, notably Salman Khan as Chulbul Pandey in *Dabangg*. A hairy chest is now seen as unattractive, and so the male star is hair-free and muscled with trimmed eyebrows, a look most admired on Salman Khan. This look has not been emulated by fans, except in the elites, and most young men in north India continue to sport moustaches.

Indians usually dress neatly, however poor they are. They have combed hair, wear pressed clothes and have a fondness for matching. However, the style among the elite for ripped jeans, faded clothes and a casual look has taken off among a few, at least outside of work. Some women, such as actor Soha Ali Khan and director Zoya Akhtar, wear a more bohemian look. The move to wearing Western clothes except for formal occasions has been one of the greatest shifts over the last decades and film has been one of the sources for this change alongside the adoption of other Western cultural forms.

The sari retains its hold for weddings and formal occasions, although the fashion sari is seen as glamorous while the traditional saris, such as those worn by the star Vidya Balan, are often regarded as 'mumsy'. The *salwar kameez* (trousers with tunic) became glamorous when it lost its middle as it changed into a midriff-baring crop top, its sleeves transformed into spaghetti straps, or it changed shape into tight-fitting tops with Pathiali

Romance in Germany with Shah Rukh Khan and Madhuri Dixit in *DTPH*.

*salwars* or short *kurtas* worn with *churidars*, tunics with tight trousers with gathered ankles. The traditional form has largely faded as a major fashion item, seen as suitable only for middle-aged women.

Men who until recently wore Western suits for formal occasions now wear them mostly in business environments, where the spread of air conditioning allows a jacket to be worn year round. For weddings, men have abandoned the Western suit to wear Indian outfits, usually *Jodhpuris* (short 'Nehru jackets') and trousers or *sherwanis* (long 'Nehru jackets') and *churidars* (tight leggings) or *kurtas* (tunics), scarves and *churidars*. *Dhotis*, lower unstitched garments, are rarely seen. The male *kurta* has become the badge of the intellectual while the safari suit of the 1960s onwards is now a comedy item.

Even changing jewellery fashions may be inspired by film stars. Most women wear some jewellery, whether gold or silver, with or without precious stones, or just costume jewellery. Fashions change, with big earrings and no necklace currently in favour. Indian men also wear jewellery, including stones (often for astrological reasons), and working-class male jewellery such as chain bracelets is seen as chic – especially as Salman Khan wears one.

Katrina Kaif's dance in the tunnels in *JTHJ*.

While some models have become film stars, film stars are now modelling, even though many of them have a different shape from the usual requirements. The endorsement of a star is important for many designers,

who also seek to have their clothes worn in films as this will increase their market value – especially for weddings, where vast amounts of money will be spent whenever possible.

## Food, Drink and Intoxicants

Finally, there is also much consumption of food, drink and stimulants in Hindi films. India is yet to have a food movie, although it has had heroes who are chefs: *Cheeni kum, Salaam namaste/Hello and Hi* (dir. Siddharth Anand, 2005).

India is one of the few countries where vegetarianism (that is, eating food that does not contain meat, fish, eggs and so on) is assumed by outsiders to be the norm, although India is actually mostly non-vegetarian and many people are only vegetarian some of the time. Vegetarianism is the default respectable position, so a 'non-vegetarian joke' means one not suitable for the family. In *Cheeni kum*, it is a joke that the chef cooks non-vegetarian food but does not eat it while the woman is non-vegetarian, so they give each other the nicknames Ghaas Poos ('straw') and Tangdi Kebab ('chicken kebab').

Vegetarianism is also equated with Hinduism more broadly than being just a practice of some high castes (Brahmins and merchants in particular),

'Chikni Chameli' whose lyrics prompt a cigarette health-warning in *Agneepath* (2012).

CIGARETTE SMOKING IS INJURIOUS TO HEALTH.

as seen in *Jodhaa Akbar*, where Jodhaa makes Akbar a vegetarian feast which everyone recognizes as a Marwari (merchant) feast and not a Rajput (approx. 'royal') one. In *Ajab Prem ki ghazab kahani*, the vegetarian Prem tries to eat non-vegetarian food as he assumes that his beloved, as a Christian, is non-vegetarian – only to find out that she is a vegetarian.

Characters in films undertake fasts, including the famous *karva chauth* fast for the long life of the husband, while any important occasion is marked by an offer of sweets to '*muh meetha kijiye*'/'sweeten your mouth'. Maternal women cook for and feed men; in HAHK, Sooraj Barjatya shows women frequently in the kitchen, but one of the women tries to cook for the first time and mistakes salt for sugar – all-round hilarity follows as she demonstrates her lack of womanliness. Junk foods favoured by the youth are celebrated in *Band baaja baaraat*, notably the famous vow: '*Bread pakode ki kasam*'/'I swear on a bread fritter'.

India has stringent anti-smoking rules and since 2005 a health warning appears at the beginning of any film that shows smoking. The authorities can even ban smoking in films if it is shown to be glamorous. *Agneepath* (2012) carried an anti-smoking warning on screen that one of its songs, 'Chikni chameli'/'Soft Jasmine', contained the lyric 'Beedi chillum jalaane aayi'/'She has come to light cigarettes and pipes'.

Although there are traditions of drinking in classical Sanskrit literature, alcohol consumption is now frowned on by many conservatives in India, with prohibition enforced on certain days or in certain states. In older films, the villain and the vamp drink while the hero or heroine drink only as a sign of going off the rails, often on the way to a tragedy such as Devdas or in *The Dirty Picture*. Drunken episodes are shown to allow people to express themselves more openly, as with Raja in *Raja Hindustani*, or for fun and fantasy in drunken songs such as 'Samjho ho hi gaya'/'Understand What Happened' in *Lage raho Munnabhai*. In *Kal ho na ho*, the reserved heroine lets her hair down after a few drinks by singing, 'It's the time to disco.' Drugs are shown much less frequently and only as a sign of mental disintegration as in *DevD*.

# SEVEN

# Agneepath/The Path of Fire, 1990–2012

The changes in the film *Agneepath/The Path of Fire*, first made in 1990 and remade in 2012, illustrate many of the changes in Hindi cinema during the period discussed in this book. The original, made by Mukul Anand, is a personal favourite as it was one of the first Hindi films I saw (at the time of its release) and one which made me realize the need to engage with the wider context of the film. The narrative of *Agneepath* was universal. Smugglers led by Kancha Cheena frame a Gandhian schoolteacher, Dinnath Chauhan, who is killed by a mob, which sends his family into exile. The son, Vijay, makes it his life's goal to restore his family honour, making the village apologize to his mother. He realizes the law will not help and becomes a gangster, but has his own high moral standards, including respect for and protection of all women, especially his mother, his sister and his wife. He achieves his goal but dies in the process, having atoned for all his sins.

There were many features about the film which intrigued me. The poetry was an instant point of entry, partly because of its rhythmic declaration and the use of words that were familiar from Sanskrit (*agneepath* itself; *vrksha*/'tree' and *shapath*/'curse'). The idea of a Hindi poem setting the scene for the film went against the widely held view of cinema as the 'opium of the masses', especially because the author was a celebrated poet, Harivanshrai Bachchan, who had written a doctoral thesis on Yeats at Cambridge University and who was the father of the film's hero, Amitabh Bachchan. The literary connections of the film and the link between the worlds of poetry and film were intriguing, too.

*Agneepath* undermined the idea of the 'formula' film as it involves little or no dancing around trees. One of the big set-piece dances was about Alibaba and the 40 thieves, featuring a girl in a leather miniskirt dancing around a swimming pool in a smuggler's den; there was also some strange disco – long after disco had vanished elsewhere – which included singing about wearing a *lungi*; and finally a catchy song to celebrate the Ganpati immersion festival.

Another deviation, this time from the standard happy-ending formulas, was the hero dying in the arms of his mother in a sort of pietà. This would have been familiar to audiences, because Amitabh Bachchan, or rather Vijay, often had to die to atone for his sins, so the film's viewers would feel a sense of justice as well as sadness. Although Amitabh Bachchan was a famous name, the nature of his stardom was new to me, requiring me to see more of his earlier films to know who Vijay was and what that white suit meant. This launched me into further film viewing, finding gems such as *Deewaar/The Wall* (dir. Yash Chopra, 1973) and following up on stories about the off-screen Amitabh Bachchan, both of which involved some effort in the pre-Internet and pre-DVD days and much of which was done under curfew during the riots in Bombay in 1992.

Mithun Chakraborty was familiar to me from art cinema, notably *Mrigayaa/The Royal Hunt* (dir. Mrinal Sen, 1976), but I did not know of his massive subsequent stardom as a disco dancer. In *Agneepath*, he played the role of an adopted brother, a figure found in most of the Amitabh/Vijay films. He was Krishnan Aiyar, MA, with a strong south Indian accent and pride in his roots, his education and his *lungi*. One of the villains, Terry, known as Terylene, had a thick English accent and bemoaned the state of the country, while Kancha Cheena's east Asian origins were evident but their wider meaning unclear.

Mauritius featured as the villain's lair, although it was usually considered a desirable holiday location by Indian audiences, and there were echoes of Bond films. These echoes were emphasized by the set-piece with a song which occurs when Amitabh stands on the front of a speedboat, which was blown up and set on fire (one of the many literal depictions of the *agneepath*) by a coconut bomb dropped from a helicopter, as well as by his subsequent Ursula Andress-like emergence from the sea, fully dressed in his white suit. There was also a Bond quality to his sly apology for being a little late for his meeting with his would-be assassin, followed by a complete reverse gear as he handed the scantily clad woman his jacket for decency.

No knowledge of Hindi was required to understand that the style of dialogue delivery was to declaim rhetorically rather than be realistic and

that Amitabh Bachchan had adopted the style of speaking used by Marlon Brando as Don Vito in *The Godfather*, though his character also had close associations with *Scarface* (dir. Brian de Palma, 1983). The Ganpati procession at the end of the film was spectacular and again reminded me of the celebration of the Feast of San Gennaro in *The Godfather, Part II* (dir. Francis Ford Coppola, 1974), whose massive popularity among Indian film-makers was then unknown to me. Jean-Michel Jarre's music was familiar but seemed defamiliarized in the context of this film.

*Agneepath* opens with the villagers of Mandwa hoping for an electricity connection, but the generic baddies/smugglers want to shut off the

Vijay (Amitabh Bachchan) arrives at Mandwa on a boat in *Agneepath* (1990).

village's access to the world of progress, which is ironic given that the baddies are associated with modern technology: endlessly ringing telephones, endless telephone conversations and then, of course, their cars (Vijay is often filmed sitting in a car, and the first assassination attempt is in a car), helicopters and boats. These all emphasize the ill-gotten gains of crime, while they are empowered further by their control of communications at a time when access to them was severely restricted.

The older *Agneepath* film was a commercial failure, even though it was critically acclaimed and won Amitabh his first National Award, while Mithun won Best Supporting Actor. Subsequently, this *Agneepath* became almost a cult movie and has had a rich afterlife. These issues were part of what sparked my curiosity. I talked to the producer, Yash Johar, about the film, and it seemed he was quite saddened by its lack of commercial success. Perhaps this was what lay behind the remake, produced by his son, Karan Johar, whose subtle and accurate reading of the film audience ensured that the new version was a massive hit.

The later version of *Agneepath* (dir. Karan Malhotra, 2012) has the same storyline but its many changes turn it into a 'Bollywood' film. The handsome and muscled superstar Hrithik Roshan plays Vijay but now has a feisty love interest in the person of the star and former Miss World, Priyanka Chopra. The film introduced another female star, Katrina Kaif, for a big song-and-dance 'item number', filmed with the bright colours and quick editing typical of today's Bollywood style. The framing of the father is changed from an encounter with a *tawaif*/dancer to the rape and murder of a young girl, a more contemporary evil which is very much in the public mind in India.

Hrithik Roshan's Vijay is not as remote and cool a figure as Bachchan's; Roshan's is sadder and less angry but more of a physical fighter than a godlike figure: machine-gun fire hospitalizes Bachchan's Vijay but he is soon back in his white suit and white shoes to exact revenge. The later film has much more dastardly villains, no longer baddies controlling their business empires but truly evil men. Vijay has a new enemy in Rauf Lala, a butcher and a pimp, played by veteran superstar Rishi Kapoor in his first negative role. Kancha (Sanjay Dutt) is massive, muscled, scarred, tattooed and bald, with animal-like nails. He hates his own ugliness and bans mirrors from his house, which he has decorated with tantric paintings. He holds a cigar in one hand and a *Bhagavad Gita* in the other, which he quotes from in Sanskrit. The *Gita* was Gandhi's favourite text and that of Vijay's father, the schoolmaster whom Kancha framed, who used to quote Gandhi's 'An eye for an eye makes the whole world blind.' Kancha has elements of Brando as Kurtz in *Apocalypse Now* (dir. Francis Ford Coppola, 1979), reminding one of Amitabh Bachchan's Brando manner of talking in the original *Agneepath*, while he also recalls Ravan, Mandwa being his island Lanka, although his obsession with hanging bodies on trees is reminiscent of the Vetal, a kind of demon who himself hangs from trees.

The second film lost the glamorous Mauritius locations which were popular in the early 1990s to become more Mumbai-centric, with the non-villainous characters seeming much more Maharashtrian: Hrithik breaks a *dahi handi* (a pot of yoghurt tied to a wire to remind one of Krishna's pranks); the 'item' song 'Chikni chameli'/'Soft as Jasmine'; Hrithik lives in a *chawl* (traditional mill labourers' tenement); and the beauty-parlour owner Kaali Gawde also has a Maratha name. The Ganpati festival remains as a spectacular and dangerous event in which unknown forces move among the devotees who are making their city holy for the festival.

This is part of a wider move in the film towards a less multicultural Bombay to one which is more Maharashtrian. Vijay loses a friend, Krishnan Aiyar, MA, the coconut-water seller, his close friendship now being his love interest, Kaali, while *hijras*/eunuchs are his protectors. His love interest is now a fellow Maratha, unlike the Christian nurse, Mary Matthew (Madhavi), of the first film. Although Mandwa itself was mostly realistically shot in the coastal town of Diu, on spectacular sets designed by Sabu Cyril, the use of known locations in Mumbai was cut, replaced mostly by studio sets, as with Vijay's *chawl*. The Gothic elements of Kancha Cheena's palace on Mandwa and his demonic nature are highlighted by the dramatic storms with lightening flashes around the building. (Mandwa is now well

The hanging of Kancha Cheena (Sanjay Dutt) in *Agneepath* (2012).

A dance in the chawl (workers' housing) in *Agneepath* (2012).

known as the jetty at Alibaug where ferries from the 'Gateway of India' whisk wealthy Bombayite or Mumbaikar Mumbaiites off to their weekend homes across the water.)

The new film is set not in the present but, as it begins with Vijay's childhood in 1977, it seems that the second film is not set in 2012, the year of its making, but rather in the 1990s. This is because it begins with Vijay's childhood in 1977 and Vijay appears younger here than in the first film. Both films play out the old melodramatic values of the revenge drama, where a boy has to look after a mother and sister whose honour

is in peril after his father is framed by a villain. The notion of a man being motivated by family honour is not seen as antiquated and remains a powerful story even today.

The changing nature of the imagined worlds of Hindi cinema is well illustrated in these two film versions. Although the duo would not stand alone as an example of changing values, especially as they could be considered to be specifically about the changing imagination of the Johar family rather than wider imaginations, they do work within the broad context of the other films in this book and the significance of Karan Johar as a major cultural figure. For example, we see a shift away from the exaggerated multiculturalism of the first film's Bombay (Mumbai since 1995), where Inspector Khan is corrupt but Vijay (whose name is Hindu) is praised for building a mosque and romances a Christian; the only community that is abused is that of the Goras, the Whites, who are traitors. The new film features a more Maharashtrian city which has seen the rising power of Maharashtrian nationalists or regionalists, the Shiv Sena and the Maharashtra Navnirman Sena. However much one is charmed by Rauf Lala's alluring villainy, it raises worrying questions about the image of the Muslim as a seller of women (not a known feature of Mumbai) and a butcher in a city which, while it may no longer fear communal riots as it did in the early 1990s, has experienced Islamist terrorism in the form of train bombings and the 26/11 attacks. The shift from the mixture of communities, intercommunal romance and the adoption of a south Indian into the family to the more regional shows this divide clearly, even though the new film is set at the same time as the old one. The present always shapes the past.

The heroine in the older film was a Christian nurse who tends to Vijay, looking after him in an almost maternal way (he curls up like a baby to sleep in her house), and they later become proud parents. In the new film, she is the feisty Kaali Gawde, who runs a beauty parlour and maintains order with her sharp tongue. Other women are abused, from those sold by Rauf Lala and the girl used to frame the father to the one who is part of Kancha's empire of desire, a woman who consumes alcohol and dances for men. The idea of evil has changed, too, with Kancha not just a villain but a fantastic demonic, psychotic power who sits just outside the city but within sight of it, and who uses the sacred texts in the service of evil and tortures and torments his victims with no conscience.

These two films frame the changes of our period in many ways, showing continuities and disruptions. The new film does not remake the old but adapts it, changing the way in which the story is imagined but keeping the central narrative and character motivation. *Bollywood's India* aims to demonstrate more widely how the Indian imagination of the world depicted in films of the last two decades has changed radically during this period, in part as a reaction to the transformations that modern India itself has undergone.

*Bollywood's India* has investigated recent Hindi cinema to provide a way of understanding how some of contemporary India's people see themselves and their country's changing culture through the narratives, images and music of the films. Hindi films eschew realism, creating imaginary worlds which allow ways of reflecting on how the new India could or should be – reflecting on the social order, the everyday, the way people think, feel and relate to one another, and also how they are entertained. This study deciphers such movies in order to demonstrate why they are an important guide to how people understand the world. The films show certain kinds of people, motivations, lives and behaviour, creating worlds that allow audiences to imagine other worlds, predicaments and challenges of their own without the films reflecting or necessarily representing these other worlds.

Cinema itself shows many ways of imagining the world, and these change over time, almost from film to film. Hindi films look forward to the future, being mostly optimistic but also afraid of what is being lost. Sometimes they seem to be replete with nostalgia, trying to blend an earlier era characterized by an emphasis on family with a present which offers greater financial and personal freedom. While modern Hindi films frequently refer back to older films, no desire to return to the past is evident, only a move to the future. This consideration of what the route and the destination might be invites the audience to imagine how the trajectories of their own lives may be shaped by broader forces beyond their control.

Even the films from the early 1990s seem as though they were made in another world. *DDLJ* seemed completely new and fresh in 1995 and changed the industry as the diaspora film came to dominate, with Karan Johar as the driving force behind the Bollywoodization of the film industry, for which he became a spokesman. The diasporic film now seems outdated and often hackneyed, as films explore new subjectivities and new ways of being Indian and seek ways to keep some of the old while engaging with the new.

Just as India has been transformed during the last few decades, the Hindi film itself has changed in all areas – technology, marketing, viewing practices, audiences and consumption, as well as content, narrative, image and sound. The old school of film-makers has nearly all gone now, and a new generation has established itself (albeit often second-generation (or more) descendants of the old makers) in companies such as Yash Raj Films and Dharma Productions. Yash Raj Films is still a family business but with a corporate structure, while Ronnie Screwvala has sold his company, UTV, to Disney.

Bollywood has dominated the last couple of decades, but its films are not homogenous. It is striking that often the most popular films are those which resist the other trends: *DDLJ* made the diaspora as Indian, if not more Indian, than Indians; the Munnabhai films created a new Indian everyman – mixed up, crazy and problematic but with a heart of gold, who knows what life's true values are; *Raajneeti* replayed the themes of the *Mahabharata*, a perennial source of 'Indianness' whose central text adapts and bends with the times; while *3 Idiots* was the most popular of a host of films which show young people seeking to understand themselves and their desires.

New imaginary worlds have appeared in the *hatke* or 'indie' cinema such as that of Dibakar Banerjee, showing the formation of new audiences with different interests and concerns. Bollywood speaks to India's new middle classes but remains popular across many social groups. The new middle classes may not be fans of the films which poke fun at them, such as *Delhi Belly*, whose central characters are urban slackers who reject upward mobility and mock it though still seem to find it intimidating. Even when they find the jobs they want in the creative and cultural industries (journalist, cartoonist, photographer), they realize that they are on the bottom layer, as even these professions are controlled by traditional business people.

Although relatively few biopics have been made, the constant talk of planning more reveals a continuing interest in this form, which reconsiders what lives are, how to live them and the mixed rewards of success as they act as guides to life, often of lives gone awry.

Hindi films often focus on dreams of success, as in one of the perennial features of the Hindi film, where someone walks onto a stage to receive rounds of applause, revealing the desire to be acknowledged, to be recognized and not seen just as one among many.

The film industry creates the biggest stars of all, and the lives of film stars remain some of the most studied and discussed. Their lives are no longer confined to film; indeed, Shah Rukh Khan can barely be contained by film as he is an all-round media star – in adverts, promoting his cricket team, appearing on television shows and even playing 'himself' as a star in films such as *Luck by Chance* (dir. Zoya Akhtar, 2009). Aamir Khan has harnessed the power of his stardom to develop skills in production and marketing, transforming himself into a social critic through his television work.

Other media are competing for film audiences, but even the mighty television industry does not create the glamour of cinema, which still pervades all the other media, thereby strengthening and continually reinventing itself.

Research on film and television in India remains in its infancy. It is impossible to make predictions about their future any more than one can about India itself. Will India become more cosmopolitan, more Americanized, more nativist? How will it continue to imagine itself and its future?

The other media have taken key roles in middle-class protests about the way the country is run, whether that be within anti-corruption movements or in demonstrations against rape and the mistreatment of women in society. But will such vociferous and powerful groups, harnessing the new media, change anything? Hindi film seems to stand apart from such movements since it is neither activist nor overtly political in style, so it may not affect events directly. What it does allow, and seems likely to continue to allow, is the creation of a new space within which Indian men and women can imagine how they may live their lives.

# Filmography

*3 Idiots*, dir. Rajkumar Hirani, 2009

*A Wednesday*, dir. Neeraj Pandy, 2008

*Aaja nachle/Come Dancing*, dir. Anil Mehta, 2007

*Aan/Savage Princess*, dir. Mehboob Khan, 1952

*Aankhen/Eyes*, dir. David Dhawan, 1993

*Aap ki kasam/My Promise to You*, dir. J. Om Prakash, 1974

*Acchut Kanya/The Untouchable Girl*, dir. Franz Osten, 1936

*Agent Vinod*, dir. Sriram Raghavan, 2012

*Agneepath/The Path of Fire*, dir. Mukul Anand, 1990

*Agneepath/The Path of Fire*, dir. Karan Malhotra, 2012

*Ajab Prem ki ghazab kahani/The Amazing Story of Wonderful Prem*, dir. Rajkumar Santoshi, 2009

*Albela/Darling*, dir. Master Bhagwan, 1951

*Amar Akbar Anthony*, dir. Manmohan Desai, 1977

*Andaz apna apna/To Each His Own Style*, dir. Rajkumar Santoshi, 1994

*Ankur/The Seedling*, dir. Shyam Benegal, 1974

*Apaharan/Kidnapping*, dir. Prakash Jha, 2005

*Asoka*, dir. Santosh Sivan, 2001

*Awaara/The Tramp*, dir. Raj Kapoor, 1951

*Baazigar/The Gambler*, dir. Abbas Mastan, 1993

*Bachna ae haseeno/Run, My Beauties*, dir. Siddharth Anand, 2008

*Baghban/The Gardener*, dir. Ravi Chopra, 2003

*Bal Gandharva/Sound of Heaven*, dir. Ravi Jadhav, 2011 (Marathi)

*The Ballad of Mangal Pandey/The Rising*, dir. Ketan Mehta, 2005

*Band baaja baaraat/Bands, Horns and Revelry*, dir. Maneesh Sharma, 2010

*Bandit Queen*, dir. Shekhar Kapur, 1994

*Barsaat/The Rains*, dir. Raj Kapoor, 1949

*Bawarchi/The Cook*, dir. Hrishikesh Mukherjee, 1972

*Beta/Son*, dir. Indra Kumar, 1992

*Bhool bhulaiya/The Maze*, dir. Priyadarshan, 2007
*Bilat pherat/England Returned*, dir. D. N. Ganguly, 1921 (Silent)
*Billu*, dir. Priyadarshan, 2009
*Bobby*, dir. Raj Kapoor, 1973
*Bombay*, dir. Mani Ratnam, 1995
*Border*, dir. J. P. Dutta, 1997
*Bunty aur Babli/Bunty and Babli*, dir. Shaad Ali Sehgal, 2005
*Burfi!*, dir. Anurag Basu, 2012
*Chak de! India/Go for It, India!*, dir. Shimit Amin, 2007
*Chakravyuh/Battle Formation*, dir. Prakash Jha, 2012
*Chameli*, dir. Sudhir Misra, 2004
*Chandni Bar*, dir. Madhur Bhandarkar, 2001
*Chandni Chowk to China*, dir. Nikhil Advani, 2009
*Cheeni kum/Less Sugar*, dir. Balki, 2007
*Chennai Express*, dir. Rohit Shetty, 2013
*Chhalia/The Cheat*, dir. Raj Kapoor, 1960
*Chhatrapati Shivaji*, dir. Bhalji Pendharkar, 1952
*Chintuji*, dir. Ranjit Kapoor, 2009
*Chori chori chupke chupke/Stealthily, Secretly*, dir. Abbas Mustan, 2001
*Chupke chupke/Secretly*, 1975
*Company*, dir. Ram Gopal Varma, 2002
*Coolie*, dir. Manmohan Desai, 1983
*Coolie No. 1*, dir. David Dhawan, 1995
**Dabangg/Fearless**, dir. Abhinav Kashyap, 2010
*Dabangg 2/Fearless 2*, dir. Arbaaz Khan, 2012
*Damini Lightning*, dir. Rajkumar Santoshi, 1993
*Damul/Bonded until Death*, dir. Prakash Jha, 1984
*Darr/Fear*, dir. Yash Chopra, 1993
*Deewaar/The Wall*, dir. Yash Chopra, 1975
**Deewaar/Let's Bring Our Boys Home**, dir. Milan Luthria, 2004
*Delhi Belly*, dir. Abhinay Deo, 2011
*DevD*, dir. Anurag Kashyap, 2009
*Devdas*, dir. Bimal Roy, 1955
*Devdas*, dir. Sanjay Leela Bhansali, 2002
*Devrai/Sacred Grove*, dir. Sumitra Bhave and Sunil Sukthankar, 2004 (Marathi)
*Dhadkan/Heartbeat*, dir. Darmesh Darshan, 2000
*Dharamputra/Son of Religion*, dir. Yash Chopra, 1961
*Dhoom/Blast*, dir. Sanjay Gadhvi, 2004
*Dil/Heart*, dir. Indra Kumar, 1990
*Dil chahta hai/The Heart Desires*, dir. Farhan Akhtar, 2001
*Dil se/From the Heart*, dir. Mani Ratnam, 1998
*Dil to pagal hai/This Crazy Heart*, dir. Yash Chopra, 1997

*Dilwale dulhania le jayenge (DDLJ)/The Braveheart Takes the Bride*, dir. Aditya
    Chopra, 1995

*The Dirty Picture*, dir. Milan Luthria, 2011

*Do dhooni char/Two Twos Are Four*, dir. Habib Faisal, 2010.

*Don*, dir. Chandra Barot, 1978

*Don: The Chase Begins*, dir. Farhan Akhtar, 2006

*Don 2*, dir. Farhan Akhtar, 2011

*Dor/The Thread*, dir. Nagesh Kukunoor, 2006

*Dostana/Friendship*, dir. Taran Mansukhani, 2008

*Dr Babasaheb Ambedkar*, dir. Jabbar Patel, 2000

*Duplicate*, dir. Mahesh Bhatt, 1998

*Ek tha Tiger/Once Upon a Time There Was a Tiger*, dir. Kabir Khan, 2012

*English Vinglish/English, Whatever*, dir. Gauri Shinde, 2012

*Fanaa/Oblivion*, dir. Kunal Kohli, 2006

*Fashion*, dir. Madhur Bhandarkar, 2008

*Firaaq/Separation*, dir. Nandita Das, 2002

*Fiza*, dir. Khalid Mohamed, 2000

*Gabhricha paus/The Damned Rain*, dir. Satish Manwar, 2009 (Marathi)

*Gadar – ek prem katha/Turmoil: A Love Story*, dir. Anil Sharma, 2001

*Gandhi My Father*, dir. Feroz Abbas Khan, 2007

*Gangaajal/Holy Water*, dir. Prakash Jha, 2003

*Gangs of Wasseypur*, Parts I and II, dir. Anurag Kashyap, 2012

*Ghajini*, dir. A. R. Murugdoss, 2008

*Ghatak/Lethal*, dir. Rajkumar Santoshi, 1996

*Ghayal/Wounded*, dir. Rajkumar Santoshi, 1990

*Golmaal/Confusion*, dir. Hrishikesh Mukherjee, 1979

*Golmaal 3/Confusion 3*, dir. Rohit Shetty, 2010

*Gulaal/Vermilion*, dir. Anurag Kashyap, 2009

*Gunga Jumna*, dir. Nitin Bose, 1961

*Guru*, dir. Mani Ratnam, 2007

*Haqeekat/Reality*, dir. Chetan Anand, 1964

*Haseena man jayegi/The Beautiful Woman Will Consent*, dir. David Dhawan,
    1999

*Hera pheri/Monkey Business*, dir. Priyadarshan, 2000

*Hero No. 1*, dir. David Dhawan, 1997

*Hey Ram*, dir. Kamal Hassan, 2000

*Housefull*, dir. Sajid Khan, 2010

*Hum/Us*, dir. Mukul Anand, 1991

*Hum aapke hain koun . . .!/What Am I to You?*, dir. Sooraj Barjatya, 1994

*Hum dil de chuke sanam/I've Given My Heart, Beloved*, dir. Sanjay Leela Bhansali,
    1999

*Hum saath saath hain/We Stand United*, dir. Sooraj Barjatya, 1999

*Hum tum/Me and You*, dir. Kunal Kohli, 2004
*I Am*, dir. Onir, 2010
*I Am Kalam*, dir. Nila Madhab Panda, 2010
*Jaane tu . . . ya jaane na/Whether You Know or Not*, dir. Abbas Tyrewala, 2008
*Jab jab phool khile/Whenever Flowers Bloom*, dir. Suraj Prakash, 1965
*Jab pyaar kisi se hota hai/When Someone Falls in Love*, dir. Deepak Sareen, 1998
*Jab tak hai jaan/As Long as I Live*, dir. Yash Chopra, 2012
*Jab we met/When We Met*, dir. Imtiaz Ali, 2007
*Jagte raho/Stay Awake*, dir. Amit Mitra and Sombu Mitra, 1956
*Jai Santoshi Maa*, dir. Vijay Sharma, 1975
*Jeet/Victory*, 1996, dir. Raj Kanwar
*Jhansi ki rani/The Tiger and the Flame*, dir. Sohrab Modi, 1952
*Jo jeeta wohi Sikandar/The Winner Is the Hero*, dir. Mansoor Khan, 1992
*Jodhaa Akbar*, Ashutosh Gowariker, 2008
*Judaai/Separation*, dir. Raj Kanwar, 1997
*Judwaa/Twin*, dir. David Dhawan, 1997
*Kaagaz ke phool/Paper Flowers*, dir. Guru Dutt, 1959
*Kabhi alvida naa kehna* (KANK)/*Never Say Goodbye*, dir. Nikhil Advani, 2006
*Kabhi khushi kabhie gham* (K3G)/*Sometimes Joy, Sometimes Sorrow*, dir. Karan
    Johar, 2001
*Kahaani/The Story*, dir. Sujoy Ghosh, 2012
*Kaho na pyaar hai/Tell Me It's Love*, dir. Rakesh Roshan, 2000
*Kal ho na ho* (KHNH)/*Whether or Not There's Tomorrow*, dir. Nikhil Advani, 2001
*Kandukondein Kandukondein/I Have Found It*, dir. Rajeev Menon, 2000 (Tamil)
*Karan Arjun*, dir. Rakesh Roshan, 1995
*Kartik Calling Kartik*, dir. Vijay Lalwani, 2010
*Khakee/Uniform*, dir. Rajkumar Santoshi, 2004
*Khalnayak/Antihero*, dir. Subhash Ghai, 1993
*Khoobsurat/Beautiful*, dir. Hrishikesh Mukherjee, 1980
*Khosla ka ghosla/Khosla's Nest*, dir. Dibakar Banerjee, 2006
*Krrish*, dir. Rakesh Roshan, 2006
*Kuch kuch hota hai* (K2H2)/*Something's Happening*, dir. Karan Johar, 1998
*Kurbaan/Sacrifice*, dir. Rensil D'Silva, 2009
*Kya kehna/What Can I Say?*, dir. Kundan Shah, 2000
*Lagaan/Once Upon a Time in India*, dir. Ashutosh Gowariker, 2001
*Lage raho Munna Bhai* (LRMB)/*Carry on Munna Bhai*, dir. Rajkumar Hirani, 2006
*Lakshya/The Target*, dir. Farhan Akhtar, 2004
*Lamhe/Moments*, dir. Yash Chopra, 1991
*Love aaj kal/Love Today*, dir. Imtiaz Ali, 2009
*Madras Café*, dir. Shoojit Shircar, 2013
*Mahal/The Mansion*, dir. Kamal Amrohi, 1949
*Main hoon naa/I'm Here for You*, dir. Farah Khan, 2004

*Maine Gandhi ko nahin maara/I Didn't Kill Gandhi*, dir. Jahnu Barua, 2005

*Maine pyar kiya/I've Fallen in Love*, dir. Sooraj Barjatya, 1989

*Mammo*, dir. Shyam Benegal, 1994

*Mee Sindhutai Sapkal/I Am Sindutai Sapkal*, dir. Ananth Narayan Mahadevan, 2010 (Marathi)

*Mission Kashmir*, dir. Vidhu Vinod Chopra, 1998

*Mohabbatein/Loves*, dir. Aditya Chopra, 2000

*Mother India*, dir. Mehboob Khan, 1957

*Mr India*, dir. Shekhar Kapur, 1987,

*Mrigayaa/The Royal Hunt*, dir. Mrinal Sen, 1976

*Mrityudand/Death Sentence*, dir. Prakash Jha, 1997

*Mughal-e-Azam/The Great Mughal*, dir. K. Asif, 1960

*Mujhse shaadi karogi/Will You Marry Me?*, dir. David Dhawan, 2004

*Mumbai meri jaan/Mumbai, My Love*, dir. Nishikant Kamath, 2009

*Munimji/The Clerk*, dir. Subodh Mukherjee, 1955

*Munnabhai MBBS*, dir. Rajkumar Hirani, 2003

*Murder*, dir. Mahesh Bhatt, 2004

*My Brother Nikhil*, dir. Onir, 2005

*My Friend Ganesha*, dir. Rajiv S. Ruia, 2007

*My Name Is Khan* (*MNIK*), dir. Karan Johar, 2010

*Namastey London/Hello London*, dir. Vipul Amrutlal Shah, 2007

*Naseem*, dir. Saeed Akhtar Mirza, 1995

*Nastik/The Atheist*, dir. I. S. Johar, 1954

*Natrang/Actor*, dir. Ravi Jadhav, 2010 (Marathi)

*New York*, dir. Kabir Khan, 2009

*No Entry*, dir. Anees Bazmee, 2005

*OMG: Oh My God!*, dir. Umesh Shukla, 2012

*Om Shanti Om*, dir. Farah Khan, 2007

*Omkara*, dir. Vishal Bharadwaj, 2006

*Once Upon a Time in Mumbai*, dir. Milan Luthria, 2010

*Paa/Dad*, dir. R. Balki, 2009

*Padosan/Neighbour*, dir. Jyoti Swaroop, 1968

*Page 3*, dir. Madhur Bhandarkar, 2005

*Parasakthi*, dir. R. Krishnan and S. Panju, 1952

*Pardes*, dir. Subhash Ghai, 1997

*Parineeta/The Married Woman*, dir. Pradeep Sarkar, 2005

*Partner*, dir. David Dhawan, 2007

*Parzania/Heaven and Hell on Earth*, dir. Rahul Dholakia, 2007

*Peepli (Live!)*, dir. Anusha Rizvi and Mahmood Farooqui, 2010

*Phir hera pheri/More Monkey Business*, dir. Neeraj Vora, 2006

*Pukar*, dir. Sohrab Modi, 1939

*Purab aur Pachhim/East and West*, dir. Manoj Kumar, 1970

*Pyaasa/The Desirous One*, dir. Guru Dutt, 1957

*Raajneeti/Politics*, dir. Prakash Jha, 2010

*Raaz/The Secret*, dir. Vikram Bhatt, 2002

*Rab ne bana di jodi/A Match Made by God*, dir. Aditya Chopra, 2008

*Race*, dir. Abbas Mustan, 2008

*Raja babu/His Lordship*, dir. David Dhawan, 1994

*Raja Hindustani/Indian King*, dir. Dharmesh Darshan, 1996

*Ram Lakhan*, dir. Subhash Ghai, 1980

*Ram Rajya/The Kingdom of God*, dir. Vijay Bhatt, 1943

*Rang de Basanti/Colour It Saffron*, dir. Rakeysh Omprakash Mehra, 2006

*Ra.One/The Demon*, dir. Anubhav Sinha, 2011

*Ready*, dir. Anees Bazmee, 2011

*The Rising: Ballad of Mangal Pandey*, dir. Ketan Mehta, 2005

*Road to Sangam*, dir. Amit Rai, 2009

*Roadside Romeo*, dir. Jugal Hansraj, 2008

*Rocket Singh: Salesman of the Year*, dir. Shimit Amin, 2009

*Rockstar*, dir. Imtiaz Ali, 2012

*Roja/Rose*, dir. Mani Ratnam, 1992

*Saajan chale saasural/Double Trouble (lit.: The Lover Has Gone to His In-laws)*, dir. David Dhawan, 1996

*Saawariya/Beloved*, dir. Sanjay Leela Bhansali, 2007

*Sagina*, dir. Tapan Sinha, 1974

*Sandwich*, dir. Anees Bazmee, 2006

*Sardari Begum*, dir. Shyam Benegal, 1996

*Sarfarosh/The Willing Martyr*, dir. John Matthews Matthan, 1998

*Sarkar*, dir. Ram Gopal Varma, 2005

*Sarkar Raj*, dir. Ram Gopal Varma, 2008

*Satya*, dir. Ram Gopal Varma, 1998

*Sholay/Embers*, dir. Ramesh Sippy, 1975

*Shree 420/The Trickster*, dir. Raj Kapoor, 1955

*Silsila/The Affair*, dir. Yash Chopra, 1981

*Sikandar*, dir. Sohrab Modi, 1941

*Singh is Kinng*, dir. Anees Bazmee, 2008

*Soldier*, dir. Abbas Mustan, 1998

*Stanley ka dabba/Stanley's Lunchbox*, dir. Amole Gupte, 2011

*Student of the Year*, dir. Karan Johar, 2012

*Sujata/The High-born*, dir. Bimal Roy, 1959

*Supermen of Malegaon*, dir. Faiza Ahmad Khan, 2008 (documentary)

*Swades/We the People*, dir. Ashutosh Gowarikar, 2004

*Taare zameen par/Stars on Earth*, dir. Aamir Khan, 2007

*Tamas/Darkness*, dir. Govind Nihalani, 1986

*Tanu Weds Manu*, dir. Anand L. Rai, 2011

*Tere naam/In Your Name*, dir. Satish Kaushik, 2003
*Terrorist*, dir. Santosh Shivan, 1999
*Trishul/The Trident*, dir. Yash Chopra, 1978
*Udaan/Flight*, dir. Vikramaditya Motwane, 2010
*Uttarayan/Journey to the Other Side*, dir. Bipin Nadkarni, 2005
*Veer Zara*, dir. Yash Chopra, 2004
*Vicky Donor*, dir. Shoojit Sarcar, 2012
*Vivaah: A Journey from Engagement to Marriage*, dir. Sooraj Barjatya, 2006
*Wake Up Sid*, dir. Ayan Mukherji, 2009
*Waqt/Time*, dir. Yash Chopra, 1965
*Welcome*, dir. Anees Bazmee, 2007
*Welcome to Sajjanpur*, dir. Shyam Benegal, 2008
*Woh Lamhe/Those Moments*, dir. Mohit Suri, 2006
*Zindagi na milegi dobara/You Only Live Once*, dir. Zoya Akhtar, 2011
*Zubeidaa*, dir. Shyam Benegal, 2001

Abbreviated film titles in common use:
APGK – *Ajab Prem ki ghazab kahani*
DDLJ – *Dilwale dulhania le jayenge*
DTPH – *Dil to pagal hai*
HAHK – *Hum aapke hain koun . . .!*
HDDCS – *Hum dil de chuke sanam*
JTHJ – *Jab tak hai jaan*
K3G – *Kabhi khushi kabhie gham*
KANK – *Kabhi alvida na kehna*
KKHH – *Kuch kuch hota hai*
MNIK – *My Name Is Khan*
RNBDJ – *Rab ne bana di jodi*
ZNMD – *Zindagi na milegi dobara*

# Further Reading

Boo, Katherine, *Behind the Beautiful Forevers: Life, Death and Hope in a Mumbai Slum* (London, 2012)

Dé, Shobhaa, *Superstar India* (New Delhi, 2008)

Deb, Siddhartha, *The Beautiful and the Damned: Life in the New India* (London, 2012)

Desai, Santosh, *Mother Pious Lady: Making Sense of Everyday India* (New Delhi, 2010)

Giridharadas, Anand, *India Calling: An Intimate Portrait of a Nation's Remaking* (New York, 2011)

Guha, Ramchandra, *India after Gandhi: The History of the World's Largest Democracy* (London, 2007)

Jaffrelot, Christophe, *Religion, Caste and Politics in India* (London, 2011)

——, *India since 1950: Society, Politics, Economy and Culture* (Delhi, 2012)

Khilnani, Sunil, *The Idea of India* (London, 1997)

Luce, Edward, *In Spite of the Gods: The Strange Rise of Modern India* (London, 2006)

Mishra, Pankaj, *Butter Chicken in Ludhiana: Travels in Small Town India* (New Delhi, 1995)

Nilekani, Nandan, *Imagining India: The Idea of a Renewed Nation* (New Delhi, 2009)

Nussbaum, Martha, *The Clash within: Democracy, Religious Violence and India's Future* (Cambridge, MA, 2007)

Sen, Amartya, *The Argumentative Indian: Writings on Indian History, Culture and Identity* (London, 2005)

Verma, Pavan, *Being Indian* (London, 2005)

## Introduction

Dwyer, Rachel, '*Zara hatke!*: The New Middle Classes and the Segmentation of Hindi Cinema', in *A Way of Life: Being Middle-class in Contemporary India*, ed. Henrike Donner (London, 2011), pp. 184–208

Jaffrelot, Christophe, *Religion, Caste and Politics in India* (London, 2011)
—, *India since 1950: Society, Politics, Economy and Culture* (Delhi, 2012)

*The Imaginary, Imagination*

Anderson, Benedict, *Imagined Communities: Reflections on the Origin and Spread of Nationalism*, 2nd edn (London, 1991)
Appadurai, Arjun, *Modernity at Large: Cultural Dimensions of Globalization* (Delhi, 1997)
Castoriadis, Cornelius, *The Imaginary Institution of Society* (Cambridge, MA, 1998)
Chakrabarty, Dipesh, 'Nation and Imagination', in *Provincializing Europe: Postcolonial Thought and Historical Difference*, Dipesh Chakrabarty (Princeton, NJ, 2000), pp. 149–79
Gaonkar, Dilip Parameshwar, 'Toward New Imaginaries: An Introduction', *Public Culture*, XIV/1 (2002), pp. 1–19
Inden, Ronald, *Imagining India* (London, 1990, 2000)
Kracauer, Siegfried, *Theory of Film: The Redemption of Physical Reality*, intro. Miriam Bratu Hansen (Princeton, NJ, 1997)
Shulman, David, *More Than Real: A History of the Imagination in South India* (Cambridge, MA, 2012)
Taylor, Charles, *Modern Social Imaginaries* (Durham, NC, 2004)

*Entertainment and Stars*

Dyer, Richard, 'Entertainment and Utopia', *Movie*, 24 (1997), pp. 2–13
—, *Stars*, Supplementary chapter by Paul McDonald (London, 1998)

*Background to Hindi Cinema*

Dwyer, Rachel, *100 Bollywood Films* (London, 2005)
—, and Divia Patel, *Cinema India: The Visual Culture of Hindi Film*, Envisioning Asia series, ed. H. Bhabha (London, New Brunswick, NJ, and Delhi, 2002)
Ganti, Tejaswini, *Bollywood: A Guidebook to Popular Hindi Cinema* (London, 2004)
—, *Producing Bollywood: Inside the Contemporary Hindi Film Industry* (Durham, NC, 2012)
Gopal, Sangita, and Sujata Moorti, eds, *Global Bollywood: Travels of Hindi Song and Dance* (Minneapolis, MN, 2008)
Kavoori, Anandam, and Aswin Punathambekar, eds, *Global Bollywood* (New York, 2008)
Nandy, Ashis, ed., *The Secret Politics of Our Desires: Innocence, Culpability and Popular Cinema* (London, 1998)
Prasad, M. Madhava, *Ideology of the Hindi Film: A Historical Construction* (Delhi, 1998)

Rajadhyaksha, Ashish, and Paul Willemen, *An Encyclopaedia of Indian Cinema*, 2nd edn (London, 1999)

Thomas, Rosie, 'Melodrama and the Negotiation of Morality in Mainstream Hindi Film', in *Consuming Modernity: Public Culture in a South Asian World*, ed. C. A. Breckenridge (London, 1995), pp. 157–82

*Songs*

Booth, Greg, 'Religion, Gossip, Narrative Conventions and the Construction of Meaning in Hindi Film Songs', *Popular Music*, 19 (2000), pp. 125–46

Gopal, Sangita, and Sujata Moorti, eds, *Global Bollywood: Travels of Hindi Song and Dance* (Minneapolis, 2008)

Morcom, Anna, *Hindi Film Songs and the Cinema*, SOAS Musicology Series, (Aldershot, 2007)

*'Bollywood'*

Dwyer, Rachel, '*Zara Hatke!*: The New Middle Classes and the Segmentation of Hindi Cinema', in *A Way of Life: Being Middle-class in Contemporary India*, ed. Henrike Donner (London, 2008), pp. 184–208

Rajadhyaksha, Ashish, 'The "Bollywoodization" of the Indian Cinema: Cultural Nationalism in a Global Arena', *Inter-Asia Cultural Studies*, IV/1 (2003), pp. 25–39

Vasudevan, Ravi, 'The Meanings of Bollywood', in *Beyond the Boundaries of Bollywood: The Many Forms of Hindi Cinema*, ed. Rachel Dwyer and Jerry Pinto (New Delhi, 2011), pp. 3–29

*National Cinema, Trans-national Cinema*

Higson, Andrew, 'The Concept of National Cinema', *Screen*, XXX/4 (1989), pp. 36–47

Rajadhyaksha, Ashish, *Indian Cinema in the Time of Celluloid: From Bollywood to the Emergency*, South Asian Cinemas series, ed. Rachel Dwyer (Bloomington, IN, 2010)

Vitali, Valentina, and Paul Willemen, eds, *Theorising National Cinema* (London, 2006)

*Hindi Cinema beyond India*

Dwyer, Rachel, '*Zara Hatke!*: The New Middle Classes and the Segmentation of Hindi Cinema', in *A Way of Life: Being Middle-class in Contemporary India*, ed. Henrike Donner (London, 2011), pp. 184–208

——, 'Bollywood's Empire: Indian Cinema and the Diaspora', in *Routledge Handbook of South Asian Diaspora*, ed. Joya Chatterji and David Washbrook (London, 2013), pp. 409–18

*Other Media in India*

Athique, Adrian, *Indian Media: Global Approaches* (Cambridge, 2012)
——, and Douglas Hill, *The Multiplex in India: A Cultural Economy of Urban Leisure* (New York, 2010)
Banaji, Shakuntala, ed., *South Asian Media Cultures: Audiences, Representations, Contexts* (London, 2010)
Batabyal, Somnath, *Making News in India: Star News and Star Ananda* (New Delhi and London, 2012)
——, Angad Chowdhury, Meenu Gaur and Matti Pohjonen, eds, *Indian Mass Media and the Politics of Change* (New Delhi and London, 2011)
Brosius, Christiane, and Melissa Butcher, eds, *Image Journeys: Audio-visual Media and Cultural Change in India* (New Delhi, 1999)
Butcher, Melissa, *Transnational Television, Cultural Identity and Change: When* STAR *Came to India* (New Delhi, 2003)
Jeffrey, Robin, *India's Newspaper Revolution: Capitalism, Politics and the Indian Language Press, 1977–1999* (London, 2000)
——, and Assa Doron, *The Great Indian Phone Book: How the Mass Mobile Changes Business, Politics and Daily Life* (London, 2013)
Mankekar, Purnima, *Screening Culture, Viewing Politics: An Ethnography of Television, Womanhood, and Nation in Postcolonial India* (Durham, NC, 1999)
Mazzarella, William, *Shoveling Smoke: Advertising and Globalization in Contemporary India* (Durham, NC, 2003)
Mehta, Nalin, *India on Television: How Satellite News Channels Have Changed the Way We Think and Act* (New Delhi, 2008)
Rajagopal, Arvind, *Politics after Television: Religious Nationalism and the Reshaping of the Indian Public* (Cambridge, 2001)

*Modernities and Public Culture*

Chatterjee, Partha, 'Critique of Popular Culture', *Public Culture*, xx/2 (2008), pp. 321–44
Dalmia, V., and R. Sadana, eds, *The Cambridge Companion to Modern Indian Culture* (Cambridge, 2012)
Dwyer, Rachel, and Christopher Pinney, *Pleasure and the Nation: The History, Consumption and Politics of Public Culture in India* (Delhi, 2000)
Eisenstadt, Shmuel Noah, ed., *Multiple Modernities* (New Brunswick, NJ, 2002)
Gaonkar, Dilip Parameshwar, ed, *Alternative Modernities* (Durham, NC, 2001)

## 1 Unity: The Nation, Its History and Trans-nationalism

Appadurai, Arjun, *Modernity at Large: Cultural Dimensions of Globalization* (Delhi, 1997)

Bakshi, Rajni, *Bapa Kuti: Journeys in the Rediscovery of Gandhi* (New Delhi, 2000)
Boym, Svetlana, *The Future of Nostalgia* (New York, 2001)
Dyer, Richard, *Stars*, supplementary chapter by Paul McDonald (London, 1998)
Nehru, Jawaharlal, *The Discovery of India* (New Delhi, 1946, 1989)
Pinney, Christopher, *'Photos of the Gods': The Printed Image and Political Struggle in India* (London, 2004)

*The Nation*

Anderson, Benedict, *Imagined Communities: Reflections on the Origin and Spread of Nationalism*, 2nd edn (London, 1991)
Chatterjee, Partha, *Nationalist Thought and the Colonial World: A Derivative Discourse?* (London, 1986)
Chatterjee, Partha, *The Nation and Its Fragments: Colonial and Postcolonial Histories* (Delhi, 1993)
Nandy, Ashis, *The Intimate Enemy: Loss and Recovery of Self under Colonialism* [1983] (Delhi, 1988)

*Nationalism and Indian Cinema*

Chakravarty, Sumita S., *National Identity in Indian Popular Cinema, 1947–1987* (Austin, 1993)
Rajadhyaksha, Ashish, *Indian Cinema in the Time of Celluloid: From Bollywood to the Emergency* (Bloomington, IN, 2009)

*History, Myth; Historical and Mythological Films*

Bhaumik, Kaushik, 'The Emergence of the Bombay Film Industry, 1913–1936', unpublished DPhil, University of Oxford, 2001
Chakravarty, Dipesh, 'Postcoloniality and the Artifice of History: Who Speaks for "Indian" Pasts?', *Representations*, XXXVII (1992), pp. 1–26
Dwyer, Rachel, *Filming the Gods: Religion and Indian Cinema* (London, New York and Delhi, 2006)
——, 'The Hindi Film Biopic', in *The Blackwell Companion to Historical Film*, ed. Robert Rosenstone and Constantin Parvulescu (Oxford, 2013)
——, 'The Biopic of the New Middle Classes in Hindi Cinema', in *The Biopic in Contemporary Film Culture*, ed. Belen Vidal and Tom Brown, American Film Institute Readers series, ed. Edward Brannigan and Charles Wolfe (London and New York, 2014), pp. 63–83
Guha, Ramachandra, 'The Challenge of Contemporary History', *Economic and Political Weekly*, XLIII/26–7 (2008), pp. 192–200
Hansen, Kathryn, 'The *Inder Sabha* Phenomenon: Public Theatre and Consumption in Greater India (1853–1956)', in *Pleasure and the Nation: The History, Politics and Consumption of Public Culture in India*, ed. Rachel Dwyer and Christopher Pinney (Delhi, 2000), pp. 76–114

Jain, Kajri, *Gods in the Bazaar: The Economies of Indian Calendar Art* (Durham, NC, 2007)

Mankekar, Purnima, *Screening Culture, Viewing Politics: An Ethnography of Television, Womanhood, and Nation in Postcolonial India* (Durham, NC, 1999)

Mukhopadhyay, Urvi, 'The Perception of the "Medieval" in Indian Popular Films: 1920s–1960s', unpublished PhD, SOAS, University of London, 2004

Pinney, Christopher, *'Photos of the Gods': The Printed Image and Political Struggle in India* (London, 2004)

Richman, Paula, *Many Ramayanas: The Diversity of a Narrative Tradition in South Asia* (Berkeley, CA, 1991)

Sarkar, Bhaskar, *Mourning the Nation: Indian Cinema in the Wake of Partition* (Durham, 2009)

Sen, Amartya, 'On Interpreting India's Past', in *Nationalism, Democracy and Development: State and Politics in India*, ed. Sugata Bose and Ayesha Jalal (Oxford, 1998), pp. 10–35

*Kashmir in Film*

Gaur, Meenu, 'Kashmir on Screen: Region, Religion and Secularism in Hindi Cinema', unpublished PhD thesis, SOAS, 2010

Kabir, Ananya Jahanara, *Territory of Desire: Representing the Valley of Kashmir* (Minneapolis, MN, 2009)

*The Diaspora and Film*

Chopra, Anupama, *Dilwale dulhaniya le jayenge* (London, 2003)

Dwyer, Rachel, 'Bollywood's Empire', in *Routledge Handbook of South Asian Diaspora*, ed. Joya Chatterji and David Washbrook (London, 2013), pp. 409–18

Uberoi, Patricia, 'The Diaspora Comes Home: Disciplining Desire in *DDLJ*', in *Contributions to Indian Sociology* (n.s.), XXXII/2 (1998), pp. 305–6

## 2 Diversity: Region, Caste and Class

Adiga, Aravind, *The White Tiger* (New York, 2008)

Boo, Katherine, *Behind the Beautiful Forevers: Life, Death and Hope in a Mumbai Undercity* (New Delhi, 2012)

Guha, Ramchandra, *India after Gandhi: The History of the World's Largest Democracy* (London, 2007)

Nandy, Ashis, ed., *The Secret Politics of Our Desires: Innocence, Culpability and Popular Cinema* (London, 1998)

Nehru, Jawaharlal, *The Discovery of India* (New Delhi, 1946, 1989)

*Language and Hindi Cinema*

Kesavan, Mukul, 'Urdu, Awadh and the Tawaif: The Islamicate Roots of Hindi Cinema', in *Forging Identities: Gender, Communities and the State*, ed. Zoya Hasan (New Delhi, 1994), pp. 244–57

Kothari, Rita, and Rupert Snell, eds, *Chutneyfying English: The Phenomenon of Hinglish* (New Delhi, 2011)

Trivedi, Harish, 'All Kinds of Hindi: The Evolving Language of Hindi Cinema', in *Fingerprinting Popular Culture: The Mythic and the Iconic in Indian Cinema*, ed. Vinay Lal and Ashis Nandy (New Delhi, 2006), pp. 51–86

Vasvani, Kishor, *Cinemai bhasha aur Hindi samvadon ka vishleshan* (New Delhi, 1998)

*Village India*

Bijapurkar, Rama, *We Are Like That Only: Understanding the Logic of Consumer India* (New Delhi, 2007)

Inden, Ronald, *Imagining India* (London, 1990, 2000)

*Caste, Tribe*

Arnold, David, and Peter Robb, *Institutions and Ideologies: A SOAS South Asia Reader* (London, 1995)

Blackburn, Stuart, 'The Formation of Tribal Identities', in *The Cambridge Companion to Modern Indian Culture*, ed. Vasudha Dalmia and Rashmi Sadana (Cambridge, 2012), pp. 30–48

Dumont, Louis, *Homo Hierarchicus: The Caste System and Its Implications*, trans. Mark Sainsbury, Louis Dumont and Basia Gulati, complete revd edn (Delhi, 1998)

Fuller, Christopher J., ed., *Caste Today* (New Delhi, 1996)

Gupta, Dipankar, 'Caste and Politics: Identity over System', *Annual Review of Anthropology*, 34 (2005), pp. 409–27

Inden, Ronald, *Imagining India* (London, 1990, 2000)

Jaffrelot, Christophe, *India's Silent Revolution: The Rise of the Lower Castes* (London, 2000)

Rao, Anupama, *The Caste Question: Dalits and the Politics of Modern India* (Berkeley, CA, 2009)

Shah, Ghanshyam, ed., *Dalit Identity and Politics* (California, London and New Delhi, 2001)

*Class*

Bourdieu, Pierre, *Distinction: A Social Critique of the Judgement of Taste*, trans. Richard Nice (Cambridge, MA, 1984)

Donner, Henrike, *Being Middle-class in India: A Way of Life* (London, 2011)

Dwyer, Rachel, *All You Want Is Money, All You Need Is Love: Sex and Romance in Modern India* (London, 2000)

Fernandes, Leela, *India's New Middle Class: Democratic Politics in an Era of Economic Reform* (Minneapolis, MN, 2006)

Ghosh, Avijit, *Cinema Bhojpuri* (New Delhi, 2010)

Gupta, Akhil, *Red Tape: Bureaucracy, Structural Violence and Poverty in India* (Durham, NC, 2012)

Jeffrey, Robin, and Assa Doron, *The Great Indian Phone Book: How the Mass Mobile Changes Business, Politics and Daily Life* (London, 2013)

Luce, Edward, *In Spite of the Gods: The Strange Rise of Modern India* (London, 2006)

Panagiriya, Arvind, *India: The Emerging Giant* (New York, 2011)

Stancati, Margherita, 'India is Not a Superpower', http://blogs.wsj.com, 13 March 2012

## 3 Religion: Myths, Beliefs and Practices

Chatterjee, Partha, *Nationalist Thought and the Colonial World: A Derivative Discourse?* (London, 1986)

Das, Gurcharan, *The Difficulty of Being Good: On the Subtle Art of Dharma* (London, 2009)

Dwyer, Rachel, *Filming the Gods: Religion and Indian Cinema* (London, New York and Delhi, 2006)

Roy, Olivier, *Holy Ignorance: When Religion and Culture Part Ways*, trans. Ros Schwartz (London, 2010)

*Hinduism*

Doniger, Wendy, *The Hindus: An Alternative History* (London, 2009)

Dwyer, Rachel, *What Do Hindus Believe?* (London, 2008)

*Islam in India Today*

Jaffrelot, Christophe, and Laurent Gayer, eds, *Muslims in Indian Cities: Trajectories of Marginalisation* (London, 2012)

*Hindutva*

Dwyer, Rachel, 'The Saffron Screen?: Hindi Movies and Hindu Nationalism', in *Religion, Media and the Public Sphere*, ed. Birgit Meyer and Annalies Moors (Bloomington, IN, 2006), pp. 422–60

Hansen, Thomas Blom, *The Saffron Wave: Democracy and Hindu Nationalism in Modern India* (Princeton, NJ, 1999)

Jaffrelot, Christophe, *The Hindu Nationalist Movement and Indian Politics, 1925 to the 1990s* (London, 1996)

*Religion and Media*

Dwyer, Rachel, *Filming the Gods: Religion and Indian Cinema* (London, New York and Delhi, 2006)

——, 'The Goddess in Indian Film', in *Goddess: Divine Energy*, ed. Jackie Menzies (Sydney, 2006), pp. 153–5

Eck, Diana, *India: A Sacred Geography* (New York, 2012)

Lutgendorf, Philip, 'All in the (Raghu) Family: A Video Epic in Cultural Context' in *Media and the Transformation of Religion in South Asia*, ed. Lawrence Babb and Susan Wadley (Philadelphia, PA, 1995), pp. 217–53.

Mankekar, Purnima, *Screening Culture, Viewing Politics: An Ethnography of Television, Womanhood, and Nation in Postcolonial India* (Durham, NC, 1999)

Rajagopal, Arvind, *Politics after Television: Religious Nationalism and the Reshaping of the Indian Public* (Cambridge, 2001)

Richman, Paula, *Many Ramayanas: The Diversity of a Narrative Tradition in South Asia* (Berkeley, CA, 1991)

Uberoi, Patricia, 'Imagining the Family: An Ethnography of Viewing "Hum aapke hain koun . . .!"', in *Pleasure and the Nation: The History, Consumption and Politics of Public Culture in India*, ed. Rachel Dwyer and Christopher Pinney (Delhi, 2000), pp. 309–51

*Islamicate Films*

Bhaskar, Ira, and Richard Allen, *Islamicate Cultures of Bombay Cinema* (New Delhi, 2009)

Dwyer, Rachel, *Filming the Gods: Religion and Indian Cinema* (London, New York and Delhi, 2006)

——, 'I Am Crazy about the Lord: The Muslim Devotional Film', *Third Text: Special issue: Cinema in Muslim Societies*, XXIV/1 (2010), pp. 123–34

*Islamism in South Asia*

Tankel, Stephen, *Storming the World Stage: The Story of Lashkar-e-Taiba* (London, 2012)

*Christians in Hindi Cinema*

Pinto, Jerry, *Helen, the H-bomb* (New Delhi, 2005)

## 4  Emotions: Sadness, Anger and Happiness

'Amitabh Bachchan Gets Lifetime Achievement Award at Dubai Fest', www.dearcinema.com, 9 December 2009.

*Emotions, Texts and Melodrama*

Caroll, Noël, 'Art, Narrative and Emotion', in *Emotion and the Arts*, ed. Mette Hjort and Sue Laver (Oxford, 1997), pp. 190–211

Meyer, Leonard B., *Emotion and Meaning in Music* (Chicago, IL, 1996)

Oatley, Keith, *The Passionate Muse: Exploring Emotion in Stories* (New York, 2012)

Smith, Murray, *Engaging Characters: Fiction, Emotion and the Cinema* (Oxford, 1995)

*Melodrama and Hindi Cinema*

Thomas, Rosie, 'Indian Cinema: Pleasures and Popularity: An Introduction', *Screen*, XXVI/3–4 (1985), pp. 161–81. Reprinted in *The Bollywood Reader*, ed. Rajinder Kumar Dudrah and Jigna Desai (Maidenhead, 2008), pp. 21–31

Vasudevan, Ravi, *The Melodramatic Public: Film Form and Spectatorship in Indian Cinema* (Ranikhet, 2010)

*Melancholy and Depression*

Bhugra, Dines, *Mad Tales from Bollywood: Portrayal of Mental Illness in Conventional Hindi Cinema* (London, 2006)

Dwyer, Rachel, 'Yeh shaadi nahin ho sakti! (This Wedding Cannot Happen!)', in *(Un)tying the Knot: Ideal and Reality in Asian Marriage (Asian Trends 2)*, ed. G. W. Jones and Kamalini Ramdas (Singapore, 2004), pp. 59–90

——, 'Bombay Gothic: 60 Years of Mahal/The Mansion, dir. Kamal Amrohi, 1949', in *Beyond the Boundaries of Bollywood: The Many Forms of Hindi Cinema*, ed. Rachel Dwyer and Jerry Pinto (New Delhi, 2011), pp. 130–55

Lutz, Tom, *Crying: A Natural and Cultural History of Tears* (New York, 2001)

Nandy, Ashis, 'Invitation to an Antique Death: The Journey of Pramathesh Barua as the Origin of the Terribly Effeminate, Maudlin, Self-destructive Heroes of Indian Cinema', in *Pleasure and the Nation: The History, Politics and Consumption of Public Culture in India*, ed. Rachel Dwyer and Christopher Pinney (Delhi, 2000), pp. 39–160

Neale, Steve, 'Melodrama and Tears', *Screen*, XXVII/6 (1986), pp. 6–22

*Anger*

Dwyer, Rachel, 'Ich mag es, wenn du zornig wirst: Amitabh Bachchan, Emotionen und Stars im Hindi-film (I Love It When You're Angry: Amitabh Bachchan, the Emotions and Stars in the Hindi film)', in *Fokus Bollywood: das indische Kino in wissenschaftlichen Diskursen*, ed. Claus Tieber (Münster, 2009), pp. 99–115; English version to appear in *Stars in World Cinema*, ed. Andrea Bandhauer and Michelle Royer (2013)

Gopalan, Lalitha, 'Avenging Women in Indian Cinema', *Screen*, XXXVIII/1 (1997), pp. 42–59

*Happiness*

Ben-Shahar, Tal, *Happier* (New York, 2007)

Dwyer, Rachel, 'Happy Ever After: Hindi Films and the Happy Ending', in
    *The Topography of Happiness from the American Dream to Postsocialism/*
    Топография счастья от Американской мечты к пост-социализму,
    ed. Nikolai Ssorin-Chaikov (Moscow, 2013), pp. 357–402

Foley, Michael, *The Age of Absurdity: Why Modern Life Makes it Hard to be
    Happy* (London, 2010)

Gilbert, Daniel, *Stumbling on Happiness* (London, 2006)

Graham, Carol, *Happiness around the World: The Paradox of Happy Peasants and
    Miserable Millionaires* (Oxford, 2009)

Narwekar, Sanjit, *Eena meena deeka: The Story of Hindi Film Comedy*
    (New Delhi, 2005)


## 5 Home: Romance, Love and the Family

Dwyer, Rachel, *All You Want Is Money, All You Need Is Love: Sex and Romance in
    Modern India* (London, 2000)

Orsini, Francesca, ed., *Love in South Asian Traditions* (Cambridge, 2006)

Uberoi, Patricia, *Freedom and Destiny: Gender, Family and Popular Culture
    in India* (Delhi, 2006)

*Gender Studies in India*

Chopra, Radhika, Caroline Osella and Filippo Osella, eds, *South Asian
    Masculinities: Context of Change, Sites of Continuity* (New Delhi, 2004)

Derné, Steve, *Movies, Masculinity, Modernity: An Ethnography of Men's Filmgoing
    in India* (Westport, CT, 2000)

Gabriel, Karen, *Melodrama and the Nation: Sexual Economies of Bombay Cinema
    1970–2000* (New Delhi, 2010)

Henniker, Charlie, 'Pink Rupees or Gay Icons?: Accounting for the Camp
    Appropriation of Male Bollywood Stars', *South Asia Research*, XXX/1 (2010),
    pp. 25–41

Nandy, Ashis, *The Intimate Enemy: Loss and Recovery of Self under Colonialism*
    [1983] (Delhi, 1988)

Osella, Caroline, and Filippo Osella, *Men and Masculinities in South India*
    (London, 2006)

Ray, Raka, ed., *Handbook of Gender* (Delhi, 2012)

*Love, Sex and Romance in Indian Film*

Dwyer, Rachel, *All You Want Is Money, All You Need Is Love: Sex and Romance in
    Modern India* (London, 2000)

——, 'The Erotics of the Wet Sari in Hindi Films', *South Asia*, xxiii/2 (2000), pp. 143–59

——, 'Yeh shaadi nahin ho sakti! (This Wedding Cannot Happen!)', in *(Un)tying the Knot: Ideal and Reality in Asian Marriage (Asian Trends 2)*, ed. G. W. Jones and Kamalini Ramdas (Singapore, 2004), pp. 59–90

——, 'Kiss and Tell: Expressing Love in Hindi Movies', in *Love in South Asian Traditions*, ed. Francesca Orsini (Cambridge, 2006), pp. 289–302

Gopal, Sangita, *Conjugations: Marriage and Forming New Bollywood Cinema* (Chicago, il, 2011)

Kasbekar, Asha, 'Hidden Pleasures: Negotiating the Myth of the Female Ideal in Popular Hindi Cinema', in *Pleasure and the Nation: The History, Consumption and Politics of Public Culture in India*, ed. Rachel Dwyer and Christopher Pinney (Delhi, 2000), pp. 286–308

*Servants*

Ray, Raka, and Seemin Oayum, *Cultures of Servitude: Modernity, Domesticity and Class in India* (Stanford, ca, 2009)

## 6 The World: Education, Work and Lifestyle

Jaffrelot, Christophe, *Religion, Caste and Politics in India* (London, 2011)

——, *India since 1950: Society, Politics, Economy and Culture* (Delhi, 2012)

Luce, Edward, *In Spite of the Gods: The Strange Rise of Modern India* (London, 2006)

Nilekani, Nandan, *Imagining India: The Idea of a Renewed Nation* (New Delhi, 2009)

Panagiriya, Arvind, *India: The Emerging Giant* (New York, 2008)

## 7 Agneepath/The Path of Fire, 1990–2012

Brosius, Christiane, *India's Middle Class: New Forms of Urban Leisure, Consumption and Prosperity* (London, 2010)

Desai, Santosh, *Mother Pious Lady: Making Sense of Everyday India* (New Delhi, 2010)

Dwyer, Rachel, *All You Want Is Money, All You Need Is Love: Sex and Romance in Modern India* (London, 2000)

Haynes, Douglas, Abigail McGowan, Tirthankar Roy and Haruka Yanagisawa, eds, *Towards a History of Consumption in South Asia* (New Delhi, 2010)

Majumdar, Ranjani, 'Aviation, Tourism and Dreaming in 1960s Bombay Cinema', *BioScope: South Asian Screen Studies*, ii/2 (2011), pp. 129–55

Mazzarella, William, *Shoveling Smoke: Advertising and Globalization in Contemporary India* (Durham, nc, 2003)

# Acknowledgements

The idea behind this book began with my inaugural lecture at soas, University of London, entitled 'Bollywood's India' (given 5 February 2008). This formed the basis of a paper published in 2010 as 'Bollywood's India: Hindi Cinema as a Guide to Modern India', *Asian Affairs*, XXXI/3, pp. 381–98. Chapter Two was written as I worked on a paper about the biopic, published in *Shah Rukh Khan and Global Bollywood*, ed. Robert Rosenstone, Elke Mader, Rajinder Dudrah and Bernhard Fuchs (forthcoming). Chapter Five draws on two published papers written by me on the emotions. First, 'Happy Ever After: Hindi Films and the Happy Ending', in *The Topography of Happiness from the American Dream to Postsocialism/* Топография счастья от Американской мечты к пост-социализму, ed. Nikolai Ssorin-Chaikov (Moscow, 2013), pp. 357–402. The second paper is 'Ich mag es, wenn du zornig wirst: Amitabh Bachchan, Emotionen und Stars im Hindi-film' ('I Love You When You're Angry: Amitabh Bachchan, the Star and Emotion in the Hindi Film'), in *Fokus Bollywood: das indische Kino in wissenschaftlichen Diskursen*, ed. Claus Tieber (Münster, 2009), pp. 99–115; English version to appear in *Stars in World Cinema*, ed. Andrea Bandhauer and Michelle Royer (2014).

Thanks are due to many. Special thanks to Faisal Devji, David Lunn and Bhaskar Mukhopadhyay. In Mumbai: Pamela and Yash Chopra, Subhashini Ali, Shaad Ali Sehgal, Gautam Pemmaraju, Udita Jhunjhunwala and Arun Janardhan, Naresh Fernandes, Nandini Ramnath, Javed and Farah Gaya, Ajay Kejriwal, Jerry Pinto, Kamalbir and Rano Singh, Vikram Doctor, Sidharth Bhatia and Meera Mehta. In Delhi: Ashis and Uma Nandy, Ravi Vasudevan, Radhika Singha, Pankaj Pachauri, Pramila Phatarphekar, Julian Parr, Valay Gada and Narayani Gupta. In Bangalore: Priya Ramani, Samar Harlankar and Babyjaan; Girish Karnad; and Ashish Rajadhyaksha.

Thanks to Excel Entertainment for images from *Don* (p. 232) and *ZNMD* (p. 188), Vidhu Vinod Chopra Films for an image from *3 Idiots* (p. 227), and Madras Talkies for an image from *Guru* (p. 230).

Amir Curmally, Maqbool and the staff at Rhythm House, Mumbai, have kept me supplied with DVDs over many years, as has Rishika Lulla of Eros International.

Thanks to Georgie Williams for helping to format the Further Reading and Josh Bryson for help with the Index.

I should like to thank my former and present students at SOAS, undergraduate, postgraduate and research, from whom I always learn so much. You are too numerous to name individually but a special thanks to those on our Facebook page, Madame Bollywood.

And Michael.

# Index

Bharat (character) 38; family of 217
Bharati, Subramnia, songs of 59
Bharatiya Janata Party (BJP) 50, 116,
    122–3
Bhatt, Mahesh, *Duplicate* (1998) 218;
    *Murder* (2004) 155
Bhatt, Vijay, *Ram Rajya* (1942) 43, 124
Bhatt, Vikram, *Raaz* (2002) 155; *Raaz
    3* (2012) 155
Bhave, Sumitra, *Devrai* (2004) 20
Bhojpuri cinema 22; expansion of 25
Blyton, Enid 224
Bollywood 7, 12, 16, 19, 22, 28, 31,
    37, 42, 47–8, 52, 62–3, 69, 87,
    89, 103, 128, 163, 191, 202, 207,
    219, 237, 251, 256; expansion
    of 22, 63; local community
    responses to 25; traditions
    developed in 53–4
Bombay Riots (1992–3) depictions of
    57, 62
Bombay Talkies 83, 105
*Bombay Talkies* (anthology film) 202
Boo, Katherine, *Behind the Beautiful
    Forevers* 111
Bose, Nitin, *Gunga Jumna* (1961) 84,
    217
Boyle, Danny, *Slumdog Millionaire*
    (2009) 26, 111
Boym, Svetlana 41
Brando, Marlon, influence of 252
Bronson, Charles 164
Buddhism 42, 119; conversion to 44;
    Four Noble Truths 161
Business Processing Outsourcing
    (BPOS) 16

Cameron, James, *Titanic* (1997) 41–2
capitalism, global 64–5
caste 64–5, 74, 80–81, 97, 120, 149,
    235; Brahmin 57, 91, 97–100,
    105, 118, 136, 235, 246; Dalit

15, 98–103, 119, 125; *dhobi* 80;
discrimination 97; Kayasths 99;
Khatri 97, 99; initial lack of
depiction of 78, 80, 97, 102,
118; inter-caste marriage 101,
118, 201; Mallah 100; NMCs,
relationship with 102; Other
Backward Castes (OBCs) 15, 98;
reservations for 15–16;
Scheduled Castes (SCs) 97–8;
Scheduled Castes and Tribes 15;
Scheduled Tribes (STs) 97–8;
Seths 99, 104, 230; sub-caste
118; Thakur 99, 104;
Untouchables 97, 99
Censor Board (CBFC) 61–2
Chakrabarty, Mithun 249
Charles, prince of Wales, depictions of
    77, 179
Chatterjee, Saratchandra, *Devdas*
    (1917) 162–3, 199, 209;
    *Parineeta* (1914) 199
China: Hong Kong 28, 240; tech-
    nology imported from 18
Chopra, Aditya, *Dilwale dulhania le
    jayenge* (*DDLJ*, 1995) 7, 22–4, *23*,
    67, *88*, 89, 138, *138*, 148, 157,
    159, *192*, 193–4, 197, 199, 207,
    213–14, 225, 241, 256; family of
    197; *Jab tak hai jaan* (*JTHJ*, 2012)
    58, 59, 78, 198, *245*;
    *Mohabbatein* (2000) 159, 166,
    201, 214, *215*, 221, 225; *225*;
    *Rab ne bana di jodi* (2000) 89,
    129, 137, 149, *149*, 159, 172,
    *173*, 203; *Silsila* (1981) 72
Chopra, B. R. 105; *Mahabharata*
    (TV series) 37–8
Chopra, Priyanka 243, 251
Chopra, Ravi, *Baghban* (2003) 214
Chopra, Vidhu Vinod, *Mission
    Kashmir* (1998) 59, 212

Farooqui, Mahmood, *Peepli* (*Live*)
(2010) 18, 96, 112, 167–8
Farsi (language) 84
fashion: jewellery 245; male 245;
*salwar kameez* 244–5; sari 244
Fazl, Abu'l, *Akbarnama* 45
feminism 185
First Indo-Pakistani War (1947–8)
depictions of 55
food 246; fasting 247; vegetarianism
246–7
Freud, Sigmund, theories of 185, 212
friendship (*dosti*) 194, 202, 219–20,
252; casual 219; love as 198

Gadhvi, Sanjay, *Dhoom* (2004) 147,
156, 234; *Dhoom 2* (2006) 156,
190, 234
Gandhi, Indira 49, 60, 110, 127, 235;
family of 126
Gandhi, Mohandas K. 43–4, 51–2,
60, 68, 97, 126–7, 168, 175,
184, 225–6, 248, 252; background of 69; depictions of
50–51, 53–4, 60, 100
Gandhi, Rajiv, assassination of (1991)
13, 56–7
Gandhi, Sonia, family of 126
Ganesh (deity), depictions of 135–6
Ganges, river 122
Ganguly, D. N., *Bilat pherat* (1921)
66
Garib Nawaz, shrine of 120
gender 185, 201–2; femininity 191;
gender alignment 191; gender
roles 186; masculinity 188–90;
payment inequality 187; physical
appearance 186–9
Germany, Berlin 96; education system
of 223
Ghai, Subhash, *Khalnayak* (1993)
148, 211, 232; *Pardes* (1997) 68,

122; *Ram Lakhan* (1980) 95,
101, 124, 211; *Taal* (1999) 220
Ghosh, Sujoy, *Kahaani* (2012) 185
Gilbert, Daniel, theory of happiness
variants 171, 173–4
globalization 65, 119
Godhra train fire (2002) 15, 117, 144;
Gujarat Riots (2002) 62, 117,
144
Golden Temple, use as filming
location 137, 149
Govinda 107, *108*, 177, *179*, *181*, 191,
230; cultural image of 94–5,
107–8; film genres associated
with 156, 177, 180–81; political
career of 60
Gowariker, Ashutosh, *Jodhaa Akbar*
(2008) *45*, 46–8, *46*, 50, 99, 107,
*136*, *140*, 142, 166, 190; *Once
Upon a Time in India* (2007) 42;
*Swades: We the People* (2004) 68,
*69*, 112
Green Revolution 13
Gujarati (language) 10, 83
Gujaratis 83, 89, 92, 105, 107, 179,
201; cultural image of 89
Gulzar, *Aandhi* (1975) 60; *Maachis*
(1996) 62
Gupte, Amole, *Stanley ka dabba*
(2011) 219
Guru Dutt 21, 111, 118, 176; *Kaagaz
ke phool* (1959) 206; *Pyaasa*
(1957) 172–3

Hansraj, Jugal, *Roadside Romeo* (2008)
28
Hanuman (deity), depictions of 136
Hassan, Kamal 88; *Hey Ram* (2000) 51
Hazare, Anna, anti-corruption
campaign (2001) 17, 60, 168
Hindi (language) 71, 79, 84, 86–7,
90, 139, 197, 250; as cultural

Ibrahim, Dawood, alleged depictions of 232
independent (*hatke*) cinema 8, 21, 23, 28, 35–6, 93, 105, 256
India 7–10, 17–19, 22, 27, 29, 32, 42–3, 45, 51–3, 55, 67–70, 72, 74, 76–7, 81–2, 84–5, 87, 92–3, 105, 114, 116–17, 119, 123, 154, 200, 204, 214, 239, 241, 256–8; Ajmer 120; Amritsar 89, 137, 149; Bhatinda 94; Bihar 22, 62–3, 84, 96, 98, 113; Bombay 10, 22, 57, 82–3, 254; British Raj (1858–1947) 50, 77–8, 97; Calcutta 83, 94, 134; Chandigarh 82; Christian population of 147; Constitution of (1950) 13–14, 97, 100, 164, 223; Delhi 54, 70, 83, 89, 93, 98, 109, 140, 168, 230; economic liberalization in 13, 64, 234; economy of 13; education system of 223–4; Goa 107; Godhra 62; government of 15, 17, 66; Gujarat 15, 62, 83, 144; Haridwar 109; Haryana 82, 227; Hindi Belt 79; Hindu population of 55, 72, 82; Hyderabad 90; Independence of (1947) 13–14, 21, 37, 43, 47, 50, 54, 78–9, 81–3, 117, 143; Jhansi 47; Jharkhand 62; Maharashtra 41, 83, 90, 93, 113, 252; military of 89, 230; Mumbai 16–17, 22, 60, 62, 82, 84, 88, 91, 93, 96, 98, 121, 134, 142, 145, 147, 149, 180, 226, 229, 240, 252, 254; Muslim population of 45, 55–6, 72, 90, 117, 147; Official Language Act (1963) 85; Parliament, 92; Partition (1947) 42, 54–6, 117–18, 143; population of 14, 102, 104–5; Pune 19, 44; Punjab 49, 80, 82, 88, *88*, 94, 193; Research and Analysis Wing (RAW) 233; Sikh population of 82; State of Emergency (1975–7) 164; Tamil Nadu 57, 88; Tirupati 137; Uttar Pradesh (UP) 50, 79, 82, 84, 94, 98, 114, 210; Varanasi 94, 138; World Heritage Sites in 77
Indian Congress Party 49, 59–60; members of 107
Indian identity 37–8, 258; development of 64, 73–4, 78, 80–81; discussion in Hindi cinema 37, 80, 82; 'sources' of 256
Indian Peace-keeping Force (IPKF) 56
Indian Penal Code Article 377, 201
Indian Premier League (IPL) 19, 27, 65, 122
International Monetary Fund (IMF), adjustment loans provided by 13
Irani, Boman 178
Islam 44, 72, 142, 162; conversion to 55, 98; Eid 121; *fatwas*, 120–21; Hajj 93, 137; *haraam* 149; Quran 56; Shariat 120; Sufism 140, 150, 162
Islamicate cinema 61–2, 117, 139–41; depiction of Muslims as terrorists 144–6; depiction of women in 141–2; Mughals on film 44–5; role of songs in 139–40; use of overseas locations in 145–7
Islamism 15, 59, 117; terrorism 61, 144, 254
Islamophobia 15, 72, 117, 145; global 146; growth of 144
Italy 241; Venice 179, 202

Jadhav, Ravi, *Natrang* (2010) 21; *Story of Balgandharva, The Sound of Heaven*, 21

199, 201, 237; production credits
of 96, 167–8; *Satyamev jayate* (TV
series) 168; *Taare zameen par*
(2007) 167

Khan, Arbaaz 209

Khan, Faiza Ahmad, *Supermen of
Malegaon* (2008) 25, 113

Khan, Farah, *Main hoon naa* (2004)
84; *Om Shanti Om* (2007) 127,
173, 179, 189, 224–5

Khan, Feroz Abbas, *Gandhi My Father*
(2007) 51

Khan, Imran 101, 213

Khan, Irrfan 240

Khan, Jiah 167

Khan, Kabir, *Ek tha Tiger* (2012) 113,
144, 200, 233; *Kurbaan, New
York* (2009) 145, 226

Khan, Kader 177

Khan, Kamaal 140

Khan, Mansoor, *Jo jeeta wohi
Sikandar* (1992) 197, 225

Khan, Mehboob 111; *Aan* (1952)
104; *Mother India* (1957) 21, 92,
111, 168, 185, 223–4

Khan, Nusrat Fateh Ali 140

Khan, Saif Ali 89, 199; background of
90, 101

Khan, Sajid, *Housefull* (2010) 77–8, *77*,
89, 177–9, *180*, 204, 213, 241

Khan, Salim 84, 164

Khan, Salman 27, 84–5, *114*, 120,
127, *128*, 189, 194, 209, 217,
232, 234, 243–5; background of
113; family of 120; film genres
associated with 156, 180

Khan, Shah Rukh (SRK) 23, 27, 43,
*43*, 68–9, 71–2, *73*, *78*, 81,
100, 120–22, 127, *128*, 131,
*134*, 138, *138*, 145–6, 154,
159–60, *160*, *163*, 172, *173*,
183, 189, 201–2, 211–12,

218, 224–5, 231–2, *232*, *233*,
*244*; background of 67–8;
common attributes of characters
portrayed by 74–6, 82, 192,
196; film genres associated
with 156; media image of 257;
*Ra.One* (2011) 90; songs
of 74–5

Khan, Soha Ali 244

Khanna, Akshaye 199

Khanna, Vinod 209; political career
of 60

Kher, Anupam 178

Kher, Kirron *146*, 202, 212

Khosla, Raj, family of 112

Khosla, Vijay, family of 112

Khote, Durga, background of 105

Kohli, Kunal *Fanaa* (2006) 59; *Hum
tum* (2004) 201

Kondke, Dada 177

*Koun banega crorepati?* (*Who Wants
to Be a Millionaire?*, TV series)
214

Kracauer, Siegfried view of cinema
30

Krishna (deity) 125, 134–5, 252;
avatar of 123; depictions of 129

Krishnan, R., *Parasakthi* (1952) 118

Kubera (deity) 229

Kukunoor, Nagesh, *Dor* (2006) 217

Kulkarni, Sonali 212

Kumar, Akshay 129, *130*, 177–8, 191;
common attributes of characters
portrayed by 76; film genres
associated with 156

Kumar, Dilip 84, 121

Kumar, Indra, *Beta* (1992) 125, 205,
215, 231; *Dil* (1990) 231

Kumar, Manoj 121, 226; *Purab aur
Pacchim* (1970) 226; *Upkar*
(1967) 60

Kunti 125

multiplex cinema 8, 23–4, 35, 105, 201; as part of consumerism 240; impact of 26

Mumbai Attacks (2008) 15, 117, 144, 254; depictions of 62; records of 149–50

Mumbai Train Bombings (2006) 144, 254

Munna Bhai (character) 53, 84, 91, 100, 109, 181–2, 219; as Indian Everyman 91, 256; concept of 91; depictions of 51, 91–2, 225–6; relationships of 84, 201

Murugadoss, A. R., *Ghajini* (2005) 166, *167*; *Ghajini* (2008) 163, 166

music 34, 195; *bhajans* (hymns) 118, 137; emotional power of 153–4; *ghazal* 56, 139; *Holi* 133; instruments 154; *qawwalis* 139–40; songs 34–5, 59, 74–5, 96, 100, 133, 194, 196, 204, 236, 247; soundtracks 57; Western 154

Muslim Personal Law 120

Nadkarni, Bipin, *Uttarayan* (2005) 21

Nandy, Ashis 28, 53

Nargis 185; family of 92

National Film and Television Institute 19

National Film Development Corporation 19

nationalism 21, 40, 44, 48, 59–60, 76, 79, 97; Hindu (Hindutva) 38, 47, 50, 57, 59–61, 65, 100, 116, 122–3, 129; Indian 69, 71; regional 79; religious 116

Nehru, Jawaharlal 12, 29, 49, 60, 126, 184, 224, 235; depictions of 60; *Discovery of India, The* (1946) 37, 79; linguistic policies of 83–4; planning policies of 110

New Middle Classes (NMCs) 63; lifestyle of 235–6; position in Indian diaspora 66; relationship with caste system 102–3; satirizing of 257

New Theatres 83

News Corporation, acquisitions made by 18

Nolan, Christopher, *Memento* (2000) 166

Onir, *I Am* (2010) 59, 201; *My Brother Nikhil* (2005) 201

Orientalism 116

Osten, Franz, *Acchut Kanya* (1936) 99

Pakistan 54–6, 59, 83, 200; Independence of (1947) 42, 54, 56, 143; military of 42, 55, 166; Muslim population of 89

Palma, Brian de, *Scarface* (1983) 250

Panda, Nila Madhab, *I Am Kalam* (2010) 219

Pandey, Chulbul *232*, *234*, 244

Pandey, Mangal, depictions of 50

Panju, S., *Parasakthi* (1952) 118

Parsi 105

Parsi theatre 39, 45

Pasta, Akhri (character), as example of stereotyping 92, 179

Patel, Jabbar, *Dr Babasaheb Ambedkar* (2000) 100

Pendharkar, Bhalji *Chhatrapati Shivaji* (1952) 49

Persian (language) 82

Persian literature 82

Phalke, D. G. 42–3

Plato, *Republic* 163–4

piracy 26; online 26

poverty 64, 73, 76, 111, 229; association with crime 112; character tropes associated with

21–2, 103; depictions of 21,
110–12, 232; rural 112, 231;
urban 96; as virtue 110, 128
Prabhat Studios 44
Prakash, J. Om, *Aap ki kasam* (1974)
153, 206
Prakash, Suraj *Jab jab phool khile*
(1965) 104
Prasad, M. Madhava 164
Priyadarshan 90, 177; *Bhool bhulaiya*
(2007) 96, 136, 178; *Billu*
(2009) 80; *Hera pheri* (2000) 109
Punjab Insurgency, depictions of 62
Punjabi (language) 87
Punjabis 90, 92–3, 143–4, 149, 216;
*karva chauth* (ritual) 119–20,
133; presence in Indian public
culture 88–9; Punjabiyat 89;
wedding ceremonies 132
Puri, Amrish 7, 214

Al Qaeda 117

racism 72, 78, 219; internal 82;
stereotypes 92
Radha-Krishna (deity) 71
Raghavan, Sriram, *Agent Vinod* (2012)
76, 233
Rahman, A. R. 26
Rai, Aishwarya 46, 212
Rai, Amit, *Road to Sangam* (2009) 51
Rai, Anand L., *Tanu Weds Manu*
(2011) 94
Rajan, Chota, alleged depictions
of 232
Rajni 88
Rajput 47
Ram Setu, depictions of 43
Rama (Ram) (deity) 38, 71, 136;
avatar of 123; family of 217;
Ram Rajya 130;
Ramjanmabhoomi (Birthplace of

Rama) 116–17; relationship with
Lakshman 124
*Ramayana* 43, 71; depiction of family
in 185; depictions of 123–4;
figures of 124, 217–18
Rampal, Arjun 125
Ranade, Mahadev 44
Rao, P. V. Narasimha, Indian prime
minister 13
*Ra.One* 136
Ratnam, Mani 28, 90; *Bombay* (1995)
57, 61–2, 91, 141, 143–4;
criticisms of 57; *Dil se* (1998)
57; *Guru* (2007) 42, 138, 197,
215, *230*; *Roja* (1992) 57, *58*, *59*
Rawal, Paresh 177–8
Ray, Satyajit 21, 102
realist cinema 21, 67, 100
regionalism 88, 91, 115, 254;
exaggerated depictions of 92
Rehman, A. R., soundtracks
composed by 57
religion 121, 138–9, 148–50, 169, 211;
caste as 119; devotional films
117–19, 142; fundamentalist 119;
influence on depiction of cities in
film 134; inter-faith romance
141–3, 145, 148; naming changes
121; pilgrimage 137; reincarnation
127–8; role of family in 131–2;
satire of 129; temples 137–8
Rizvi, Anusha, *Peepli* (*Live*) (2010) 18,
96, 112, 167–8
romance 193–6; adultery 206; consumerism in depictions of 241;
development in depictions of
198–200; gay 191, 196, 201;
Hindi cinematic ideal of 192;
language of 193–6; marriage 101,
118, 184, 192–3, 199–200,
202–6; stages of 193–4, 210–11,
241; role of dance in depiction of

Vetal (demon) 252
violence against women 63, 168
Vishnu (deity) avatar of 123
Vora, Neeraj, *Phir hera pheri* (2006)
    109

Walt Disney Company, investment in
    UTV Motion Pictures 24, 28, 256
'War on Terror' 145
Warsi, Arshad 182
women 27, 50, 81, 121, 164, 179,
    191, 204, 248, 254; bar girl 142;
    depiction of employment of
    228–30; depiction of in
    Islamicate cinema 141–2;
    depiction of role in family 124,
    185–6, 205–6, 242, 247;
    development in image of 89,
    187–8, 212, 243–5; industrial
    inequality 187–8; men as 141;
    Muslim 141–2, 145; popular

consumption of television among
    106; vamps 147; violence against
    61, 63, 168, 258
work: consumerism 236–8, 240,
    242–3; criminal 232–3; *dharma*
    228; housing 242; images of
    wealth aspiration 229–32, 237–8;
    women 228–30
World Bank Extreme Poverty Line,
    110–11

Yadav, Rajpal 178
Yash Raj Films 24, 97, 172, 256; films
    distributed by 24, 159, 172, 201;
    wealthy lifestyles depicted by
    230–31
Yuddhisthira 125

Zemeckis, Robert, *What Lies Beneath*
    (2000) 155
Zinta, Preity 199, 211–12